CUBA

A Revolution in Motion

Isaac Saney

Fernwood Publishing • Zed Books

Editing: Brenda Conroy
Cover image: Ahmed Velázquez, Granma International
2003 May Day Rally, Havana, Cuba
Design and production: Beverley Rach
Printed and bound in Canada by Hignell Printing Limited

Published in Canada by Fernwood Publishing
Site 2A, Box 5, 8422 St. Margaret's Bay Road
Black Point, Nova Scotia, B0J 1B0
and 324 Clare Avenue, Winnipeg, Manitoba, R3L 1S3
www.fernwoodbooks.ca

Published in the rest of the world by Zed Books Ltd
7 Cynthia Street, London N1 9JF, UK
and Room 400, 175 Fifth Avenue, New York, NY 10010, USA

Distributed in the USA exclusively by: Palgrave, a division of St Martin's Press LLC
175 Fifth Avenue, New York, NY, 10010, USA

Zed Books ISBN: 1 84277 362 3 hb   ISBN: 1 84277 363 1 pb

Fernwood Publishing Company Limited gratefully acknowledges
the financial support of the Department of Canadian Heritage,
the Nova Scotia Department of Tourism and Culture
and the Canada Council for the Arts for our publishing program.

A catalogue record for this book is available from the British Library.

National Library of Canada Cataloguing in Publication
Saney, Isaac
Cuba: a revolution in motion / Isaac Saney.

Includes bibliographical references and index.
ISBN 1-55266-114-8

1. Cuba—Economic conditions—1990-. 2. Cuba—History—1959-.
3. Cuba—Social conditions—1959-. I. Title.

F1788.S23 2003   972.9106'4   C2003-903818-1

Reprinted: March 2005

Dedicated to

my loving parents

Clifton and Joan Saney

and

the Cuban people

whose struggle for a better world is an inspiration

CONTENTS

ACKNOWLEDGEMENTS

This work would not have been possible without the encouragement, advice and assistance of various individuals. Professor Henry Veltmeyer, Saint Mary's University, provided the initial impetus. Errol Sharpe of Fernwood Publishing was unwavering in his support of this project. I wish to extend my gratitude to the Travel Committee of Henson College, Dalhousie University, who funded many of my trips to Cuba. Appreciation is also extended to Dr. Sam Scully, Vice President-Academic, Dalhousie University, who provided a critical grant to complete this book.

Over the last decade, I have benefited from numerous rich and intense discussions, debates and correspondences. While these exchanges did not always arrive at a point of agreement, they were always fruitful. I wish to draw particular attention — and not necessarily in this order — to: Jesús Garcia Brigos (Institute of Philosophy, Cuba), Arnold August (author of *Democracy in Cuba and the 1997–98 Elections*), Mark Rushton (colleague and fellow member of the Nova Scotia Cuba Association, who provided invaluable comments and technical assistance), Gary Zatzman (Research Associate, Dalhousie University), Tony Seed (publisher/editor *Shunpiking Magazine*), Samuel Fure Davis (Faculty of Foreign Languages, University of Havana), Cliff Durand (Morgan State University and coordinator of the Annual Conference of North American and Cuban Philosophers and Social Scientists), Susan Hurlich (a tireless journalist/scholar resident in Cuba for more than ten years), Fernando Garcia Bielsa (formerly with the Central Committee of the Communist Party of Cuba and now with the Cuban Interests Section, Washington, D.C.), Al Campbell (University of Utah), Carlos Fernández de Cossío (Ambassador of Cuba to Canada), Michael Lebowitz (Simon Fraser University), John Kirk (Dalhousie University), Brenda Conroy (an exemplar for all editors), Anton Allahar (University of Western Ontario), David Austin (friend and scholar), Isaac "Ike" Nahem (an activist and writer who, as he so poignantly puts it, also drives a train "from New York — the financial capital of imperialism— to Washington — the political capital of imperialism"), Jonathan Suorvell (a very promising young intellectual) and many others whose names do not appear solely because of reasons of space and the failings of my memory. Also, I wish to thank the journal *Socialism and Democracy* for allowing me to use and reconfigure previously published material. I would be remiss if I did not extend my sincerest gratitude to the very many "ordinary" Cubans whom I interviewed and conversed with, especially those who had to endure my idiosyncratic Spanish.

However, while a great debt is owned to others, in the end this work — shortcomings and all — is solely my responsibility.

INTRODUCTION

Since the collapse of the Soviet Union and the Eastern Bloc in the early 1990s and the strengthening of the United States' economic blockade, many "experts" have predicted the imminent collapse of the Cuban Revolution. Some have even seen this "inevitable collapse" as a regional threat (Dominguez 1995: 8). However, "clearly defying" the logic of the specialists and perplexing them "the world over" (Kirk 2000: xii), not only has the Cuban Revolution and the government of President Fidel Castro continued to defy conventional wisdom and survive, Cuba has also been able to develop and grow economically. Indeed, probably the most ironic commentary came from James Wolfensohn, President of the World Bank, who acknowledged, "Cuba has done a great job on education and health" and "it does not embarrass me to admit it." He added, "We just have nothing to do with them in the present sense, and they should be congratulated on what they've done" (Lobe 2001).

Yet, despite this admission, the island continues to be ignored by both development theorists and the technocrats in charge of implementing and administering the programs that are supposed to lead to the improved well-being of the world's people. A 1997 World Bank Discussion Paper, "Poverty Reduction and Human Development in the Caribbean," contains not a single mention of Cuba (Baker 1997). In neither *Globalization and the Developing Countries* (Bigman 2002) nor *Latin America: Its Future in the Global Economy* (Gray 2002), does Cuba merit even a solitary comment. In *Society, State and Market* (Martinussen 1999: 230) Cuba warrants one parenthetical remark. In a *New Internationalist* issue on the topic of "The Liberation of Latin America," which focuses on the region's burgeoning challenges to the nostrums of neoliberalism, Cuba's development model and experience are not discussed (May 2003). Oswald de Rivero's *The Myth of Development* dismisses Cuba, in a brief note, as marginal in today's world (2001: 183).

However, in spite of this almost universal dismissal, the development trajectory of the Cuban Revolution represents a profound challenge to conventional approaches. Cuba highlights, as no other country does, the debate surrounding the necessary conditions and instrumentalities to achieve development (e.g., the strong and interventionist state versus the

1

free market, privatization and neoliberal prescriptions). The Cuban Revolution offers not only a different conception of development but also a unique model of development. On one hand, the island demonstrates the limitations that external geopolitical and economic conditions and internal material constraints impose on the socio-economic transformation paths available to countries of the South. On the other, the Cuban Revolution indicates the possibilities open to those countries that pursue radical development models.

In 1959, in the months immediately following the triumph of the Cuban Revolution on January 1st, there was a poignant and telling exchange between Fidel Castro and Che Guevara. While studying various designs for the construction of spacious apartment buildings and housing developments, Guevara argued that the government could not afford to implement such ambitious plans. Castro emphatically retorted: "But that's why we had a revolution, so every Cuban can have such a place to live!" (Glazer 1989: 76). Despite the tempering of this early exhilaration, Cuba offers an important — and unique — example of a Third World country that has undergone a remarkable transformation that benefits the people. The standard of living has significantly improved for the vast majority of Cubans. Critical to this Cuban metamorphosis have been the creation of universal healthcare and education systems and the establishment of comprehensive social security. Thus, hundreds of schools, hospitals, clinics, industrial complexes, resort facilities and recreational parks were, and continue to be, constructed (Glazer 1989: 77). Of course, both success and frustration have characterized the Cuban revolutionary experience. Economic constraints have framed the Cuban goal of achieving justice for all. With the advent of the crisis of the 1990s, many problems have come to the forefront. Some are new, while others have slumbered — albeit not always quietly — under the surface. Yet even in these regards, this small island has profound lessons for humanity.

The central contention of this book is that the Cuban experience offers significant insights into not only a different paradigm, but a paradigm that has been largely successful — especially given the objective limitations of a small, poor, underdeveloped island nation — in utilizing the country's resources and wealth for the public good. This book, intended as an introduction for students and the general reader, explores Cuba as it enters the twenty-first century, a lone island of anti-imperialism, anti-capitalism and socialism in the so-called "age of globalization." This work seeks to explain what some have called the "miracle" of the Cuban Revolution's survival in the face of an unprecedented economic contraction. Chapter

One contextualizes this discussion by providing an overview of Cuban history, the Cuban Revolution and the economic crash of the early 1990s. It surveys the economic measures enacted to meet the crisis and the ensuing results and impact. Chapter Two raises the most controversial and, for some, unsettling, proposition: that the "explanation" for the Cuban "miracle" is to be found in the Cuban political system, in its own unique democracy. Cuba is invariably portrayed as a totalitarian regime, a veritable "gulag" guided and controlled by one man, Fidel Castro. However, this stance, as Chapter Two argues, cannot be sustained once the reality of Cuba is assessed.

Chapter Three examines inequality and racism. It analyzes the successes and shortcomings of Cuban policy in this area and extrapolates the meaning of the Cuban experience for the rest of the world. Chapter Four covers the Cuban criminal justice system and the rising problem of crime. Chapter Five focuses on U.S.–Cuba relations, locating the Cuban Revolution's relationship with the U.S. within the context of Washington's historical engagement with the island. Chapter Six discusses Cuba's experience with foreign investment and government policy and practice on environmental matters. It also examines Cuba's internationalist policies, particularly its roles in securing Namibian independence and accelerating the end of the apartheid system in South Africa. The chapter concludes with a brief discussion of Cuban socialism.

The central questions that preoccupy the vast majority of Cuba watchers are: Who will succeed Fidel Castro and what will happen to Cuba after he is gone? Many Cuba specialists predict instability and the disintegration of the Revolution in the wake of Castro's death. While the integral and historic role of Fidel Castro is undeniable, these two interconnected questions reflect a certain "Fidel-centrism" that permeates the musings on Cuba. The Cuban Constitution establishes a very definite and clear line of succession if Castro were to die suddenly or become incapacitated while in power. In the case of incapacitation or death, the First Vice-President of Cuba will temporarily assume the position of President. At present, the First Vice-President is Raul Castro. An emergency session of the National Assembly — the island's elected parliament — would then be convened to select a new national President. Speculation on possible successors often focuses on Ricardo Alarcón (head of the National Assembly), Carlos Lage (often referred to as the economic czar) and Felipe Pérez Roque (the young Foreign Minister). What is missed in this concentration on individual succession is the reality that a generational transition and transfer of power — as discussed in Chapter

Two — have been underway. Increasingly — as a direct and conscious decision of the Cuban leadership — all levels of government on the island are run by people in their thirties and forties. It is this generation that will carry on the tasks of the Cuban revolutionary project.

One cannot discuss Cuba without reference to the United States, especially its relentless efforts to undermine and ultimately destroy the Cuban Revolution. Chapter Five outlines this history. What have been most misunderstood and misconstrued have been the internal dimensions of U.S. strategy: the determination, as discussed in Chapter Two, to create a domestic opposition movement in Cuba. The Cuban government's actions — the arrest, trial and sentencing of seventy-five individuals in April/May 2003 — to deal with exogenously generated and funded figures and organizations have been extremely controversial, leading to widespread condemnation by Western governments and the media.

The European Union instituted diplomatic sanctions, limiting official travel to and contacts with the island. Cuba responded by holding mass demonstrations that denounced these sanctions as unacceptable interference in the island's internal affairs, asserting its determination to preserve and defend its independence and sovereignty. Also, several renowned intellectuals — among them Eduardo Galeano, Jose Saramago and Howard Zinn — wrote and/or signed letters of protest against what they deemed to be unjustifiable repression and the imposition of savage prison sentences (see Galeano 2003). While many of these intellectuals acknowledged continuing U.S. hostility, they argued that the Cuban response was a drastic overreaction and a suffocation of legitimate dissent.

The debate centred on Cuba's right to defend itself against the danger posed by Washington. Those who supported Cuba countered by arguing that the Cuban Revolution does not exist in a world of its own choosing but must grapple with an undeclared war being waged against it by U.S. imperialism. Furthermore, Cuba's response was reasonable, understandable and justified in the wake of the U.S. drive for global hegemony, especially as it was waging war on Iraq. Some have viewed Cuba's actions as the first open rebellion against the Bush Doctrine's goal of cementing U.S. supremacy (Sandels 2003; see also Office of the President 2002). A resolute response was judged to be required in order to demonstrate that Cuba would not be an easy target for the U.S. military. Whether the Castro government was accurate in its assessment of the imminence of an attack, it was clear that it could not fail to respond in a definitive manner. In a telling exchange this author had with the acclaimed documentary maker and journalist Saul Landau on this issue, Landau finally admitted: "Unlike scholars, statesmen cannot afford to be wrong" (Landau 2003).

Thousands of international figures rallied around Cuba, endorsing the *Conscience of the World*, a declaration in defence of Cuba against U.S. aggression (Porcuba 2003). Perhaps, James Petras delivered the most incisive commentary on the intellectuals who abandoned Cuba and

> who prefer the luxury of issuing moral imperatives about freedom everywhere for everyone, even when a psychotic Washington puts the knife to Cuba's throat.... Is it moral cowardice to pick up the cudgels for the empire and pick on Cuba when it faces the threat of mass destruction over the freedom of paid agents, subject to prosecution by any country in the world? What is eminently dishonest is to totally ignore the vast accomplishments of the revolution in employment, education, health, equality, and Cuba's heroic and principled opposition to imperial wars — the only country to so declare — and its capacity to resist almost 50 years of invasions.... They cannot claim they don't know the repercussions of what they are saying and doing. They cannot pretend innocence after all they have seen and read and heard about U.S. war plans against Cuba.... It is easy for critical intellectuals to be a "friend of Cuba" in good times at celebrations and invited conferences in times of lesser threats.... It is much harder to be a "friend of Cuba" when a totalitarian empire threatens the heroic island and puts heavy hands on its defenders. It is in times like this — of permanent wars, genocide and military aggression, when Cuba needs the solidarity of critical intellectuals, which they are receiving from all over Europe and particularly Latin America. (Petras 2003)

Probably no country has faced a greater and more concerted campaign of disinformation than the Republic of Cuba. The image of Cuba's social reality has been so distorted that for most people — both lay and academic — Cuba appears to be an unmitigated "hell." This book does not portray Cuba as a perfect society, a paradise. Nor does it present the island's revolutionary process as a universal model for Third World development. But, as an example, the Cuban experience has much to offer. As noted by Carlos Fernández de Cossío, Cuba's Ambassador to Canada, Cuba is:

> a nation going through real difficulties, with insufficient answers to meet all its problems immediately and with an even approach. Mistakes are made and corrected. There is no blueprint or

> previous experience to draw on, even though there is indeed a
> clear idea of the direction to follow.... The 1990s shall rightly be
> registered as one more crucial decade in Cuba's rich history of
> struggle for the protection of its full sovereignty and to pursue José
> Martí's dream of achieving "all justice." (Fernández de Cossío
> 2001: 5)

Cuba exhibits none of the chronic and, in some cases, epidemic problems (e.g., social and political instability, death squads, high levels of crime, social violence, drug trafficking and drug use, homelessness, massive inequalities and government corruption) that confront the rest of Latin America. It is this author's observation — based on more than fifteen extended visits — that Cuba is bereft of the social phenomenon of homeless children that besets the region. Indeed, if by state practice there is a deliberately privileged group, it is children (Green 1998: 165; Lutjens 2000a: 55–63 and 2000b: 149–59). Moreover, Cuba, a so-called under-developed country, is actually a living refutation in the Americas of everything that Washington has mandated as essential for the region to modernize and develop. A poignant illustration is Washington's own predictions on the consequences of the re-establishment of U.S. he-gemony over the island. A series of prescriptions — necessitating a return to the situation that prevailed in Cuba before the Revolution — have been laid down as the basis for the "normalization" of relations. Among the measures advocated by the U.S. government is wide-ranging privatiza-tion, encompassing industry, agriculture and education. In anticipation of the social toll and dislocation the entire social security would be "com-pletely restructured to protect citizens during the transition to a market economy and beyond" (U.S. Congress 1998). The Cuban experience, particularly the Special Period, shatters and exposes the various imperialist dogmas: from Rostow's "take-off" thesis to the necessity for foreign capital to lead, drive and control a nation's development path. Cuba is, perhaps, best captured by President Castro, who mused:

> Cuba is neither a heaven nor a hell. So let's say it's purgatory,
> where they say people go; and from where, with a little patience
> and the help of a few prayers and whatever else can be done for
> the poor souls in purgatory, they can move on to heaven. They
> say there is a way out of purgatory, but there's never a way out
> of hell. If we are in purgatory, we are not going back to hell. At
> least we have escaped Satan, and are patiently waiting for the
> moment of reaching heaven. (1996a: 90)

1. FROM COLUMBUS TO REVOLUTION

Christopher Columbus established Spanish dominion over Cuba in 1492 (Pérez Jr. 1988; Franklin 1997; Canton Navarro 2000; and Le Riverend 1997). The consequences for the indigenous peoples were catastrophic. Forced by the Spanish conquerors to work in the gold mines, in only two decades the entire indigenous population was virtually exterminated, a result of the forced labour regime, frequent massacres and the introduction of diseases. Cuba remained under Spanish control for the next four centuries, with a brief interruption when Britain occupied Havana for eleven months in 1762–63. During the sixteenth century, Cuba and Puerto Rico were considered "the pride of Philip II of Spain" (Thomas 1988: 17).

Spanish domination of the island was met with tenacious resistance from the indigenous inhabitants. In the sixteenth century, Hatuey, an indigenous leader who had escaped to Cuba from the island of Hispaniola, observed:

> These Europeans worship a very covetous sort of god. They will exact immense treasures of us and will use their utmost to reduce us to a miserable state of slavery or else put us to death. (McManus 1989: 17–18)

Hatuey was eventually captured and burnt at the stake. Other revolts against Spanish rule occurred but ultimately the Spanish military prevailed. The virtual extermination of the native population led to the large-scale importation of African slaves — first to mine for gold and then to work the sugar plantations, which became the mainstay of the Cuban economy, especially after the Haitian Revolution. At least a million slaves were imported from 1791 to 1840, with more than 600,000 alone imported between 1821 and 1831 (Davidson 1980: 91; McManus 1989: 21). As Eric Williams observed, it was "strange that an article like sugar, so sweet and necessary to human existence, should have occasioned such crimes and bloodshed!" (1983: 27). With the attendant brutality and oppression of the plantation system, the stage was set for resistance, including several rebellions against the slave system. Ironically, the most successful and dramatic rebellion against slavery in the Americas — the Haitian Revolution — catapulted Cuba into the forefront of slavery sugar production. When Haiti was seized by the enslaved African population in the 1790s, French landowners fled "to Cuba, creating more plantations with subsequent increased demand for slaves" (Franklin 1997: 2). With historical poignancy, the experience of an independent Haiti presaged that of the Cuban Revolution. And, as was to happen to "Cuba after its revolution, Haiti was subjected to an economic and diplomatic quarantine by former trading partners" (Foner 1983: 13).

Taking advantage of the disappearance of Haiti from the world market, "Cuba forged ahead to fill the gap" (Williams 1983: 149). It became the largest producer of sugar in the West Indies (Augier et al. 1971: 130; Williams 1983: 151–52). In 1865, Cuba's sugar output was more than forty times greater than it was in 1775 (Williams 1983: 151). Cuba's pre-eminence as a major sugar producer and source of profit was, thus, secured. However, this explosion in the sugar sector "distorted the island's economy by forcing the abandonment of many other activities, posing new problems and radically transforming the landscape" (Munck 1988: 48). Indeed, *"sin azucar no hay pais"* (without sugar there is no country) became an aphorism regarding Cuba. However, despite the extensive exploitation of Cuban labour, the sugar plantation was in many ways increasingly a foreign enclave within the island. By the mid-1920s, for example, 75 percent of Cuba's sugar production was foreign owned (Munck 1988: 49).

The emancipation of slaves in the British empire in the 1830s further cemented Cuba's dominant position in sugar, because British colonies suffered labour shortages and, therefore, could not compete with planta-tion slavery. To curtail competition from its rivals and reduce their advantage, Britain imposed a ban on the slave trade (Williams 1983: 151–52). This established serious constraints on the supply of African peoples to replace and renew slave populations. However, Europe's demand for sugar continued to grow. In order to meet the labour shortfall, 125,000 Chinese labourers were imported into Cuba between 1852 and 1874 (Augier et al. 1971: 201–202; Foner 1983: 23). These indentured labourers "worked side by side" with the slaves (Williams 1983: 29). In 1886, with the abolition of slavery in Cuba, there arose another labour shortage, leading to the importation of more than 200,000 workers from Haiti, Jamaica and Puerto Rico (Augier et al. 1971: 266; Williams 1983: 29).

As the Cuban economy developed, an oligarchy emerged, certain sections of which increasingly chafed under Spanish colonial control over the economics and politics of the island. In the nineteenth century, Cuban nationalists initiated a succession of insurrections to achieve Cuban independence. The two major armed struggles were the First War for Independence, also referred to as the Ten Years War, 1868–1878, and the Second War for Independence, 1895–1898. Although the Spanish were defeated in the Second War, the Cubans incurred an immense human toll during the struggle, with an estimated 400,000 fatalities (Scheer and Zeitlin 1964: 35). Under the command of General Valeriano Weyler, the Spanish forces, with the aim of crushing the rebels and destroying their support base among the population, instituted the policy of recontrado, where "the rural population was herded into concentration camps under penalty of death" and "thousands died of hunger and disease" (Scheer and Zeitlin 1964: 36; see also Augier et al. 1971: 249–50; Izquierdo Canosa 1998).

With the *mambises* — Cuban liberation fighters — on the verge of victory, the United States, with a keen eye on its economic and strategic interests, intervened. At the defeat of Spain, Washington extracted a peace treaty "that effectively transferred sovereignty over Cuba to the United States" (Michalowski 1997). Thus, a period of American domination of Cuba was initiated, lasting until the triumph of the Cuban Revolution in 1959. During this six-decade period, Cuban economics and politics were controlled by U.S. corporate and financial interests.

In the years leading up to the Revolution, U.S. investment in Cuba comprised more than 11 percent of the total U.S. investment in Latin America and the Caribbean (Ewan 1981: 13). By 1959, U.S. corporations controlled 40 percent of sugar production and 75 percent of arable land; they also owned more than 90 percent of electric and telephone utilities, 50 percent of the railways, 90 percent of mines, 100 percent of oil refineries and 90 percent of cattle ranches. They dominated the transportation, manufacturing and tourism sectors. Moreover, U.S. banks held more than one quarter of bank deposits (Barry, Wood and Preusch 1984: 268; Greene 1970: 139; Patterson 1994: 35–54). Organized crime from the U.S. — particularly the Mafia — came to have a tremendous influence in Cuban economics and politics (Cirules 2002). Consequently, corruption flourished, whether in the form of embezzlement of public funds or payoffs from the Mafia.

Pre-1959 Cuba was counted within the upper tier of Latin America, contrasting sharply with more underdeveloped countries in the region.

Indeed, it is argued that the Cuban people were relatively well off. In Latin America, for example, Cuba ranked third in life expectancy, fourth in electricity consumption per capita, and fifth in per capita income ($353 U.S. in 1958) (Williams 1984: 480). The island had one of the highest ownership levels of televisions and automobiles. However, what is hidden in these figures is the level of inequality in Cuban society at that time (Gilmore 2000: 132). The distribution of wealth and well-being was heavily skewed in favour of the rich and professional classes. In 1956, the U.S. Department of Commerce counted Cuba's per capita income at 345 pesos. However, it stated that this figure was misleading and calculated — once other indices were factored in — the actual income as 180 pesos (just over $270 U.S.) It compared this to the per capita income of $638 for the State of Mississippi, the poorest state at that time in the U.S. (Scheer and Zeitlin 1964: 18). Yet, the actual income for the majority of Cubans was even much lower. The World Bank in a 1951 study observed: "there is a very wide gap between the income of a relatively few high-income receivers at the top and the mass of low-income receivers" (quoted in Scheer and Zeitlin 1964: 18). Moreover, racial discrimination, as examined in Chapter Three in this volume, was rampant, with whites inhabiting a different Cuba than blacks. This societal fissure was delineated most starkly in the urban/rural divide, with the wealthy urbanites revelling in a lifestyle and patterns of consumption that sought to replicate the "American dream."

The reality was very different in the rural areas. More than one quarter of Cuba's population were landless peasants, dependent on unstable seasonal employment, who lived a precarious existence. The land was concentrated in the hands of a few large landowners, many of whom were U.S. companies. Before the Revolution, Cuban reflected the urban/rural divide patterns prevalent throughout the Third World. In the countryside, over 80 percent of the dwellings — called *bohios* — were thatched-roofed and mud-floored. Only 10 percent had any plumbing or electricity (Mace 1982: 121; Glazer 1989: 77). More than one-third of the rural population suffered from infestations of intestinal parasites and other diseases. Malnourishment was the reality. Meat was a dietary rarity, with only 4 percent of Cuban peasants consuming it as a regular part of their daily meals; only 1 percent had access to fish, less than 2 percent eggs, 3 percent bread, 11 percent milk, and almost none ate green vegetables. This dietary pattern reflected the level of poverty that prevailed. The average pre-1959 peasant income was less than a third of the national average. Moreover, the illiteracy rate was 45 percent, with 44 percent having no formal education.

Fifty-four percent of rural homes had no toilets and 84 percent depended on rivers or unmonitored springs and wells for water (Gilmore 2000: 132; Scheer and Zeitlin 1964: 21). However, the rural standard of was not an anomaly within Cuban society. It represented the extreme deprivation experienced by the majority of citizens. Nationally, the unemployment rate was 25 percent. While most urban dwellings had access to electricity, less than half had complete sanitary facilities, and more than 50 percent of these facilities were inadequate. In 1959, most of the 1.4 million Cuban dwellings were in substandard condition (Glazer 1989: 77). The illiteracy rate stood at 26 percent of the population (McManus 1989: 35).

REVOLUTIONARY ENTHUSIASM

On several occasions, the U.S. intervened militarily or manipulated Cuban domestic politics to ensure that governments malleable to U.S. control were established. This chain was broken on January 1, 1959, when, after a two-year struggle, the July the 26th Movement, a revolutionary movement led by Fidel Castro, mobilized workers, peasants and other sectors to topple the U.S.-supported government of Fulgencio Batista. The Movement was born in the failed July 26th, 1953, attack on the Moncada military barracks in the city of Santiago de Cuba, aimed at ending the Batista dictatorship. Its manifesto, *History Will Absolve Me* — based on Fidel Castro's defence speech at his trial — outlined the goals of national independence and social justice and became the basic program that guided the movement and the early years of the Revolution.

The Cuban revolutionary struggle was a national one, encompassing all sectors of Cuban society. However, critical to its success was the working class, which "provided a vital backdrop to the revolutionary struggle" (Munck 1988: 177). The labour movement was a dominant force in the political development and direction of the Revolution. Workers were prominent actors throughout the urban wing of the revolutionary struggle, which complemented the rural armed struggle. The rebel army relied heavily on the "rural proletariat" (the sugar plantation workers) and the *campesinos* (peasant farmers) (Munck 1988: 177). A general strike in January 1959 sealed the revolution's victory by defeating an attempt — supported by Washington — to install a new government comprised of recycled elements of the old political order, a manoeuvre designed to exclude the revolutionaries from power.

After the triumph of the Cuban Revolution, workers played a major role in shaping its trajectory. The various programs and policies that were implemented reflected not only the revolutionary leadership's initiatives but also the demands and pressures "of the working class both within the state structures and in the factories, fields and sugar mills" (Munck 1988: 177). These demands were the crystallization of objectives of the working class that could not be satisfied under capitalism. The "demands for full employment and improved and increasing social services came into conflict with the imperatives of capitalist rationality" (Petras 1981: 215). Those demands required a radical transformation of the Cuban social, economic and political terrain

> The class struggle ... became clearer, and the social dimension of the revolution became predominant — essentially through the penetration by the working class of the critical new institutions, the embryonic revolutionary state, the Rebel Army, and the popular militias ... the socialist stage of the revolution, punctured as it was by conflicts and some violence, was relatively peaceful, because the working-class role in the armed struggle for democracy had secured it a strategic position, allowing it to undermine all bourgeois opposition. (Petras 1981: 220)

This change in the balance of class forces was reflected, as the Revolution developed, in workers' attitudes and views of both themselves and their new role in production and society. A copper miner stated: "Before, a raise in production benefited the bosses. Not now" (Zeitlin 1967: 206). This was echoed by a nickel-furnace tender: "We worked for the boss before. We work for ourselves now" (Zeitlin 1967: 206). One brewery worker stated:

> The boss paid us a miserable salary. The revolution put the workers to work, and paid more. The profits of the industries are now used for schools and for highways that we build ourselves.... We don't have a boss now. We ourselves run the brewery. There are no overseers, but rather *responsables* [persons encharged with responsibility for a particular task] — because we need technical advisers.... Before I didn't want to work. Now, I work of my own will, at whatever is necessary. (Zeitlin 1967: 206)

A worker at a sugar refinery commented:

> Everything is now done as is necessary for the workers. Now we have decent human beings who work with us, as we work with

them. Before, we didn't know whom we working for or whom we were working with. When I work now, I work of my own free will [*mi propia fuerza*], not like before when I worked only out of need. (Zeitlin 1967: 206)

With the triumph of the Cuban Revolution, the long period of U.S. domination of Cuban affairs now passed into the period of implacable U.S. hostility, culminating in an imposition of a stringent economic embargo and a U.S.-sponsored and organized invasion in 1961. Thus began the process leading to the transformation of Cuba into a socialist state. The radical restructuring of society inevitably resulted in a clash with the wealthy Cuban oligarchy and, as detailed in Chapter Five, entrenched U.S. interests. The *Wall Street Journal* of June 24, 1959, observed:

> What discontent there is up to now — with Mr. Castro seems limited primarily to conservatively inclined upper-income groups.... Chat with bellhops, elevator operators, secretaries, and other working people in Havana, and you are quickly convinced Mr. Castro still has the enthusiastic, almost idolizing support of the general public. The very Castro moves which have distressed the business community have won him popular support. (quoted in Scheer and Zeitlin 1964: 100)

The initial revolutionary measures were aimed at redistribution of wealth. Castro declared:

> The problems concerning land, the problem of industrialization, the problem of housing, the problem of unemployment, the problem of education and the problem of the health of the people; these are the six problems we would take immediate steps to resolve. (quoted in Huberman and Sweezy 1960: 38)

Pharmaceutical prices were reduced by 15–20 percent and electricity rates by 30 percent. The minimum wages in the agriculture, industry and commerce sectors were raised. Taxes were lowered for the middle and working classes, while increased for the rich (Pérez Jr. 1999: 479). The new revolutionary government recognized that one of the most pressing needs of Cuban society was resolving the housing problem. This was embodied in the Moncada Program — authored by Fidel Castro — which outlined the primary objectives of the Revolution (Canton Navarro 2000:

215). Thus, the critical first steps taken were to deal with the housing crisis. These measures were an integral component of other key policy initiatives, encompassing urban reform, nationalizing banks and industries, and overhauling the education system (Glazer 1989: 77).

The housing policy of the revolutionary government was centred on the eradication of the worst shantytowns and the relocation of the residents to better housing (Eckstein 1994: 151; Glazer 1989: 79; Karol 1970: 212). The first effort, in 1960–61, at elimination of these areas was through an organized "self help" initiative, resulting in former residents of shantytowns building an estimated 3,500 homes with the help of technical assistance and loans. Each new community contained 100 to 150 dwellings and had facilities such as schools and health clinics (Glazer 1989: 79; Canton Navarro 2000: 216). This transformation of the outlying urban areas earmarked the institution of a national-scale public housing project. Integral to this thrust was focusing financial and material resources toward the transformation of the rural areas and the renovation of the island's infrastructure (Glazer 1989: 79; Mace 1982: 123–24).

In January 1959, the first housing decree was passed. The law blocked evictions and reduced rents by 30 to 50 percent (Karol 1970: 23, Glazer 1989: 77; Canton Navarro 2000: 216; Mace 1982: 121). Rates had been so exorbitant that workers consumed half of their earnings paying rent (Scheer and Zeitlin 1964: 19). The law provided protection for small landlords. A ten-year tax exemption was granted for owner-occupied houses built in the ensuing two years. The goal was the deterrence of the construction of rental properties and raising the level of home ownership (Glazer 1989: 77). In addition, owners of vacant lots of land were required to sell them to people seeking to construct their own homes (Canton Navarro 2000: 216). However, the most important legislation was the *Urban Reform Law*, passed in October 1960. Before the promulgation of this law, it was

> an impossible dream for any tenant in Cuba was to finally become the owner of his or her house or apartment. The Revolution immediately set out to try to make this popular aspiration come true. (Canton Navarro 2000: 215)

The *Urban Reform Law* permitted landlords to keep their homes and vacation houses, but required them to sell all rental property. Current tenants were given first priority in purchasing and were able to amortize the price over a specified period of time — between five and ten years, depending on whether the dwelling was built before or after 1940 (Canto Navarro 2000: 215; Glazer 1989: 78). The state collected the amortization payments from the tenants and in turn paid the former landlords instalments, providing landlords with an assured lifetime income of between 150 and 600 pesos per month, a comfortable sum, given that the average Cuban monthly income was then around 100 pesos (Canton Navarro 2000: 216; Glazer 1989: 78; Mace 1982: 122). Also in concordance with the *Urban Reform Law*, a program of government-constructed housing began. These houses were leased with lifetime occupancy rights, with rent set at a maximum of 10 percent of family income (Glazer 1989: 78). By 1972, 75 percent of Cuban homes were owner occupied (Mace 1982: 122). At the end of the 1990s, more than one million Cuban families had become homeowners (Canton Navarro 2000: 215).

The *Urban Reform Law* benefited both tenants and small landlords: tenants were guaranteed ownership of their houses within a reasonable period of time; small landlords did not have to rely on fluctuating or insecure rents, as they received monthly payments from the government. The interests that were adversely affected were those of the real estate speculators, large landlords and private mortgage lenders. (Karol 1970: 23; Canton Navarro 2000: 216).

Two basic modes of housing tenure were instituted. Most tenants became homeowners. Tenants in the new government-owned dwellings were given long-term, *usufruct* leases — a lifelong contract — allowing the tenant the advantages derived from use of the home. The rents for these leases were set at a rate not exceeding 10 percent of each family's annual income. Leaseholders did not acquire equity in the dwelling and were obligated to continue paying rent as long as they occupied the domicile. However, no other types of renting were permitted, other than in hotels or vacation apartments, although this restriction was relaxed under the 1984 *General Housing Law* (Glazer 1989: 78). In the present economic situation, families are allowed to rent rooms or apartments for extended periods of time. A licence must be obtained and annual fees and taxes paid.

This goal of home ownership remains at the heart of Cuba's housing policy. The aim of providing universal and free housing for all reflected the optimism that suffused the early years of the Revolution, primarily the belief that a rapid and unhampered transition to socialism was on the immediate agenda. Moreover, it was illustrative of the substantial constraints that objective conditions, namely limited economic resources, imposed on the development possibilities and options that are open to a nation. It was to prove to be a fecund learning and teaching experience.

Rural life was profoundly transformed by mass nationalizations and the redistribution of land to *campesinos,* which led to the formation of cooperatives, state farms and a body of small private farmers. On May 17, 1959, the first agrarian reform law, a thorough land reform program, was passed. This was followed by the agrarian reform law of 1963 (Pérez Jr. 1999: 479). Before the agrarian reform, 0.6 percent of Cuba's landowners controlled 35.2 percent of the land. Half of the land, encompassing 46 percent of the best-quality and arable land, was held by just 1.5 percent of landowners. This situation was reflected in the social reality that the vast majority of small farmers — an estimated 150,000 families — were share-croppers, tenant farmers and squatters, with an additional 500,000 agricultural workers, representing another 200,000 rural families, confined to seasonal and casual underemployment (Garcia Luis 2001: 23). They alternated between sugar and coffee plantation work and unemployment (Karol 1970: 22; Frank 1993: 99; Huberman and Sweezy 1960: 110–33).

Under the first agrarian reform, land holdings were limited to a thousand acres. The large sugar companies and the twelve thousand largest private owners were expropriated. As a result, 110,000 sharecroppers and farm tenants gained title to the land. The minimum allotment for a family of five was set at sixty-seven acres, with the right to purchase an additional hundred. In Camaguey province, 2.3 million acres were distributed in less than three weeks (Scheer and Zeitlin 1964: 97). The second agrarian reform limited land holdings to 167 acres and expropriated ten thousand large farms (Frank 1993: 99–100; Le Riverend 1997: 108–11). The large plantations and ranches were turned into state farms. Small farmers — an estimated 45,000 — were guaranteed that their properties would not be expropriated. However, they were encouraged to sell their land voluntarily to state farms. It is important to note that there was no forced collectivization in Cuba. At present, 15 percent of the land is held by private farmers (Canton Navarro 2000: 258).

One of the central objectives of revolutionary policy was to bridge and ultimately eliminate "the differences between urban and rural living" standards (Glazer 1989: 80). To fulfil this goal, the level and quality of services had to be equalized between the two areas. In order to provide services that had historically been denied in rural areas and also to optimize the use of resources, it was necessary "to concentrate residents in communities that were large enough to make the services viable" (Glazer 1989: 80). Hence, new towns and communities were created in the countryside and were equipped with, for example, schools, clinics and libraries. Residents were given fully-furnished, rent-free homes (Glazer 1989: 80).

From 1959 to 1964, the Cuban government directly built or sponsored 26,000 new homes in rural areas, representing approximately 47 percent of all new dwellings. Before the Revolution, virtually all new housing had been constructed in urban areas, particularly Havana. One hundred and fifty settlements, varying in size from several dozen houses to several hundred, were created. These new housing and community conditions were reflected in a new stability in rural employment. At the end of the fifth year of this first phase of housing construction and community development, 70 percent of agricultural workers had regular salaried positions (Glazer 1989: 80).

Development under colonialism and neo-colonialism — i.e., prior to the Revolution — had generated urban centres where wealth and services were concentrated and rural regions, particularly in the mountainous zones, where the absence of services and poverty reigned. The relationship between town and country was altered as the revolutionary government directly addressed the historical disparity in the allocation of resources. Rural needs were emphasized over urban needs, ensuring that rural areas would have priority in the allocation of material and labour resources. This policy was an integral element in Cuba's efforts to decentralize development by curtailing Havana's economic importance and share of resources. Cubans from rural areas or the east often half-jokingly claim that the rest of the country works to sustain Havana. It is a readily acknowledged fact that two Cubas exist: the more revolutionary countryside, whose development has been priortized, and Havana, which until recently had been relatively neglected.

Furthermore, it was hoped that the allure of migration to Havana would diminish. Mass migration to Havana had been a serious problem of pre-revolutionary Cuba, placing substantial demands on urban services and creating a labour shortage in the countryside (Frank 1993: 79). The revolution's policy was successful in stemming the flow of people into the large cities and in equalizing the quality of housing, health care, educational facilities and social services between urban and rural regions. Indeed, Havana has had the lowest rate of population growth of any Latin American or Caribbean capital. Between 1970 and 1988, Havana's population increased by less than 7 percent (Frank 1993: 79). Cuba has thus avoided the problems that have afflicted so many Third World cities. While Cuba classifies 80 percent of its population of eleven million as urban, it must be borne in mind that over three million of these urban Cubans live in towns that may have fewer than a thousand residents (Frank 1993; 80 and Castro 1996a: 34). These are classified as urban zones by standards applied to the demography of developing countries because they have electricity, schools, water supplies, health clinics, cultural centres and other facilities (Frank 1993: 80, Karol 1970: 351; Stubbs 1989: 138).

Rationing and the ration book — *the libreta* — are a central and misunderstood feature of Cuban life. On March 12, 1962, *Law 1015* was passed, establishing an island-wide rationing system. This was in response to the extreme shortage of food and other products that resulted after the imposition of the U.S. economic blockade. Cuba's economy, as a dependent and underdeveloped extension of the U.S., had relied heavily on imports. Indeed, "imports from foreign markets — especially from the United States — served as an umbilical cord supplying the daily needs of the people, industry, transportation and utility services" (Garcia Luis 2001: 100). Cuba imported 60 percent of its grains, 37 percent of vegetables, 42 percent of cereals, 84 percent of fat, 69 percent of canned meat, 80 percent of canned fruit and 83 percent of cookies and candy (Garcia Luis 2001: 101). The rationing system was thus a necessary response to the "undeclared war to which Cuba was subjected" (Garcia Luis 2001: 101). It was a concrete commitment to the equitable distribution of food and other goods, so that "nobody would be left out; not to allow the law of money and of supply and demand to be imposed, but to ensure justice; and not to allow intolerable inequalities to arise in the heart of society between those with smaller incomes and those with larger ones" (Garcia Luis 2001: 101). The continuance of the rationing system has guaranteed this objective within Cuban society.

OBJECTIVE CONSTRAINTS

The Cuban Revolution has passed through several phases. The period extending from 1959 to the beginning of the 1970s "was characterized by revolutionary experimentation in all areas of social organization, including comprehensive government management and control of production and distribution" (Michalowski 1997; see also Salas 1983: 47). The fundamental objective was the elimination of the old social order and the establishment of new arrangements both internally and externally. Fidel Castro described this phase as one of "iconoclasm," which necessitated that Cubans "destroy the system, destroy its laws, destroy everything" (quoted in Salas 1983: 44). However, this destruction of the old order was paralleled by the prodigious construction of a new society. The most notable instances of this experimentation involved the practice of mass democracy, the refurbishing of existing popular organizations and the creation of new ones, and a thorough renovation of the justice system.

While the existing system was not eliminated, it was bypassed as new forms and institutions were created. The new peoples' courts *(tribunales de base)* "emphasized informal procedures, and utilized ordinary citizens as lay prosecutors, lay advocates, and lay judges rather than filling these positions with formally-trained jurists" (Michalowski 1997; see also Baerg 1993: 249–50; D'Zurrilla 1981: 1275–76).

The 1960s was a period of almost boundless revolutionary enthusiasm, in which formal structures and methods were eschewed in favour of revolutionary spontaneity. The revolutionary government openly challenged the legacy of underdevelopment and dependent capitalist development by pursuing a program of rapid industrialization (Huberman and Sweezy 1960; Karol 1970; Seers 1964). Since this dependency was symbolized by sugar, the overriding goal was to free the country of its historical dependence on sugar. However, the limitations of this economic strategy became readily apparent (Blanco 1997: 19; Karol 1970: 226). Revolutionary idealism clashed against economic realities. The belief that anything could be accomplished once the social order was transformed — often critiqued as voluntarism[1] — was overtaken by the objective constraints imposed by Cuba's limited economic resources.

As experience accumulated, many argued that the attempt to rapidly industrialize had ignored the basic economic reality of Cuba. The island did not have the necessary capital, infrastructure, skilled labour, raw materials or technology to jump from being a primary producer to an industrialized country. Moreover, extensive healthcare and education systems were being established, and these were deemed to be of more importance to the national development project. In short, Cuba could not by sheer force of will alone skip stages in economic development. It would have to first create the material conditions necessary for such a transition. The Cuban experience reflects the ongoing debate about the relationship between national material conditions and the possible developmental trajectories available, especially *vis-à-vis* the construction of socialism in countries that are predominantly based on agricultural productive and social relations (Castro 1996a: 74–79; Karol 1970: 367–69).

Thus, as the 1960s drew to a close, the overall development strategy was modified. The aim of breaking structural underdevelopment and dependence within the world economy was now viewed as a much more nuanced, difficult and long-term goal. The focus was no longer on abandoning sugar but on using it as the source of earnings to finance the eventual transition to an industrial model. Indeed, sugar was the only Cuban export capable of substantial foreign exchange earnings. Hence, emphasis was put on expanding, modernizing and mechanizing the sugar sector. Out of this renewed emphasis came the objective in 1970 of achieving a ten-million-ton harvest. However, although a record 8.5-million-ton *zafra* (sugar harvest) was achieved, it resulted in a severe dislocation of the economy. For outside observers and critics of the Revolution, this setback was viewed as a failure, an example of socialist ineptitude. In Cuba it constituted a valuable learning experience.

The revolutionary leadership came to the conclusion that Cuban society could no longer operate on the basis of the existing framework. Consequently, there was a re-thinking of economic strategy and the process of decision-making. Thus, while the 1960s had been the time of "taking heaven by storm," the 1970s were characterized by the institutionalization of the new economic, social and political order (Blanco 1997: 22; Michalowski 1997). The goal was now to establish stable regulatory forms and the formal institutional setting for popular input into national decision-making. This included the passage of a the new Cuban Constitution and the reorganization of the political system, administrative structures and the legal system in order to create a structure "more suited to the ideology and practice of a socialist political economy" (Michalowski 1997; see also Evenson 1994: 13–14; August 1999: 202; Fitzgerald 1994: 56–95; Fuller 1992: 172–91; Mesa-Lago 1974; Reckford 1971: 103; Roman 1999: 68–71). The institutionalization of the Revolution was formally marked in 1976 with the establishment of the National Assembly of Peoples' Power and ratification through popular referendum of the new Constitution.

Also Cuba developed much closer economic relations with the Soviet Union and the Eastern Bloc, leading to what was later viewed as an "unnecessary overdependence" (Blanco 1997: 22). Moreover, the economic direction pursued in the 1970s moved away from the previous revolutionary goals of immediately creating a new socialist society to one in which the island was viewed as first being required to transverse several intermediary stages. Cuba implemented "an economic liberalization program based on market mechanisms, material incentives, financial accountability, private consumer markets, and greater managerial/ministerial autonomy within the overall pattern of central planning" (Petras and Morley 1992: 96). In the mid-1980s, a campaign of "rectification" was instituted to eliminate problems that had emerged from the mechanical copying and implementation of the models and policies from the U.S.S.R. and other Eastern European countries. Central to rectification was a revitalization of the political process, which had become increasingly bureaucratized (Blanco 1997: 22–26; Fitzgerald 1994: 153–69; White 1987). Also, various capitalist tendencies and practices had emerged: e.g., markets where "middle men" were able to accumulate considerable wealth at the expense of the rest of the population and the rise of an individualistic ethos that led to widespread inefficiency, pilfering and waste of resources. The new policies combated the rise of "privileged managers, party functionaries and globe-trotting technocrats on expense accounts and with access to hard currency" (Petras and Morley 1992: 96). This was epitomized by the case of General Arnaldo Ochoa and his cohorts, who in July 1989 were tried, found guilty and eventually executed for a series of illicit activities, particularly drug trafficking (Editorial José Martí 1989; Petras and Morley 1992: 97). While the process of rectification was forestalled by the economic crisis that ensued in the wake of the collapse of the Soviet Union and the Eastern Bloc ten years later, the achievements of the campaign provided the "resilience to face the problems that the 1990s were bringing to the embattled island" (Azicri 2000: 68).

THE ECONOMIC CRASH

It is difficult to truly comprehend the depths of the Cuban economic contraction of the early 1990s. In order to understand what unfolded in Cuba, it is essential to grasp the material limitations that stemmed from the disintegration of the Soviet Union and the collapse of the Eastern Bloc. As Cuba was intimately tied into the Council of Mutual Economic Assistance (CMEA) — the economic union of the Soviet Union, Eastern European countries and Mongolia — the island's economy went into a precipitous decline when it disappeared.

In October 1961, the United States imposed a trade embargo on Cuba, terminating an economic relationship in which that country was Cuba's major investor, trading partner and market for sugar. In the wake of this rupture, the Soviet Bloc became Cuba's major trading partner. The CMEA was a vital contributor to Cuba through investments and the provision of resources and technology for general development and substantial projects. This economic integration resulted in stable markets and the specialization of production. Eighty-five percent of Cuba's trade — 81 percent of exports and 88 percent of imports — was with the CMEA. Over 95 percent of Cuba's oil was imported from the Soviet Union. The main markets for sugar and citrus fruit were the U.S.S.R. and the Eastern European countries (Franklin 1997: 274; Pérez Villanueva 1997: 1). As trading relations were based on preferential rates that took into consideration Cuba's status as a lesser-developed country, the relationship under the CMEA framework promoted a relatively stable and mutually advantageous commercial intercourse. From 1971 to 1989 the economy grew at an average annual rate of 6 percent (Azicri 2000: 30–31). The Latin American growth rate for the same period was 3.6 percent (Polanyi Levitt 2000). During the 1980s, Cuba had a "qualitatively higher level of industrial development than elsewhere in the Caribbean" (Thomas 1988: 89). Indeed, during this period, compared to the rest of the region, Cuba's economic performance was "an island of sanity and stability" (Petras and Morley 1992: 95). In contrast to other developing nations whose main interactions were with the West, Cuba's relationship with the CMEA afforded Cuba "considerably more control over national economic development and more effective autonomy" (Rous Manitas 1983: 153). Hence, "whatever may have been the intrinsic motives of the Soviet Union, the structure and style of their assistance in the Cuban case helped rather than hindered the national trajectory of revolution" (Rous Manitas 1983: 153). Thus, while Cuba became dependent on the Soviet Union, this dependency was qualitatively different than the relationships other developing countries — particularly in Latin America and the Caribbean — had with the West. Nevertheless, this extensive connection with the Soviet Bloc left Cuba in an extremely vulnerable situation.

Consequently, the demise of the CMEA had a devastating impact on Cuba. The island lost its principal trading partners and sources of investment. By 1992, trade with the Eastern Bloc had declined to 7 percent of its 1989 value (Gunn 1993: 28). It is estimated that the dissolution of the CMEA cost Cuba a minimum of $10 billion U.S. (Martinez 1998). For the second time in less than forty years, Cuba faced a major rupture in economic relations. On September 28, 1990, when CMEA members failed to fulfil their trading agreements, President Fidel Castro declared that Cuba had entered "a special period during peacetime" (Franklin 1997: 271). The term referred to the scarcities caused by the collapse of the CMEA, scarcities on a magnitude similar to the levels that would be generated by a naval blockade were the nation at war. A spectacular economic crash ensued. In 1997, the United Nations Economic Commission on Latin America and the Caribbean (ECLAC) concluded that this "interruption of commercial relations with the CMEA countries constituted a loss of markets more severe than that brought about by the Great Depression" (ECLAC/ECF 1997: 34).

From 1989 to 1993, Cuba's Gross Domestic Product (GDP) declined by 35–40 percent (Martinez 1998; Canton Navarro 2000: 258; Smith

1996: 3; Susman 1998: 187). Per capita income dropped by 39 percent. From 1989 to 1992, oil imports from the former Soviet Union fell more than 85 percent: from 13.3 million tons in 1989 to less than two million tons in 1992 (Erisman 2000: 114; Martinez 1998: 1; Mesa-Lago 1993: 163). At the height of the economic crisis, because of the severe limitations on Cuba's purchasing capacity, the island could only import six million tons of oil (Castro 1998: 10). The island lost not only a supply of fuel but also an important source of foreign exchange, which had been obtained through petroleum re-export (Susman 1998: 186). Import capacity declined by over 75 percent from 1989 to 1992. In 1989, Cuba was able to import $8.1 billion U.S. worth of goods. In 1992, the island was capable of only importing $2.2 billion U.S. (Castro 1998b: 6; Susman 1998: 187). By 1993, import capacity further declined to $1.7 billion U.S. (Franklin 1997: 318). Grain imports declined by more than 50 percent, while fertilizer and pesticide imports dropped by 80 percent (Rosset 1997: 160). As a consequence, the budget deficit began to spiral out of control, amounting in 1993 to 33.5 percent of GDP (Castro 1998b: 42; Martinez 1998: 3).

This astounding contraction almost completely paralyzed the country's economy. The unavailability of oil directly affected the electricity supply, leading to frequent "*apagones*," or blackouts, that lasted several hours each day. Rationing of electricity was instituted in order to preserve and optimize energy supplies. Each neighbourhood was told when the power outages would occur, thus allowing the populace to make preparations. At the height of the crisis, the disruptions in service sometimes lasted for eighteen hours a day, seven days a week (Hernández 1997: 36; Garcia Bielsa 1997; Ross Leal 1997). The oil shortage forced the closure of over 60 percent of the factories, leaving the rest to operate at levels considerably below capacity (Castro 1998b: 7; Garcia Bielsa 1997; Ross Leal 1997). The forced closure or reduced activity of many enterprises, factories and other production and service centres left more than 100,000 people unemployed (Lage 1996: 53; Canton Navarro 2000: 258).

The dramatic fuel shortages, coupled with the inability to obtain fertilizer, animal feed and spare parts for machinery purchased in the CMEA, decimated agricultural production. The impact on the production of sugar, the largest export earner, was dramatic. In 1995, the sugar harvest was reduced to 3.3 million tons — the lowest in fifty years (Franklin 1997: 370; Ross Leal 1997). It further declined to 3.2 million tons in 1998 (Frank 2001b). Food production, especially of milk and eggs, was severely affected (Susman 1998: 189; Garcia Bielsa 1997). During the early 1990s, the average daily caloric and protein intake by the Cuban people may have been much as 30 percent below levels in the 1980s (Rosset 1997: 159). In 1992–93 there was an epidemic of optic neuropathy, which was directly attributable to a decline in nutrition. An estimated 50,000 persons suffered visual loss and associated sensory problems. Emergency imports of vitamin supplements alleviated the epidemic and facilitated the recovery of the victims (Eisenberg 1997; Roman 1995: 122, 530–33). Pregnant women were afflicted with anaemia, and birth weights began to decline.

Hence, all areas of Cuban society felt — and still feel — the drastic impact of the crash. In hospitals and various community healthcare clinics there were serious shortages of medical supplies. In 1998, it was estimated that there was a shortage of more than three hundred medicines, vaccines, surgical materials and spare parts for hospital equipment (Mesa-Lago 1998). The education system was plagued by a lack of textbooks, pens, pencils and notebooks. The cultural sphere also faced significant limitations. Television programs, the theatre, newspapers, magazines and other publications were curtailed. The extensive public transportation system was crippled. In Havana, the number of daily bus trips was reduced from over 50,000 to fewer than 7,000 (Susman 1998: 189; Garcia Bielsa 1997). As public transport was scaled back and petrol supplies diminished, one third of the city's population resorted to riding bicycles. Clothing, shoes and other personal amenities were in short supply (Hernández 1997: 36). The extreme shortage in cement, other raw materials and tools had a drastic impact on building construction. The construction industry was forced to reduce the amount of cement used to make reinforced concrete from 700 kilograms of cement per cubic metre of reinforced concrete to 304 kilograms per cubic metre (Castro 1998b: 29). Thus, housing construction came to a standstill. President Castro declared:

> If in five years we don't build housing, if that's the price for saving the Revolution, then we'll spend five years without building them. (quoted in Eckstein 1994: 99)

In short, the entire range of cultural, recreational, public and personal affairs and activities was circumscribed.

The crisis was compounded by adverse developments in the world economy during the first half of the nineties. The continuing decline of commodity prices, especially sugar and nickel, reduced the income from exports. Rising import prices, high interest rates and limitations imposed by Cuba's external debt further exacerbated the situation (Susman 1998:

186; Garcia Bielsa 1997). The fuel crisis was made worse by climbing oil prices. Unfavourable weather conditions — particularly Hurricane Georges and drier-than-usual growing seasons — contributed to the problems that beset agriculture and other sectors of the economy. The storm destroyed a significant portion of the crops in the agricultural belt that surrounds Havana and severely damaged several hotels (Blanco 1997: 35).

Another critical factor was the intensification of U.S. economic aggression. Washington stepped up its economic pressure, most notably by passage of the *Cuba Democracy Act* of 1992 (commonly referred to as the Torricelli Act) and the *Cuban Liberty and Democratic Solidarity (Libertad) Act* (the so-called Helms–Burton Bill) in 1996 (Alarcón 1997; Suarez Salazar 1991: 183–200). The legislation was fashioned as a *coup de grace*, aimed at asphyxiating Cuba's remaining sources of capital, commercial opportunities and trading links (Krinsky and Golove 1993; Murray 1993; Prada 1995; Schwab 1999; Sweig and Bird 1997; Whitney et al. 1996). It is estimated that the U.S. economic blockade of Cuba has cost the country in excess of $60 billion U.S. (Martinez 1998). One study estimated that a simple relaxation of some strictures of the economic blockade would result in such a significant increase in Cuba's import capacity that national income would rise by one quarter (Pastor Jr. and Zimablist 1998: 15).

THE ECONOMIC MEASURES OF THE SPECIAL PERIOD

Central to the initiation of a period of economic recovery and expansion was (is) the implementation of measures aimed at internal economic reorganization and the insertion of Cuba into the world economy. These measures, by promoting economic growth and efficiency, were designed primarily to protect and preserve the social gains and achievements of the Revolution — enshrined in Article 8 and Chapter VI of the Constitution of Cuba as the fundamental rights of citizens — principally employment, health care, education and social security programs. As a consequence of these rights, Cuba compares favourably with the industrialized world in many social indicators. And further, despite the precipitous economic decline of the early 1990s, no "shock" market policies have been applied. Accordingly, the Cuban government refused:

> to copy the models of deregulation, contraction of the state, privatization, reduction of social programs and adoption of the neoliberal practices tested in Eastern Europe, Latin America and many other parts of the world.... The country refused to imitate the so-called "transition" advocated by promoters of the free

market and imposed without mercy on the countries of the former socialist bloc. (Fernández de Cossío 2001: 4)

Cuba was faced with the unavoidable necessity of reinserting itself into the capitalist world economy. The island had to adjust to operating within a system of international economic relations that were based on very different principles and practices than the ones — after thirty-five years of structural integration into the CMEA — upon which it had relied and based its economy. Virtually overnight, Cuba lost its markets, source of credit and security of prices. In the search for new markets and sources of capital, the island was faced with the imperative of reorganizing its economy. This necessitated a reorientation of the development strategy and resulted in a series of measures which were implemented to reactivate the economy:

1) *The rationalization of production centred around the more efficient use of existing and available resources*: This often meant the reintroduction of old technologies and manual techniques (e.g., the use of oxen in farming). State subsidies were reduced by 70 percent, with state spending in general being substantially reduced. The strengthening of the existing regime of import substitution complemented this policy (Martinez 1998; Canton Navarro 2000: 258; Susman 1998: 191).

2) *The establishment of self-employment and small private enterprise*: In 1993, legislation was passed authorizing self-employment in over a hundred occupations, which were mostly service oriented enterprises, such as restaurants and bicycle, refrigerator and television repair shops. The size of the self-employed sector has varied from year to year. However, as the economy recovers, the number of the self-employed has dropped: from a high of 205,000 in 1996 to 160,000 in 1998 (Lage 1996: 57; Martinez 1998; Canton Navarro 2000: 259).

3) *Legalization of the possession of foreign currency, specifically U.S. dollars, in order to tap into domestic supply, and stabilize and increase the purchasing value of the Cuban peso*: In the midst of the crisis, as production and distribution declined precipitously, the underground economy thrived. Indeed, it became the indispensable source of many products and services. The currency of use was the U.S. dollar, purchasable only in the underground economy at a price, in 1993, of 150 pesos for one U.S. dollar. This had a devastating impact on the livelihood of the vast majority of Cubans, who

earned an average monthly income in the early 1990s of just under 200 pesos. The buying power of the peso was increasingly circumscribed as only the basic necessities could be purchased with it, and, as domestic production and the national economy continued to decline, even these were scarce. The objective of legalizing foreign currency possession was to increase the circulation of hard currency in the country. This resulted in more people having access to U.S. dollars and allowed the state to tap directly into this domestic source of foreign exchange. This policy, together with increased production and control of the peso supply, resulted in a dramatic drop in the peso–dollar exchange rate. Indeed, the value of the peso appreciated more than seven-fold, with the exchange rate stabilizing for several years at 20 pesos to 1 U.S. dollar (Castro 1996a: 83–84, Lage 1996: 51; Martinez 1998). At present, as a direct consequence of the downturn of the world economy — particularly the travel industry in 2001 — the exchange rate is now 26 to 1.

4) *The institution of a pricing policy and other measures in order to reduce the budget deficit and the amount of money in circulation*: Among the other measures implemented were the elimination of certain free services and the creation of taxes, which had been abolished in the early years of the Revolution. The taxes are not on wages, but only on profits and investment income. These measures in total had a profound effect on the country's internal finances. From 1994 to 1998, over 2.5 billion pesos were taken out of circulation, and the budget deficit was reduced from 33.5 percent of GDP to 2 percent. This truncation of the peso supply was a major factor in the rise of the peso's value (Castro 1998b: 42; Lage 1996: 56–57; Hernández 1997: 37; Martinez 1998).

5) *The transformation of the landholding structure*: In what can be described as a third agrarian reform, state farms were replaced by cooperatives and private farmers' markets were opened in order to stimulate food produc-tion. Former state farms became Basic Units of Cooperative Production (UBPCs), with those already working the land obtaining *usufruct* rights. The UBPCs sell a specific quota to the state and keep or sell the rest in the private farmers' markets. At present, state farms account for only one-third of agricultural land. Forty-two percent of the land is represented by UBPCs, 10 percent by other forms of cooperatives and 15 percent by private farmers. This contrasts sharply with the pre-Special Period, when 75 percent of the land was held by the state (Castro 1998b: 49; Hernández 1997: 36; Lage 1996: 48; Martinez 1998; Canton Navarro 2000: 258). The

Cuban government estimates that under these changes, 316,000 hectares have been handed over to farmers, who now hold 25 percent of the cultivatable land. At present, the National Association of Small Farmers (ANAP) has a membership in excess of 300,000, with 57,000 having joined the association since these changes to landholding structure (Pages 2003). Levels of food production, particularly of vegetables, have increased considerably (Sinclair and Thompson 2000). Additionally, urban gardening and organic farming methods have been encouraged and widely employed (Wald 1999a). The UBPCs now account for the production of 53 percent of root vegetables; 56 percent of fresh vegetables; 90 percent of tobacco; 75 percent of corn; 76 percent of beans; 73 percent of fruits; 73 percent of coconuts; 58 percent of coffee; 63 percent of cocoa; 61 percent of honey and 18 percent of sugar (Pages 2003).

6) *The reorganization and simplification of the state apparatus*: Greater autonomy was given to state companies and the decentralization of administration expanded. This involved granting wider jurisdictions and greater powers of decision-making. State enterprises were allowed to operate in foreign currency as a move toward becoming self-financing. The number of government ministries was reduced from fifty-five in 1993 to thirty-three in 1998. The planning system is being transformed from a material production basis to a financial basis. Now, costs of production must be considered by each enterprise, part of the drive to promote greater efficiency in the entire state economy (Hernández 1997: 38; Lage 1996: 48; Martinez 1998; Canton Navarro 2000: 260). As part of this policy, the armed forces implemented its own programs of self-sufficiency, engaging in, for example, the production of food. Both the Cuban armed forces and the overall military budget were considerably reduced.

7) *The large-scale development of tourism*: As the island faced a foreign exchange crunch, the expansion of tourism was accelerated, with impressive results. The earnings from tourism in 1996 were 50 percent greater than in 1995. In that year, for the first time, tourism surpassed sugar as Cuba's major revenue generator, earning $1.38 billion U.S. In 1996, an additional $300 million U.S. was invested in the tourist industry (*Cuba Business* 1997: 2; Susman 1998: 197). In 1998, 1.14 million tourists visited, bringing in over $1.5 billion U.S. (Martinez 1998). In 1999, $2 billion U.S. was generated. In both 2000 and 2001, nearly two million tourists visited Cuba (Azicri 2000: 157). The sector has achieved an annual average growth rate of 15–20 percent. The Ministry of Tourism states that the profit margin

that accrues to the state is 20 percent. In many ways, the tourism sector has become the motor of the economy, significantly contributing to the growth of light industry and artisan markets. It is estimated that 60 percent of the inputs are domestic (*Cuba Business* 2001a: 1).

8) *The promotion and pursuit of foreign investment2 for virtually all sectors of the economy*: Foreign investment was sought in a variety of sectors, with the exceptions of healthcare, education and defence. This process is controlled by the state and directed to areas of the economy where it is calculated that foreign investment will not compromise Cuba's independence, sovereignty or the future exploitation of its main resources. Significant investments have occurred in tourism, petroleum, nickel, telecommunications, biotechnology and other manufacturing industries. Foreign investment now plays a significant role in the Cuban economy, accounting for 3 percent of Cuba's GDP in 1998 (Lage 1996: 46). At present, 397 joint ventures exist with international capital (Radio Havana Cuba 2001c). In 1999, there were 36 promotion and protection agreements with 36 countries (Alvarez 1999). As of 2001, the countries with the largest number of joint ventures are Spain, with 99, Canada, with 74 and Italy, with 57. Another hundred projects are being studied (Radio Havana Cuba 2001c). Since the opening to Western capital investment, at least $5.5 billion U.S. has been pledged, with an estimated $3 billion U.S. already invested. The average annual investment from 1996 to 2001 was estimated at $288 million U.S. (*Latin American Monitor: Caribbean* 2002: 5). It is striking that Cuba was able to achieve this level despite the Torricelli Act and the Helms–Burton Bill, which were designed to paralyze and reverse the process of foreign investment. Indeed, more than 40 percent of new foreign investment occurred after the March 1996 passage of the Helms–Burton Bill (Alvarez 1999). However, the Bush administration has since intensified the economic pressures, creating a very significant impact on foreign investment. In 2001, it declined to $38.9 million U.S., down from $488 million U.S. in 2000 (*Latin American Monitor: Caribbean* 2002: 5).

THE ECONOMIC RECOVERY

The economic measures were successful not only in halting the economic decline but also in initiating a period of sustained growth. The GDP began to rise in 1994, with an increase of 0.7 percent. It grew by 2.5 percent in 1995; 7.8 percent in 1996; 2.5 percent in 1997; 1.2 percent in 1998, 4.2 percent in 1999 and 5.6 percent in 2000.[3] The noticeable drop in 1998 was due to a combination of factors: a low sugar harvest (just over 3 million

tons), a decline in world market nickel prices and bad weather —
particularly, the impact of Hurricane Georges and a prolonged drought in
the eastern part of the country, which affected agricultural production
(*Cuba Business* 1998b: 1; Martinez 1998). Thus, from 1995 to 2000, the
Cuban GDP grew at a rate slightly higher than 4.7 percent. Comparatively,
the overall growth for Latin America in the 1990s was around 3 percent
(Polanyi Levitt 2000; Veltmeyer 2001). Also, as previously noted, the
budget deficit was reduced and remained at around 3 percent of GDP, with
the Cuban peso, which had been verging on worthlessness, significantly
rebounding in value.

Imports and exports have steadily increased. For example, in 1996,
imports increased to $3.2 billion U.S., a 54-percent increase over 1995
(*Cuba Business* 1998b: 4). For the first nine months of 2001, international
trade increased by 12 percent in comparison to 1999 and 5 percent over
2000. The figures for January–September 2001 show a 3-percent and 9-
percent increase in imports and exports, respectively (*Cuba Business*
2001b: 8). While export levels did not match the recovery in import
capacity, there was continued growth. Notably, foreign trade has become
remarkably diversified. At present, Cuba has trading relationships with
166 countries (*Cuba Business* 2001b: 8). Forty-four percent of trade is with
Europe; 39 percent with the Americas; 15 percent with Asia and 1 percent
with Africa and Oceania (2001b: 8). Also, the source of income has been
restructured in terms of the ratio of goods to services. Before the Special
Period, goods accounted for 88 percent of the source of income and
services 11 percent (Martinez 1998). In 1999, goods and services were
equally balanced as sources for earning income with tourism accounting
for the bulk of services (Martinez 1998).

Labour productivity increased by 19 percent in the Special Period,
accounting for approximately 75 percent of economic growth (Castro
2001c). Present production levels in, among other things, manufacturing,
electrical power, vegetable crops, citrus fruits, pharmaceuticals and cigars
equal or exceed those achieved in 1989. Significant increases occurred in
the production of nickel, tobacco, cement, steel, fertilizers and fish, and
in oil extraction and refining. Nickel production, for example, now
exceeds pre-Special Period levels and represents Cuba's largest export
earner. It grew by 31 percent in 1996 and by 14.7 percent in 1997
(Hernández 1997: 34; Oramas 1998). In 2002, for the second consecutive
year, nickel production exceeded 75,000 tons, representing export earnings of $400 million U.S. (*Granma International* 2003b).

Cuba, like most countries, must import most of its petroleum to meet its fuel and energy needs. The island requires a minimum of 100,000 barrels of oil, with a usual requirement of approximately 150,000 barrels. This results a considerable expenditure of foreign exchange. In the first two months of 2000, for example, the rising price of oil necessitated an additional expenditure of $38 million U.S., prompting a nation-wide campaign of additional fuel-saving measures (*Cuba Business* 2001a: 1). Consequently, the Cuban government has channelled considerable investment into domestic oil production. Oil extraction has consistently increased, rising from 500,000 tons in 1989 to 3.4 million tons in 2001, a significant 7.5 percent increase over 2000 levels. Natural gas production has also risen. In 2001, 584 million cubic meters of natural gas were produced, a 2.5 percent increase over the previous year (Radio Havana Cuba 2001a). In 2002, oil and gas production reached the record level of 4.1 million tons; a 20 percent improvement on 2001 figures. Production in 2003 is projected to be more than 3.5 million tons of oil and 600,000 tons of natural gas (Frank 2002a).

However, due into its high sulphur content, Cuban oil has limited uses. Crucially, it is unsuitable for refining into petrol. Thus, even though Cuba produces the equivalent of 80,000 barrels per day, it still has to import 65 percent of its oil needs, necessitating a yearly expenditure of $1 billion U.S. (Frank 2002a). Nevertheless, as electrical plants have been modified to burn Cuban oil, it has played an increasing role in electricity production. Indeed, at the beginning of the second half of 2003, all of the island's electricity was being generated by Cuban oil (Garcia 2003). The Cuban government estimates that each ton of domestic oil and natural gas utilized in electrical power generation and other industries creates a saving of 60 percent of the costs in foreign exchange currency of importing the equivalent amount of oil (Castro 2001c).

Since 1991, the government has invested more than $1 billion U.S. in the energy sector, especially in the construction of new power plants that use natural gas and in the refurbishing of old plants to burn Cuban oil (*Granma International* 2002c). By 2005, the government hopes to meet 60 percent of Cuba's energy requirements through domestic production. A joint venture between Sherrit International, Pebecan (both Canadian companies) and Cubapetroleo (the Cuban state company) accounts for 60 percent of the oil and gas output (Frank 2002b). As the economy recovered and local oil and gas production rose, the interminable power outages receded and in some places disappeared altogether. Many factories that had ceased production began working again, some at full capacity (Castro 1998b: 37; Lage 1996: 39; Martinez 1998; Canton Navarro 2000: 259).

Cuba has also had impressive results in biotechnology. More than $1 billion U.S. was invested in the sector in the 1990s, and there are "38 biotech research centers, grouped together in a science park to the west of Havana, which integrate R&D, production and marketing" (Aitsisselmi 2002: 38). This has resulted in more than four hundred patents, with exports to over twenty countries and the World Health Organization (Aitsisselmi 2002: 38). A major impetus for developing biotechnology was the U.S. embargo, which compelled the island to initiate a regime of "import substitution and domestic production of drugs, encompassing 422 pharmaceuticals at a cost of $75 million" (Aitsisselmi 2002: 38). Important achievements have occurred in areas such as genetic engineering; the production of vaccines, monoclonal antibodies and immunochemicals; prenatal congenital and hereditary diseases; microbiology and tropical medicine; and neurophysiology. Among the key developments have been a vaccine for meningitis B and an effective drug — PPG (polycosanol) — for the reduction of cholesterol and low-density lipoprotein (Bravo 1998). An AIDS vaccine has also been developed (*Cuba Business* 2001c: 11). The Cuban Centre for Immunology has developed a product for treating different types of epithelial cancer (Radio Havana 2003). For these and other products, marketing agreements have been made with international pharmaceutical companies (Blackburn 2000: 19).

As noted, sugar has played a central role in the Cuban economy. Until it was surpassed by tourism, the export of sugar accounted for the bulk of Cuba's foreign exchange earnings. Thus, the recovery of sugar production and the revitalization of the industry has been a major focus. The sugar sector has begun a recovery from its nadir of the early 1990s, growing by 24.3 percent in 1999 and by 18 percent in the first six months of 2000 (Frank 2001c). However, despite this modest recovery, a dramatic restructuring of the sugar industry was initiated in 2002, in response to continuing and rising unprofitably, a result of the very low prices that sugar commands on the world market, prices well below the costs of production, and competition from European-produced sugar. The price of sugar fell from 8.5 cents per pound in January of 1999 to 5.99 cents in the first quarter of 2000 and rose slightly to 6.5 cents in the last quarter of 2001 (Castro 2001c). In 1999, the value of exports declined by 4 percent because of the drop in the price of sugar. Seventy-one of 156 mills were closed, resulting in the loss of more than 100,000 jobs in the sugar sector. The restructuring calls for greater efficiency and diversification, coupled with a plan to employ biotechnology to create a fructose- as opposed to sucrose-producing sugarcane. The displaced workers have received no salary cut and either have taken up new employment, are retraining or are returning to school. A portion of the land no longer devoted to sugarcane is now being used for food production and the raising of livestock (*Granma International* 2002d).

Also, as noted, tourism has had impressive growth, with an eight-fold increase in gross income between 1990 and 2000. Cuba's tourism industry is the fastest-growing in the world, averaging a growth rate of 20 percent in the 1990s. It now accounts for 8 percent of the Cuban GDP (*The Economist* 2002a: 36–37). In 1990, gross income amounted to $243 million U.S.; in 1999 it was $1.95 billion U.S. (*Prensa Latina* 2001). The role of the hospitality industry in generating funds for the country's balance of payments went from 4.1 percent to 43 percent over the same period. Moreover, domestic inputs into the tourism sector rose from 12 percent to 61 percent (*Prensa Latina* 2001). There has been a fivefold increase in the number of tourists since 1995. The main factor underlying this growth is the tripling of the number of hotel rooms and the doubling of the number of workers in the sector. The number of rooms grew from 12,900 in 1990 to 35,300 in 2000 (*Prensa Latina* 2001). Eighty-nine percent of available rooms are wholly owned by the state, with 11 percent held in fifty/fifty partnerships with foreign companies. In 2001, fifteen management groups from six countries ran fifty-three hotels containing a total of 16,463 rooms (*Prensa Latina* 2001).

Food production has rebounded. Basic foodstuffs that were once in critically short supply are now readily available. In 1998, urban farms produced 3,650 tons of meat, 7.5 million eggs and 30,000 tons of fruits (Wald 1999a). Root crop production increased 14 percent from 1994 to 1999. Also, over the same period, vegetable production increased an astounding 246 percent, citrus fruit 50 percent and beef 15 percent (Hernández 2002: 23). Moreover, there was a substantial drop in the price of food. Prices in the private farmers' markets decreased by 84 percent. For example, the price of beans — a Cuban staple — dropped from 60 pesos per pound in 1994 to around 10 pesos per pound in 1997. The price of a pound of rice dropped from 50 to less than 5 pesos (author's notes; Smith 1996: 3). A crucial factor in the decline of prices in the private farmers' markets has been the existence of the state-run farmers' markets, which charge lower average prices and thus generate a downward pressure on prices overall (Castro 2001c). As production has increased, the supply of agricultural goods to state markets has risen. Consequently, food consumption has improved across the island. The average daily per capita caloric intake improved from 1,948 calories in the early 1990s to 2,400 in

1999. In 2000, it rose to 2,578, with protein consumption rising from 47.7 grams to 68.3 grams (Castro 2001c).

Housing construction went from 22,000 per annum in the early 1990s to 40,000 in 1995, 43,000 in 2000, and an estimated 47,000 in 2001. Thus, from 1995 to 2000, an estimated 320,000 homes were built, providing housing for more than 1.2 million people (Castro 2001c; Castro 1998: 37; Lage 1996: 39; Martinez 1998; Canton Navarro 2000: 165). However, housing continues to be a major and chronic concern.

In 1996 alone, 53,000 new jobs were created; in 1999, there were 87,000. Since 1995, 712,000 jobs have been created, with 50 percent in agriculture, education, public health, sugar, agri-business, community services and gastronomy. In 2002, of the over 150,000 jobs created, more than 90 percent were in the agriculture and social services sectors. Of these new jobs, 45 percent went to women and 66 percent to youth (*Granma International* 2002a). Thus, the unemployment rate has declined, dropping from 6 percent in 1998 to 5.4 percent in 2000 (Lage 1996: 53; Martinez 1998; Canton Navarro 2000: 259). It fell to 4.1 percent in 2001 and then to 3.3 percent in 2002 (Snow 2002; Castro 2001a; *Granma International* 2002a; author's notes). For comparison purposes, the Latin American unemployment rate for 2000 was 9.3 percent, with Brazil and Argentina averaging between 15–18 percent (Petras and Veltmeyer 2001: 51). In the European Union in 2000, the rate was 8.6 percent, in the United States, 6.0 percent, and in Japan, 5.4 percent (*Cuba Business* 2001e: 7).

Significantly, the Cuban average monthly wage grew from 182 pesos in 1996 to 223 pesos in 1999 to 249 pesos in 2001 (*Cuba Business* 2001e: 7). When monetary incentives and other forms of payment-in-kind are considered, the average monthly income is expected to rise to 373 pesos in 2002. In the state sector, 82 percent of workers, a total of 1,091,200 persons, received salary increases (Castro 2001c). The increase in the purchasing capacity of the peso has led to a gradual recovery in real wages. The demand and value of the peso was — and is — maintained. Some items can only be purchased with pesos. Also, interest rates on peso bank accounts are 50 percent higher than interest rates for accounts in U.S. dollars (Castro 2002d; author's notes). The increase in the value of Cuban wages may be contrasted with Latin America as a whole, where real wages fell 15–25 percent over the same period (CEPAL 1996: 7).

It must be emphasized that Cuba has achieved its economic recovery without access to preferential loans "from any country, financial institution or bank in the world during this period" (Fernández de Cossío 2001: 5). Cuba is unable to receive long-term loans and can only borrow on the short and medium terms. Thus, it is forced to borrow at interest rates of 15–20 percent (Fernández de Cossío 2001: 5).

THE SOCIAL SPHERE

While the economic crisis of the 1990s forced Cuba to implement a stabilization program involving the incorporation of market mechanisms, these policies contrast sharply with the International Monetary Fund (IMF) policies that have been foisted on the South. As previously noted, no "shock" therapy has been imposed (Schuyler 2000; Veltmeyer 1999: 57–60). Despite the precipitous economic decline, funding for health, education, social security and sports increased (Martinez 1998). Indeed, 65 percent of the 2002 budget was allocated to healthcare, education and social security (Radio Havana Cuba 2001b). Moreover, both education and heathcare continue to be free, rights which are enshrined in the Cuban Constitution (*Constitution of the Republic of Cuba* 1993). Poignantly, not a single school, hospital, polyclinic or daycare centre was closed (Blanco 1997: 47–48; Canton Navarro 2000: 258). Consequently, Cuba has not only been able to sustain its social indicators but attain considerable improvement.

Notwithstanding the economic crisis of the 1990s, by 1996, Cuba had begun to overcome the deterioration of the public health system (Dotres 1996). The government maintained high levels of investment in the area, allocating in 2001 9.1 percent of its GDP to healthcare, a ratio equivalent to Canadian levels (IBRD 2001). One of the most remarkable results of this targeted investment is that the island has graduated an estimated 67,500 medical doctors and has the highest ratio of doctors in the world, at more than five doctors per thousand people (Castro 2001e: 101; Martinez Puentes 2003: 410). The coverage is nearly universal, with almost 99 percent of the population covered by the healthcare system (Green 1998: 157; Martinez Punetes 2003: 361). The Cuban life expectancy — bordering 75 years — is among the highest in the Third World. The World Health Organization's (WHO) new yardstick, Healthy Life Expectancy, measures the number of years that a person can be expected to live in full health. Cuba, as the WHO notes, "has the highest healthy life expectancy in the region [Latin America and the Caribbean], at 68.4 years, near U.S. levels" (2000). On its fiftieth anniversary, the WHO awarded President Fidel Castro the "Health for All Gold Medal," in recognition of Cuba's accomplishments (WHO 1998b). The award's citation acknowledged that "Cuba has in many ways become a model for other developing countries in respect of its enlightened and progressive health services" (WHO 1998a).

Cuba has consistently performed well in the annual United Nations human development reports. The reports rank countries on the basis of the Human Development Index (HDI), creating three categories for countries: high human development, medium human development and low human development. The 2002 report ranked Cuba 55th among 173 countries and placed it in the very upper end of medium human development, with an HDI of 0.795, only 0.005 outside the 0.800 value that qualifies a country for high human development status (UNDP 2002). In 2003, Cuba was ranked 52nd out of 175 nations, with an HDI of 0.806, placing it in the high human development category (UNDP 2003). However, while the HDIs aim to calibrate the performance of nations by utilizing measures other than per capita income, the national average income continues to have a significant role in its calculation and evaluation. Hence, the continuing under-valuation of per capita income in Cuba, *vis-à-vis* the extensive social supports, has resulted in a lower HDI and world ranking than is warranted.

Between 1990 and 2000, Cuba reduced its infant mortality rate from 11 per 1,000 births to 6.2. This compares very favourably with the West, placing it sixth in the world and first in the Americas (U.N. Wire 2002). In contrast, the average infant mortality rate for Latin American and the Caribbean was 30 in 1999. In Argentina it was 18 in 1999; in Chile, 10; and Costa Rica, 12. Additionally, the mortality rate for children under five in Cuba has declined from 13 to 8 per 1,000 over the 1990s. The Latin American and Caribbean average was 38 in 1999. Indeed, the island's mortality rate for children is 50 percent less than that of Chile, the Latin American country that ranks second. In Cuba, 90 percent of children are fully vaccinated against the major preventable childhood diseases, such as tuberculosis, polio and measles (Green 1998: 165).

Investment in education is 6.7 percent of GDP. This is twice the average proportion allocated regionally. The average educational level achieved by Cubans is 10th grade, surpassing the 5th grade regional average. In 1998 and 2001, UNESCO studies on education in Latin America evaluated the Cuban education system as the best in the region (Constance 2002; *Granma International* 1999b: 12). The Latin American and Caribbean illiteracy rate for youth aged fifteen to twenty-four is 7 percent. The Cuban rate is *zero*. From 1990 to 1997, the net primary enrolment for both girls and boys increased from 92 percent to 100 percent (Martinez Puentes 2003: 411). This rate not only exceeds the 80- to 90-percent regional enrolment rates, but also surpasses the United States. In 1997, the Cuban primary school teacher-to-student ratio stood at 12 to 1, placing it on par with Sweden. The average for Latin America and East Asia was 25 to 1.

Cuba continues to outstrip the entire region in the quality of primary education (Marquis 2001).

This is paralleled by a significant focus on higher education and research; thus, the number of university graduates has also continued to increase. By 1999, Cuba had produced more than 700,000 university graduates (Castro 2001e: 10). Currently, there are an estimated 24,000 university professors teaching 130,000 university students (Bravo 1998: 182). This investment in higher education is reflected in the scientific area, where, with only 2 percent of Latin America's population, Cuba has 11 percent of its scientists. The scientific infrastructure is impressive, with more than two hundred scientific research centres and institutes (Bravo 1998: 105; Hernández 1997: 100; Canton Navarro 2000: 281).

The safety net has not unravelled. Most of the unemployed workers were relocated to other enterprises, while the rest received 60 percent of their salaries and retraining (Canton Navarro 2000: 258; Lopez Vigil 1999: 13). Many of the unemployed opted for self-employment. As the state sector recovered, many of these were reabsorbed. Also, as noted, the average salary increased. In 1999, more than 60 percent of workers, particularly in the areas of health, education and the police, had significant wage increases of between 12 percent and 40 percent (*Granma* 1999a). Social security and welfare programs were expanded. Pension levels were maintained and in some cases increased. The 2002 allotment for social security was increased by 342 million pesos over the 2001 expenditure (Radio Havana Cuba 2002). More than 17 billion pesos have been paid out in pensions since the beginning of the Special Period (Castro 2001c).

While some goods and services, such as alcohol, tobacco, inter-provincial bus-fares and airfares, have increased in price, basic necessities — for example, staple foods and local transit costs — are kept at affordable prices and remain purchasable in pesos. The Cuban government provides $700 million U.S. in food subsidies (Castro 2001a; author's notes). Rents have not increased, holding at around 6–8 percent of salaries. Indeed, more than 85 percent of Cubans own their homes outright. While power rates rose, this in fact meant no increase for 52 percent of the population, as households below a certain income level were insulated from the increased rates.

Commentators often argue — using the peso–U.S. dollar exchange rate of 26 to 1 — that Cubans endure extreme privation. This is a flagrant distortion of Cuban social and economic realities. The breakdown of the average monthly expenses of a Cuban family is as follows:

Rent: 26.6 pesos ($1.02 U.S.; It must be noted that 85 percent of
Cubans own their homes and thus do not pay rent.)) (Castro
1998b: 44; Canton Navarro 2000: 268).
Electricity: 13.60 pesos ($0.52 U.S.).
Telephone: 6.25 pesos ($0.24 U.S.).
Cooking gas: 7.63 pesos ($0.29 U.S.).
Water: 1.30 pesos ($0.05 U.S.).
Monthly food ration for a family of four: 45.56 pesos ($1.75 U.S.).
This includes, among other things, rice, beans, eggs, potatoes and
powdered milk for children up to seven years old (*Cuba Business*
2001e: 7).

The total monthly costs amount to 100.98 pesos. As the average
monthly wage is 249 pesos ($9.58 U.S., the family monthly income —
assuming a two-parent home and bearing in mind that women, without
exception, receive equal pay — is 498 pesos ($19.15 U.S.). Thus, the
100.98 pesos monthly expenditure represents 20.23 percent of the family
income. It must be noted that, while the monthly food ration is not large
enough to last the entire month, items are available in the private and state
agricultural and industrial markets. Moreover, the monthly ration is
augmented by the other aspects of the generous social wage provided by
the state, which, in addition to subsidized housing, food and utilities,
includes free healthcare and education and subsidized clothing.

Thus, despite the unprecedented economic crisis that afflicted Cuba,
the island has avoided the deep social problems and political convulsions
that grip the rest of Latin America. The previously mentioned ECLAC
study stated that "contrary to what is happening in Latin America, the
liberalization of the market in a social environment of solidarity has served
to mitigate some of the regressive distortions of spreading the costs of the
so-called special period" (ECLAC/ECF 1997: 15–16). The study further
concluded, "in the face of the magnitude of the external shock, the cost
of the stabilization policy was relatively low and its distribution more
equitable in comparison with other Latin American economies, thanks to
the policy of guaranteeing employment and income for the population"
(66). Moreover, as opposed to "the experience in many countries where
the introduction of markets, privatization, and decentralization have
deepened poverty and dislocation," the Cuban working class and farmers
"have benefited from the changes" (Sinclair and Thompson 2000: 39).
Hence, while throughout Latin America, rural poverty and unemployment have increased, and inequality has grown, Cuban government

policies and measures have increased production and facilitated economic growth "but not at the cost of wealth for a few and misery for the majority" (Sinclair and Thompson 2000: 39).

THE AFTERMATH OF SEPTEMBER 11TH

Cuba, as with all countries, was profoundly affected by the aftermath of the terrorist attacks on New York City on September 11, 2001, particularly the economic fallout. Economic growth for Cuba in 2001 had been forecast at between 4 and 4.5 percent; following the attacks, growth dropped to 3 percent (Frank 2001a) and growth for 2002 was only 1.1 percent (Frank 2001a). In comparison, the average economic growth for Latin America ranged from -0.5 percent to -1 percent. The projection for 2003 for Cuba is 1.1 percent. The low growth in 2002 was the result of a decline in tourism, rising oil costs, the impact of two hurricanes and the low prices for sugar and other exports. In October 2001, the tourism sector experienced a 14 percent decline, a trend that translated into an overall drop of 5 percent for 2002 (Snow 2002). Rising petroleum prices beset the Cuban economy, with each dollar increase in the cost of a barrel of oil adding $30 million U.S. to the nation's fuel expenditures (Frank 2002b). The world market price per pound of sugar dropped from $0.09 U.S. to $0.0653 U.S. (Castro 2001c). Other products, such as tobacco, also were affected. The price of nickel declined from $8.640 U.S. to $4.715 U.S. per ton. Family remittances from abroad declined (Castro 2001c; Frank 2001b). The price of nickel has since rebounded to more than $8.000 per ton (Wroughton 2003).

Hurricane Michelle, in November 2001, was the most powerful storm to hit Cuba in more than fifty years, causing $1.86 billion U.S. in damage (Frank 2001a). More than 166,000 houses were damaged, with another 12,600 completely destroyed, at an estimated cost for repairing and rebuilding of 785 million pesos. The electrical and telecommunications systems were significantly disrupted. The sugar crop was seriously affected, with more than 50 percent of the crop damaged, causing an estimated loss of 400,000 tons. Citrus orchards were decimated. The agricultural losses and the cost recuperation have been calculated, respectively, at 260 million and 317 million pesos (Radio Havana Cuba 2001d; Frank, 2001b).

In response to the situation, the Cuban government implemented a series of cost-saving measures and continued its policy of rationalization of investment and promotion of efficiency (*Cuba Business* 2001a: 1). The program also involved a "reduction in dollar budgets and nonessential

imports and a freeze on investments that do not guarantee a quick return"
(Cawthorne 2001). Energy conservation programs have been put in place
and are complemented by tighter rationing of goods. Central to this
strategy has been the commitment to guarantee the population's heath,
educational and nutritional requirements by increasing funding to these
areas. A critical component of this approach is the determination to defend
the value of the peso and thus avoid a precipitous deterioration of citizens'
buying power. In the face of economic uncertainty and the decline in
national income, the value of the peso declined to 26 to 1 U.S. dollar.

Carlos Lage, Vice-President of Cuba and the government official in
charge of economic policy, reiterated that while "Cuba is not exempt
from the effects of the current crisis, the country is much more organized
and economically organized" than before the crisis of the early 1990s.
Hence, the country is "prepared to deal with its current difficulties in a
much more organized and efficient manner than it did in the past" (*Cuba
Business* 2001a: 1). In short, the Castro administration emphasizes that
there will not be a return to the crisis proportions of the early 1990s.

NOTES

1. Voluntarism refers to the school of Marxist thought — usually identified
   with Maoism — which argues that, once a socialist revolution unleashes the
   inherent creativity and energies of the masses, material constraints on the
   level of social transformation are no longer relevant or applicable. One of the
   frequent critiques of the early years of the Revolution focuses on the belief
   that any developmental goal could be achieved without considering the
   economic possibilities of the country. This is part of the Marxist debate about
   the proper balance between subjective and objective conditions. In Cuba,
   the debate has been over the applicability of Che Guevara's ideas of the
   superiority — and necessity — of moral over material incentives (Blanco
   1997: 18–20; Silverman 1971; Mesa-Lago 1974: 6–9). An example of this
   early unbounded enthusiasm that a new social order was imminent was
   Castro's assertion that Cuba was on the threshold of creating "a society in
   which money will become unnecessary" (quoted in Heller 1969: 109).
2. The controversial role of foreign investment is explored in greater detail in
   Chapter Six.
3. A discussion of the impact of the events stemming from September 11, 2001,
   is addressed later in this chapter.

2. GOVERNANCE IN CUBA

The central task for Cuba-watchers and specialists of all hues is to account for the resilience of the Cuban Revolution in the face of the economic collapse of the early 1990s, a "collapse which would have sunk almost any other system without a trace" (Kapica 1996: 249). At the centre of the "Cuban miracle" of survival is the island's political system. As Fidel Castro observed in 1996 at the crucial 5th Plenum of the Communist Party of Cuba, the miracle that was "worked was not economic but political" (Castro 1996b: 1). The capacity of the Cuban government to govern cannot be separated from the legitimacy of the Cuban Revolution and the political system that has arisen within that unfolding process. If the Cuban Revolution is indeed unpopular and undemocratic, how was it able to endure in the face of the precipitous decline of the economy and living standards with "few manifestations of dissent?" (Kapica 1996: 249).

Those who study "democratization" consider the political system in Cuba the antithesis of democracy but, paradoxically, acknowledge as axiomatic that regimes which do not have legitimacy "are vulnerable to collapse in periods of economic and social distress" (Diamond et al. 1990: 10). Even in the literature on the left, while emphasis is placed on Cuba's impressive achievements in "ending hunger and poverty and providing healthcare, education and old age security for all, and generally creating a society with high degrees of social equality and human solidarity" (Campbell 2001: 259), the political base — the guarantor and motive force — upon which these achievements rest is ignored and marginalized in the discourse.

THE DOMINANT MODEL OF DEMOCRACY

The dominant paradigm conceptualizes democracy as "a political system separate and apart from the economic and social system to which it is joined" (Diamond et al. 1990: 6). It must be noted that while the theorizing on this concept allows for some interface between economics and politics, the political system is treated as overriding — if not divorced from — the economy. At the heart of this model is the assertion that democracy is defined by a system of governance encompassing free, fair and competitive elections, multiple political parties, the participation of all adult groups and the protection of civil and political liberties, including freedom of expression, the press and association (Dahl 1971). Integral components of this structure are political competition and participation of the citizenry. Consequently, for a country to be deemed democratic there must be "extensive competition among individuals and organized groups (especially political parties) for all effective positions of government power" (Diamond et al. 1990: 6).

Within this model, it is essential to counterbalance and control the power of the state, ensuring that "its incumbents remain responsive and accountable to the people" (Diamond et al. 1990: 19). Thus, the existence "of a pluralistic, autonomous, vigorously organized civil society that can balance and limit state power" is an imperative (17). Indeed, civil society and an active non-state sector are seen as creating "additional channels for the articulation and practice of democratic interests" (15). Therefore, the absence of an independent non-state sector and non-state organizations or the presence of extensive state control, together with the lack of free, fair and competitive multi-party elections, are seen as the hallmarks of non-democratic regimes. These regimes are generally divided into three types: hegemonic party system, authoritarian and totalitarian.

While opposition parties are a characteristic of the hegemonic party system, effective political competition is circumscribed "through pervasive electoral malpractice and frequent state coercion" (9). A prominent example would be Mexico during the domination of the Partido Revolucionario Institucional. Authoritarian regimes establish severe limits on political pluralism and independent organization. However, they vary in form in terms of the level of independent political expression and organization that are permitted (O'Donnell et al. 1986). Hence, all political parties, except the ruling party, may be legally proscribed or operate within a closely controlled electoral process in which different parties participate. The end result is the elimination of meaningful politically competitive elections. The controlled election process is a carefully crafted project to create a façade of democratic contestation for power while attempting to mask "the reality of authoritarian domination" (Diamond et al. 1990: 8). The regimes that prevailed in Central America until the 1990s fall under this ambit. Totalitarian regimes "repress all forms of autonomous social and political organizations, denying completely even the most elementary political and civil liberties, but also demand the active commitment of the citizens to the regime" (8). This regime-type designation has usually been ascribed to the world's socialist countries, including Cuba (12).

It is clear that under the dominant model Cuba fails the "democratic test." However, it is interesting to note that while Cuba fails to satisfy the central criterion of a multi-party system, the island does meet certain other elements of the model. As this chapter illustrates, Cuba has a vibrant and active civil society, one whose organizations are not simply mere extensions of the state. Cuba's political system has been condemned because it lacks the "rules of regular, formalized political competition" (O'Donnell et al. 1986: 3). Indeed, not only has the Cuban electoral process been denounced, but its very existence has been denied. For example, Anna Louise Bardach, in her best-seller, *Cuba Confidential*, asserts that "it has been fifty-four years since an election has been held in Cuba" (2002: 351). Yet, as will be seen, local governments not only have substantial power, but their delegates are selected and elected through a competitive process in which the Communist Party of Cuba (PCC) is excluded. Indeed, the PCC is legally proscribed from any formal role in the electoral system. The municipal, provincial and national elections are governed by established rules and procedures. Up to half of the membership of the National Assembly of People's Power is comprised of delegates selected at the municipal level's competitive elections. Moreover, the Cuban government has demonstrated considerable responsiveness and accountability to the Cuban people, as evidenced, for example, by the 4th Congress of the PCC in 1991 and the workers' parliaments of 1994 (which are discussed later in this chapter). However, the determination of the democratic nature of Cuba is not dependent on whether it meets or fails to meet the requirements of the dominant model.

CRITIQUE OF THE DOMINANT MODEL

The dominant model itself has come under intense criticism, as it reduces democracy primarily to the contestation in the electoral arena between different parties for the prize of political office. In short, it reduces

> the limits and scope of democracy to the procedural arrangements by which individuals acquire the power to decide by means of a competitive struggle for the people's vote. (Boron 1995: 191)

Thus, procedural rules governing multi-party competition have "become" the *sin qua non* of democracy; its heart. This procedural model of democracy assumes that the rules themselves provide an adequate framework to allow the various sectors and groups of society "access to the seats of power" (Petras and Veltmeyer 2001: 109). It obfuscates the manner in which these rules are used, manipulated, redefined and altered to deny the majority of the polity any meaningful participation in decision-making or exercise of power. Moreover, this definition masks "the interrelationship between the political economy and the changing uses and abuses of electoral rules" (Petras and Veltmeyer 2001: 109). It generates an ahistorical conception of democracy that is then universalized as not only applicable to, but essential for, all countries. Consequently, this formulation:

> leaves in a gray area the real contents of politics, and it focuses its main attention on the organizational instrumental angle of power and silences its effective content. The conception that is pro-moted also establishes an abstract model as valid and universal, without taking into consideration the concrete economic and political national situation, as well as the social policies and national sovereignty. Democracy shows itself then as a product imposed and imported, as a political and ideological requisite and as an end in itself, independent from the society in which it develops. (Fernández 1993)

Under the dominant paradigm, democracy is conceptualized as a system divorced from the underlying economic and social relations. Its focus is on the institutional order and formal functions as opposed to substance. This rules-of-the-game approach "overlooks the overarching importance of capitalist property relations and interests" (Petras and Veltmeyer 2001: 118). In short, democracy in capitalist societies "does not exist independently of class interest and conflict" (Petras and Veltmeyer 2001: 119). By treating the electoral process as autonomous, the dominant model ignores the under-girding socio-economic spheres and forces, focusing instead on a particular conception of civil and political rights. As a result, it marginalizes the right to economic security, employment, healthcare, education, housing, liveable environment, etc.

> Without economic equality and justice, the political dimension of democracy is meaningless. As long as the means of production and systems of distribution in a society are controlled by a few people, that society will always suffer from an imbalance of power and social injustices. (Lumumba-Kasongo 1992: 4)

Consequently, genuine democracy requires "social and economic structures that support a minimal level of fundamental equality," a standard that even the most developed capitalist countries "barely meet" (Boron 1995: 192). Democracy becomes a sham when elected governments "exhibit total irresponsibility in light of the suffering of the poor" (Boron 1995: 203). This reality underscores that capitalist renderings of democracy severely limit, if not bar, popular participation in the setting of public policy. The illusion of participation is created through the ballot box, obscuring the wider and systemic disenfranchisement. Hence, the capitalist election system "only permits political parties to come to power and they serve vested interests, instead of being instruments which empower the people" (Bains 1993a: 23). Democratic rights are reduced to the exercise of the vote every few years.

Under these arrangements, political freedom is reduced to the competition between political parties for government, with the sustaining of the conditions of competition considered the life-blood of democracy. Political opposition, the revolving of parties in and out of power, guarantees the continued existence of competition and the façade of real choice for the voter. This occurs "independently of the repercussions that the resulting contest might create in the socio–economic reality of the electorate" (Fernández 1993). The faces in power change, but the economic and political realities remain untouched. Furthermore, a plutocratic logic dominates, where money determines that the spoils of political power and government are only open to the economic elite. Thus, the chimera of a contest between a plurality of options hides the reality that the existing political and economic order is never transformed. While in theory sovereignty rests in the citizen, in practice, capitalist political systems "show that the interests of the rich are what really count" (Boron 1995: 203). The unequal distribution of resources guarantees that "political equality will remain illusory" (Bains 1993a: 22). Throughout the world, especially in the South, governments "implement regressive macroeconomic policies without consulting their electorate or even the elected legislature" (Petras and Veltmeyer 2001: 69). Structural adjustment programs, cuts in social spending, retrenchment of workers and privatization of state assets and national resources are executed at the behest of the International Monetary Fund, the World Bank or some other financial institution without any input from or consultation with the vast majority of the citizenry. Thus, while democracy is treated as the "natural corollary of capitalism," in which both "are closely entwined," it is imperative to note:

When capitalist exploitation has been threatened, capitalist governments unleash special institutions to spy on, infiltrate and subvert the opposition. Whether one looks at the McCarthy era of witch-hunting, the FBI's efforts to undermine Martin Luther King in the struggle for civil rights, the official attack on the Black Panthers, the U.S. government's infiltration of anti-war movements and even churches (as in the case of the Sanctuary Movement to protect undocumented Central American refugees), it is not hard to establish that real freedoms are eroded by the establishment, when it feels itself substantially threatened. (Makhijani 1992: 52, 56–57)

In summation, capitalist democracy, the prevalent model globally, fails to meet or respond to the needs of the electorate. Sovereignty rests not with the people but with entrenched and powerful interests who utilize their control over the state and other institutions to perpetuate their domination. Thus, under capitalism, the formal electoral process generates "the illusion of majority rule" (Silber 1994: 156). While the mirage of participation in the decisions that shape society is carefully fostered, what unfolds, in reality, is the marginalization of the immense majority of individuals from actual engagement in creating the policies that impact on their lives.

THE HISTORICAL AND PHILOSOPHICAL CONTEXT OF GOVERNANCE IN CUBA

While Western political systems stem from the tradition embodied by thinkers such as Locke and Montesque, the Cuban system springs from the country's unique history and the application of Marxist-Leninist theory and praxis. The form and content of Cuban government and governance is rooted in Cuba's struggle to exercise sovereignty and attain social justice. Crucial to the realization of these goals is the work of José Martí (Cuba's national hero), other Cuban thinkers, and socialist theory and practice (Liss 1987). The necessity for a single party derives from Martí's writing on the imperative of forging national unity and his experience in building the Partido Revolucionario Cubano (Cuban Revolutionary Party — PRC). Martí's thinking was decisively shaped by his experience in the United States. His observations of the U.S. political system inured him against its multi-party arrangements and the politics that ensued. His succinct summarization of the system was:

Elections are quite costly. The capitalists and the large companies help the needy candidates with their campaign expenses; once the candidates are elected, they pay with their slavish vote for the money which the capitalists lay out in advance. (quoted in Foner 1988: 18)

Martí came to the conclusion that democracy in the U.S. "would be nothing but fraudulent while the large monopolists rule the country" (quoted in Foner 1988: 18). He further noted:

What has the Senate done to stop these evils, the Senate where the millionaires, the large landowners, the railway magnates, the mining tycoons, form the majority, despite the fact that senators are chosen by the state legislatures elected directly by the people do not own the mines, the land or the railways?… Although the country votes for it directly the House of Representatives is chosen by such corrupt methods that every election is falsified by the vast sums of money. Has a single voice been raised in the House of Representatives to denounce the danger and to speak of the needy? (quoted in Foner 1988: 19)

Martí's U.S. experience contributed "substantially to the building of the foundations of the PRC and feeding the logic of the need for one political party as the expression of the Cuban Nation" (August 1999: 95). The aim was to establish "a new party dedicated to the vast majority of Cubans, especially the most humble section from whose ranks the party emerged." The single-party system was conceptualized as "an alternative to the foreign imposed political process, in which Cubans were incited to divide themselves along the lines of one or other of the political parties each of which fought to attain political power for itself" (August 1999: 94–95). In Martí's vision, the working masses would provide the impetus for meaningful change. He declared that "profit creates worms. It is among the poor that the sincerity that drives the worms away prospers" (quoted in Foner 1988: 113).

In the wake of the Revolution, Martí's ideas were amplified by the Cuban disenchantment with the political system that prevailed from the early 1900s until 1959. Indeed, as the late Cuban Vice-President Carlos Rafael Rodríguez observed, Cuban revolutionaries consider Martí's "advice and example are so fruitful and his lesson so valid that we can consider him as the greatest among us, never distant from our side" (quoted in Foner 1988: 21). With the overthrow of Batista and the neocolonial regime, there was an "enormous democratizing effect of the revolutionary triumph which allowed ordinary people to run government" (Fernández 1993). This new experience drew heavily on the political practices and structures that emerged in the liberated areas during the rebellion. The old system was rejected by the people because they viewed it as characterized by corruption, cronyism, external dependence, racism and poverty for the broad masses, and as an instrument through which the United States, in collaboration with the Cuban *comprador* class, exercised its domination over the island. This disenchantment with the old way of doing politics was underlined by the "complete and thorough rejection of elections" by workers and peasants in the first months of the Revolution (August 1999: 184). At one of the numerous mass assemblies, Castro raised the notion of elections. It was promptly and vociferously rebuffed. Manuel Urrutia, President of Cuba at the time, observed:

> The first time I heard the promise of elections repudiated was when Castro and I attended the opening of the library at Marta Arbreu University at Las Villas. At the end of the meeting, Castro mentioned elections and a large number of his listeners shouted against them. After the speech, Castro asked, "Did you notice how they spoke against elections?" (quoted in Pérez Jr. 1988: 321–22)

To a huge and enthusiastic rally in 1960, Castro elaborated:

> Our enemies, our detractors and those who would like to see us fail, keep asking questions about general elections… as if the only democratic procedure to attain power were those often corrupted electoral processes devised to adulterate and falsify the will and interests of the people and to place in power the least qualified, the most incompetent, the most cunning, and the grafters…. As if after so many fraudulent elections, as if after so many unscrupulous political deals and combines and so much corruption, it could be possible to make the people believe that the only way to profess democracy, to live democratically is to stage one those old-fashioned electoral farces. (Greene 1970: 308–309)

Elections were connected in the minds of the people with corruption and disenfranchisement. However, as the Revolution developed, as noted in Chapter One, the mass assemblies were replaced by fresh political institutions, ones centred around a "new type of elections based on the democracy of the majority, that is, elections within the context of the majority holding power" (August 1999: 186). Thus, the Cuban Revolution and its political forms are an extension of Cuban history, particularly the struggle to attain independence and social justice. Perhaps Castro best captured this ethos when, in the aftermath of the Washington-sponsored Bay of Pigs invasion and the proclamation of the socialist character of the Cuban Revolution, he declared:

> What we have, obviously, is not the democracy of the exploiters. Do the exploiters have rights in Cuba? No [Shouts of "no."] Do the foreign monopolies have rights in Cuba? No! [Shouts of "no."] And the estate owners? [Shouts of "no."] No, and do they have a right to govern the country? [Shouts of "no."] Do they have a right to make the laws of the republic? [Shouts of "no."] ... Now we are speaking of another democracy, the democracy of the people, of the workers, of the peasants, of the humble men and women [applause], the democracy of the majority of the nation, of those who were exploited, of those who had no rights in the past. And this is the true democracy, the revolutionary democracy of the people, the democracy of the humble, by the humble and for the humble [applause]. (Castro 1961)

The Cuban Revolution is also a creative and valuable contribution to the corpus of Marxism. The tradition embodied in socialist theory and praxis is the means by which the historical aspiration of the Cuban nation is actualized. Thus, the Cuban political system is firmly rooted in the socialist tradition. Within this context, the work of Rousseau, Marx, Engels, Lenin and the legacies of the Paris Commune and the Russian Revolution have had — and continue to have — a critical influence. However, Cubans are not involved in merely replicating the experiences and forms of other socialist countries. Rather "they have rejected *copismo* [copying]" (Spalding 2003: 60). Hence, the study of socialist democracy in Cuba necessitates:

> the differentiation of the genuine Marxist paradigm from its canonized interpretations and from the discredited political practices that corrupted socialism in various other countries, through the use of technocratic methods of political direction, the pres-

ence of regimes that banished the popular masses from power or through the idea that diluted what is individual into a social concept and forgot all about individual human beings. (Fernández 1993)

The central concept of the Marxist tradition is the *mandat imperatif,* where the main function of elected representatives is to listen to their constituents, responding to complaints and suggestions (August 1999: 377–403; Roman 1999: 14–26, 155–209). Under capitalism, the formal electoral process generates the deception that it's the citizenry who exercise power. While capitalist democracy rests on a "socio-economic structure that is increasingly elitist and oligarchic," rendering the exercise of participation in decision-making a fiction, the Cuban political system has made concerted efforts to overcome and transform this "capitalistic way of life from within and without" (Lopez García 1999: 43). Toward this end, the island has an extensive political framework that ensures popular participation in the deliberations that shape and determine the decision-making process. Moreover, the participation exceeds mere consultation, establishing and exercising significant control. This is exemplified in *Poder Popular* (Peoples' Power), the system of representative government that gives each citizen the right to select, elect and be elected. This is manifested in the power of Cubans to nominate candidates for the different levels of government, the principle "that the people should nominate and the people should elect" (Madan et al. 1993: 6). This power is not vested in the Communist Party of Cuba, but rather is exercised either directly by the people, as at the municipal level, or through the various mass organizations and elected representatives. Thus, the role of the Cuban electorate extends to active participation in choosing the list of candidates, instead of having a slate foisted upon them. This contrasts sharply with the practice that prevailed in the U.S.S.R. and the Eastern Bloc, where all candidates were chosen by the various communist party committees or depended on securing their approval (Silber 1994: 159). As Olga Fernández notes, the Cuban electoral system challenges the established model in several fundamental ways:

1) It breaks with the traditional electoral models conceived with the exclusive function of legitimizing mechanisms in the form of political competition, winners or losers game of negotiations, party alliances and circumstantial compromises with electoral goals; 2) at the same time a different concept is introduced

regarding elections in which there are two very new and original elements: it is not a competitive battle, or a political objective by itself, and 3) it revolutionizes the means and mechanism of running candidates, as they are not nominated by party machineries but through a complex of consultations and interrelations in which diverse popular and community organizations have a great weight. (Fernández 1993)

The goal in socialism is to extend democracy to both the political and economic spheres, in contrast to the claims and expressed intentions of capitalist democratic theory. Within class society, particularly capitalism, not only is the public authority separated from the people but "set up against it" (Engels 1985: 273); the state is a public power distinct from the mass of people. Hence, the task is to bridge the divide between public authority and the citizenry. Consequently, socialist conceptions of democracy go beyond the mere proclamation of the rights and freedoms of citizens, moving "from formal equality to actual equality" (Lenin 1977: 477). Therefore, socialist democracy rests on four bases: political participation, economic equality, the merging of civil and political society and the *mandat imperatif* (Campbell 2001: 260).

THE WORKERS' PARLIAMENTS

In December 1993, at a meeting of the National Assembly of People's Power, the Ministry of Finance proposed a series of far-reaching measures, such as a reduction of subsidies to state enterprises and increases in prices of specific goods and services. The most controversial measure was the proposed personal and business tax system, which would encompass the entire country and include a tax on wages. The proposed package, while not constituting the "shock therapy" of the various structural adjustment programs implemented in the South at the behest of the International Monetary Fund, was seen as a series of austerity measures that "would entail sacrifices on the part of many" (Fitzgerald 1994: 186). Representatives of the unions vigorously opposed adoption of this "package" — particularly the tax on wages — on the basis that the workers had not had a chance to discuss any of the proposed measures. Therefore, the National Assembly decided "to delay making any decisions until these and related issues had been thrashed out in a truly national debate" (Fitzgerald 1994: 186). President Castro argued:

Economists frighten me. There is only one thing I know a little about and that is politics. That has been my job, and the most important job I have had. I believe that things must be viewed through politics. The ideas presented by the specialists must be analyzed from a political viewpoint.... A technocratic approach cannot be used to solve these problems. (quoted in Waters 1994: 44)

Thus, the proposed package was set aside and a nation-wide period of broad and popular discussion of the economic situation and the possible solutions initiated (Fitzgerald 1994: 186).

From January to March1994, more than 80,000 meetings (workers' parliaments) in different workplaces — involving more than three million workers (85 percent of the workforce) — were held throughout the country. People expressed their opinions, debated, discussed and proposed solutions to the economic crisis (Lopez Vigil 1999: 76–77; Peter Roman 1995). Difficult proposals were eventually accepted: for example, eliminating government subsidies to many state-run factories and consequently reducing the number employed in many of those workplaces. Also, the decision to confiscate goods accumulated by "underground marketeers" was the direct result of a workers' parliament's recommendation. Instead of raising prices on the basic rationed foods, the workers' parliaments supported price increases on items like rum and cigarettes, and, for the first time, a small charge for sports and cultural events to help raise needed revenue (Lopez Vigil 1999: 77).

The outcomes of the workers' parliaments were decisive. National policy decisions clearly reflected and responded to the viewpoints and positions expressed. Indeed, it was these discussions that provided the primary input for the special session of the National Assembly — the unicameral body that is the highest and only legislative body in Cuba — which was convened from May 1–2, 1994. As the workers had expressed an overwhelming consensus against a tax on wages, the May 1994 Assembly deliberations adopted a resolution calling for further "study of the selective introduction of a tax on personal income, excluding wages." At the August 1994 National Assembly meeting, an income tax law was adopted, with the understanding that it would be applied chiefly to the self-employed rather than waged workers (Evenson 2002b: 11; Peter Roman 1995: 44). Thus, the changes initiated in the Cuban economy occurred within the context of broad and active participation of the population. This massive nation-wide popular consultation clearly distinguishes the Cuban experience and sets it apart from other countries, where the adjustment programs adopted were imposed without any input from their citizenry.

PODER POPULAR

Extensive popular participation is at the centre of the Cuban model of governance and is manifested not only in the form of workers' parliaments. Moreover, this participation impacts on the everyday issues that confront ordinary Cubans. The official organs of government in Cuba are the municipal, provincial and national assemblies of the *Poder Popular* (people's power) structures. In 1992, the electoral system was altered in order to facilitate more effective and efficient popular participation and input into decision-making. The National Assembly is the sole body with legislative authority, with delegates — as in the provincial and municipal assemblies — directly elected by the Cuban electorate.

The National Assembly chooses from amongst its members the Council of State, which is accountable to the National Assembly and carries out its duties and responsibilities, such as the passage and implementation of decrees, when the Assembly is not in session. The Council's decisions and decrees must be ratified at subsequent sittings of the National Assembly. The Council of State also determines the composition of the Council of Ministers, and both bodies together constitute the executive arm and cabinet of the government. The President of the Council of State serves as head of both the government and state.

In reviewing the Cuban electoral system, four striking points emerge: First, Cubans are not preoccupied with a mere mechanical implementation of a rigid, unchanging model. Contrary to dominant preconceptions, the Cuban political system is not a static entity. Cubans are involved in an intense learning process whose hallmark has been experimentation and a willingness to correct mistakes and missteps by periodic renovation of the project. Thus, the system responds to popular demands for adjustment. One of the challenges the system wrestles with is that "excessive centralization of power and paternalism have reduced the efficacy of the public's participation and self-management" (Roman 1999: 96–97). Consequently, a number of measures and changes have been enacted to enhance and "remove obstacles to political participation in the process of socialist development" (Cole 1998: 127). Thus, in 1992, the Constitution and electoral laws were modified to require the direct popular election of all members of the national and provincial assemblies. Previously, only the municipal assemblies were directly elected, with the make-up of the provincial assemblies determined by a vote of municipal delegates and, in

turn, the National Assembly composition established by provincial representatives. Also, the creation of the popular councils in the early 1990s (see
below) was directly aimed at increasing the power of local government
and reducing the impact of bureaucracy. The political system and process
is "always in flux" and evolving "in response to the creative actions of its
citizens (Lappe and Du Bois 1994: 14–15).

Second, the function of the Communist Party of Cuba (PCC) is
significantly circumscribed, as it does not operate as an electoral party. It
is proscribed by law from playing any role in the nomination of candidates.
This is integral to harmonizing

> the concept of a single party with the idea that the people should
> nominate and the people should elect. We had to make it work
> in practice, because what was known to exist in the world when
> there wasn't a single party was a multiplicity of parties, and this
> was the only known procedure for carrying out elections. So we
> had to create something new, something more just, more equi-
> table, more democratic, more pure, because our main concern
> was to preserve the purity of our electoral process and prevent any
> politicking or corruption from filtering in. (Castro as quoted in
> Madan et al. 1993: 6–7)

At the municipal level, the nominations occur at street meetings,
where it is the constituents who directly participate in and control the
selection. Each municipality is divided into several *circumscriptions,* or
districts, comprised of a few hundred people. Each *circumscription* nominates candidates and elects a delegate who serves in the local municipal
assembly. On October 20, 2002, in "14,946 *circumscriptions,* 13,563
municipality delegates were elected from a total of 32,585 candidates"
(*Granma International* 2002b). There is a high degree of popular participation in the selection of candidates, marked by active and uncoerced citizen
interaction and involvement. The members of the community first make
their decisions about who would be appropriate candidates, and then those
people are nominated as candidates. The elections at the municipal level
are competitive and the casting of ballots is secret. By law, there must be
at least two candidates and a maximum of eight. If no candidate receives
more than 50 percent of the vote, then a run-off election is held between
the two candidates who obtained the most votes. Consequently, in order
to complete the 2002 local government elections, a second round was held
in 1,383 constituencies (*Granma* 2002).

At the provincial and national levels, candidacy commissions select and sift through thousands of people. The commissions are comprised of representatives from the various mass and grassroots organizations and are presided over by workers' representatives chosen by the unions (August 1999: 226; Roman 1999: 133–38). The PCC is prohibited from participation in the work of the commissions, ensuring "that the grassroots delegates are nominated without any intervention from the Party" (Cole 1998: 122). Indeed, "in principle and practice a peasant or taxi driver can be member of these Commissions" (Hurlich 2002). The commissions' recommendations are then presented to the municipal assemblies for final approval. For example, on December 1, 2002, in preparation for the 2003 elections, the municipal assemblies approved 1,199 candidates for the provincial assemblies and 609 for the National Assembly. The candidates had:

> been selected from an original of 57,340 proposals, of which 32,585 were made at constituency level; 7,273 in provincial plenary sessions of the mass and student organizations, the Central Organization of Trade Unions and the Association of Small Farmers, and 15,857 in those organizations' national plenary sessions. (Valencia 2002)

Thus, it is the Cuban citizenry that both nominates and elects its representatives. By law, up to 50 percent of National Assembly deputies can be municipal assembly delegates. In the 1998–2003 National Assembly, 46.3 percent of the delegates were from the municipal assemblies (August 1999: 366). The other members of the National Assembly are "national or provincial figures, politicians, managers, scientists, doctors, workers, teachers, intellectuals, peasants, athletes, artists and leaders from religious and other spheres" (Hurlich 2002: 4). The selection process ensures a broad representation of society as:

> the electoral commission made up of all civic organizations and sectors of the population spends over a year going from province to province, town to town, sifting through tens of thousands of proposed candidates to come up with the most representative slate of candidates to make sure that every sector of the population is truly represented. That slate is then presented to the population to vote up or down (as occurs in other countries, as well). But even then, citizens can choose to vote yes or no, one by one, for

each of the 601 candidates. (Wald 2003a)

Each member of the National Assembly, including Fidel Castro, is directly elected and must receive more than 50 percent of the vote in her or his constituency (August 1999: 226). In Cuban municipal, provincial and national elections, the turnout is very high, usually in the ninetieth percentile. The high turnout is a product not only of "political reasons [i.e., one's feeling of civic responsibility] but also cultural reasons. These include a highly developed sense of community and *'vamos para la calle!'* [Let's go to the street!] of which the social aspect of voting is one part" (Hurlich 2002: 6). Also, although a single national delegate list is put to the electorate, "not every candidate on the slate receives the same number of votes, an indication that Cuban voters are both aware of and exercise their right to vote only for those they feel will adequately represent them" (Wald 1999b: 88).

There is no formal campaigning, which curtails the role of money in Cuban elections (August 1999: 261–98; Roman 1999: 106–29). Instead, a month before the election, a biography of each candidate is displayed in various public places, where they can be perused at the convenience of the entire electorate. The objective of circumscribing formal campaigning is "to avoid the emergence of a 'class' of politicians" (Cole 1998: 39). Elections in Cuba are free of the commercial advertising that dominates and has come to denote the political system in capitalist countries. Professional politicking and politicians are viewed as symbolic of the corrupt past and marginalization of the citizenry that characterized pre-revolutionary Cuba. Consequently, the sons and daughters of workers and peasants comprise virtually all the delegates of the national, provincial and municipal assemblies. As Ernesto Freire, president of the National Candidacy Commission, stated, the goal is to establish for all Cuban citizens "the space and opportunity in equality of conditions" (Valencia 2002). To become a member of the governing structures, individuals

> don't have to be rich, they don't have to be landowners, or great industrialists, or multi-millionaires. They don't need money, they don't need anything except decency and civic worth…. We wanted to avoid politicking at all costs, we wanted to have a fair, really fair, process in which a person's worth, a person's personal history, a person's qualities would be the deciding factor. (Madan et al. 1993: 7, 29)

Third, a rare closeness exists between the elected municipal delegates and the people they serve. Each delegate must live in the electoral district (usually comprising a maximum of two thousand people). The municipal assemblies, which meet four times a year, elect from their membership a president, vice president and a secretary. These are the only full-time, paid positions in Cuban local government; all other members of the municipal assemblies are unpaid and continue in the jobs they had before they were elected. Delegates have a high degree of familiarity with their constituency and are constantly on call. Every six months, there is a formal accountability session at which complaints, suggestions and other community interests (*planteamientos*) are raised with the delegates. Issues at these sessions include a constellation of problems, such as "the repair of public fencing; a leaking water main; the need for more recreational and sports facilities; the lack of public lighting; a problem at work that has not been solved at the local level, etc." (Hurlich 2002: 3). The delegate must then attempt to resolve the matter or provide an explanation at the following accountability session. In short, the delegate must account for her or his work carried out since the previous session. Each *planteamiento* is carefully recorded, and approximately 70 percent are resolved. For example, in October 1999, the Camito Municipal Assembly, in the province of Havana, "reported that of the 583 problems presented to them by that date, some 81 percent have already been solved" (Hurlich 2002: 4). These *planteamiento* sessions have resulted in local issues being taken to the national level where they are examined and discussed, thus ensuring popular input into government policy (Roman 1999: 238). If constituents are dissatisfied with the performance of their representative, then she or he can be recalled or voted out in the next round of elections (Roman 1999: 128). In 1989, for example, only "45 percent of delegates were re-elected and 114 were recalled" (Cole 1998: 38). In the 2002 municipal elections, 47.87 percent were re-elected (*Granma International* 2002b).

In the working and meetings of the provincial assemblies and the National Assembly, the goal of achieving "unity and concensus" is central. The unanimous votes that occur "do not represent, as critics charge, imposition by the PCC, but rather legitimate consensus worked out in lengthy discussion at several levels" (Spalding 2003: 60). The National Assembly, for example, has ten permanent commissions. At the end of 2002, it met from December 16th to 20th to discuss more than forty topics, including the fishing industry, the environment, the restructuring of the sugar sector, the production of medicine and links between Cuba and the European Union, particularly Cuba's decision to apply to join the

Cotonou Agreement, an economic accord between the EU and African, Caribbean and Pacific states (*New York Times* 2002).

Fourth, the *consejo populares* (popular councils) serve as a real basis for solving problems. Article 103 of the Cuban Constitution establishes the municipal assemblies as the highest local organizations of state power (*Constitution of the Republic of Cuba* 1993). Their mandate is primarily exercised through the *consejo populares*, which represent a form of neighbourhood government. The *consejo populares* emerged as an important innovation in the early 1990s and were primarily aimed at enhancing the power of the municipal and provincial assemblies and at curbing corruption and the growing underground market. The *consejo populares* have decentralized some of the powers of the governmental system, providing a more substantive connection between local government and upper echelons of the state (Roman 1999: 238). This is part of the considerable decentralization in administrative decision-making that was initiated in the 1990s. By organizing community forces, the councils are an important source of self-government. The *consejo populares* are invested with considerable administrative and decision-making power. Their objectives are to work towards "meeting the population's welfare, economic, educational, cultural and social needs," while promoting efficiency in the production and service industries (*Constitution of the Republic of Cuba* 1993). Each *consejo popular* has the responsibility for the economics of their particular neighbourhood (Roman 1999: 215–56). Consequently, the role of people in affecting and transforming the conditions of their lives is amplified.

THE NATIONAL ASSEMBLY ELECTIONS OF 1993, 1998 AND 2003

During the Special Period there have been three national elections. These elections are, therefore, particularly significant in assessing the popular support for the Revolution and the government. The 1993 election was held just two and a half years into the Special Period, in the midst of the harshest phase. The 1998 and 2003 elections occurred well into the Special Period when, despite the economic recovery, the economic situation was still quite difficult, and the political and ideological impact of the crisis and the measures implemented would have had time to seep into and undermine popular support for socialism and the revolutionary project.

In fact, the national election of 1993 ended up being transformed into a plebiscite on the Revolution, socialism and the leadership of Fidel Castro. While the election was not centred on a contest between rival candidates or parties, voters could render a protest vote by boycotting the election or by ballot nullification (spoiling or leaving the ballots blank). The Cuban exile community in Miami broadcast hundreds of hours of programming into Cuba exhorting voters to do just that. In the run-up to the vote, radio stations broadcast an estimated combined total of 1,112 hours (the equivalent of more than forty-six days) per week into the island, urging an electoral boycott (Azicri 2000: 340). Even Lawton Chiles — then governor of Florida — called for Cubans to annul their vote (August 1999: 359–60, Vigil Lopez 1999: 5; Roman 1999: 146). On the island, the election was treated as a *de facto* referendum. An intense campaign was launched, calling for a *Voto Unido* (unified vote): a vote for the entire slate of candidates. Thus, the TV, press and mass organizations urged both a *Voto Unido* and *Si Por Cuba* (Vote for Cuba) (August 1999: 344–51, Lopez Vigil 1999: 6; Roman 1999: 139–42).

On February 24, 1993, Cubans went to the polls. It must be emphasized that this was a secret vote; neither was there any military presence at the polling stations. Foreign journalists or any foreign visitor could and did observe the voting process and the vote count (August 1999: 357–58). More than a hundred journalists from twenty-one countries witnessed the elections (Cole 1998: 122). Furthermore, children guarded the ballot boxes. It is instructive to note that there was not one accusation of voting fraud. The Miami based magazine *Contrapunto* stated: "The counting of votes was impeccable. It was open and public, and since over 120,000 people were involved in 30,000 polling stations, the results could not be tampered with" (Cole 1998: 122). In the face of Miami predictions that up to 50 percent of the ballots would be spoiled or blank, Cubans overwhelmingly demonstrated their support for the Revolution, social-ism and the leadership of Fidel Castro. A Cuban friend explained that when each person was alone in the voting booth with their conscience, the vast majority chose to demonstrate their support for the national project embarked upon in 1959.

The result? Of the eligible electorate of more than 7.5 million, 99.6 percent voted. It must be emphasized that in Cuba voting is not compulsory, as it is, for example, in Argentina. Of the votes cast, 92.97 percent were valid, with 94.99 percent of valid ballots cast as a unified vote. In short, 87.96 percent of the electorate overwhelmingly expressed their support for the Revolution (August 1999: 360–61, Lopez Vigil 1999: 6; Roman 1999: 146). Elizardo Sanchez, the most prominent "dissident" and government opponent in Cuba and President of the Cuban Commis-sion for Human Rights and National Reconciliation, accepted the validity and legitimacy of the vote, acknowledging that the mandate of the Cuban government had been renewed (*Latin American Weekly Report* 1993: 18).

On January 11, 1998, Cubans again went to the polls. Once again, the election was treated as a plebiscite and "political forces opposing the electoral process became active" and called for a boycott (Azicri 2000: 116). Of the eight-million-plus electorate, 98.35 percent voted; 94.98 percent of the cast ballots were valid, with 99.38 percent being a unified vote. Thus, 92.83 percent of the voters voted in favour of the Revolution, an increase over 1993. The negative vote — blank and spoiled ballots — decreased, declining from 7.03 percent in 1993 to 5.02 percent in 1998. Significantly, the negative vote in the capital, Havana, dropped from 10.34 percent to 3.42 percent (August 1999: 360–63; Roman 1999: 146). Elizardo Sanchez, once again, acknowledged that the 1998 election "signified the renovation of the mandates and the legitimacy of the government" (Roman 1999: 146). The January 2003 national elections had a voter turnout of 97.16 percent, with 91.35 percent casting a united vote. Blank and spoilt ballots amounted to 3 percent and .86 percent respectfully, despite renewed calls from opposition groups for Cubans to shun the entire process (*Granma International* 2002e).

WORKERS AND THE UNION MOVEMENT

It is frequently advanced that there are no workers' rights in Cuba and that the existing unions are merely an extension of a despotic government. However, as the workers' parliaments have demonstrated, workers in Cuba have very definite and concrete rights. They have considerable input and say in their workplaces and in major societal decisions. Central to this promotion and exercise of rights are the unions. The Cuban union movement encompasses more than 98 percent of Cuba's workers through the nineteen national unions (Evenson 2002b: 9, 16). The unions are autonomous — a requirement prescribed by law — and are completely self-financed through monthly dues (Evenson 2002b: 16–17). Thus, while they work closely with the Communist Party of Cuba (PCC) and the government, unions are independent. Indeed, unions exercise considerable influence on these institutions, as both the PCC and the National Assembly have significant representation from unions and the working class. The function of Cuban unions is twofold: "1) to further the economic, political and social interests of the country as a whole and 2) to protect the rights and advance the standard of living of Cuban workers" (Evenson 2002b: 9).

Among the different relationships the unions develop with employers, the most significant is with the government (Evenson 2002b: 1–13;

Fuller 1992; Zeitlin 1967). As the discussion of the workers' parliaments illustrates, workers in Cuba have a definite role in shaping national policy. The government must consult the unions on all matters involving labour policy (Evenson 2000b: 10–12). If the government intends changing, for example, the labour code, it must go to the workers for approval. The workers conduct meetings amongst themselves, debate the proposals by the government and then decide whether they are amenable to the changes to the legislation.

On many occasions, workers have accepted some proposals while rejecting others. For example, in 1995, proposed alterations to social security were rejected by the Cuban Confederation of Workers (CTC), resulting in the legislation being sent back to be reworked. In 1995, a provision in the *Foreign Investment Act* that would have allowed joint ventures with foreign investors to directly hire Cuban workers was abandoned in the face of opposition from the CTC (Evenson 2000b: 11). As mentioned in the discussion of the workers' parliaments, the unions also effectively challenged the 1994 proposal to tax workers' wages. By law, workers meet in their work-centres twice-yearly to participate in discussions on the economic plan of their company or enterprise. Agreements from the previous round of meetings are reviewed, reports from the administrators are discussed and examined, future plans and objectives are analyzed, and measures are implemented if deemed necessary. Workers have the option of rejecting the proposals proffered by management, necessitating a round of negotiation between the workers' representatives and the administrators. The resulting new proposal must be submitted to a workers' assembly for ratification. Workers' assemblies also determine the production norms and rates and thus, the work pace (Evenson 2000b: 13–16; Lorimer 2000: 26).

In the case of labour for joint ventures with foreign capital, the Cuban Ministry of Labour and Social Security operates a special office, run somewhat like a union hiring hall. Foreign companies cannot directly hire or fire workers. If a problem with a worker develops, the company must discuss it with the Cuban manager and the union. The worker returns to the Ministry of Labour office if he or she needs retraining or replacement. Cubans working for a foreign investor have the same benefits and protection as other Cuban workers (*Foreign Investment Act* 1995). Foreign companies are bound by Cuban social legislation. Thus, discrimination on the basis of race, sex or ethnicity is prohibited. A worker can challenge a dismissal as unfair or discriminatory, with the Ministry of Labour and Social Security acting as the final arbiter (Garcia Bielsa 1997; Ross Leal

1997). While workers in foreign enterprises must be Cuban or permanent residents, individuals who are not permanent residents can fill management and administrative positions.

Wages are paid directly to the state agency, which in turn pays the workers. The foreign employer pays the state agency in hard currency, while the Cuban workers receive their wages in Cuban pesos (*Foreign Investment Act*). This labour regime has been criticized as exploitative because the workers receive only a fraction of the wage paid by the foreign company (Lago 1997: 4; Susman 1998: 198). Cuban officials — both government and union — have countered that it is necessary for the state to manage the salaries in order to avoid the creation of a privileged stratum of workers (August 1999: 230). In addition, the management of wages allows the state access to a source of hard currency, which is used to maintain the healthcare, education and the social security systems (August 1999: 230). It is also argued that, while the wages workers receive are low — when U.S. dollars are used as the gauge — workers' basic needs are met by the state, and they are protected by extensive labour and social legislation, effectively rendering real wages much higher.

The primary work of the Cuban union movement is organized through the Confederation of Cuban Workers (CTC), which unites all unions. The CTC organizes, on a periodic basis, national congresses where Cuba's working-class democracy is most publicly put into practice. During the Special Period, there have been two such congresses: one in 1996 and the other in 2001. The 1996 congress was held five years into the intense economic crisis of the 1990s. The delegates discussed and debated many issues, focusing on the economic changes introduced and the national struggle to overcome the crisis. In preparation, a document dealing with many subjects pertaining to workers, *Theses for the 17th Congress*, was distributed to all of Cuba's workplaces at the end of 1995 and was discussed in the municipalities and then at grassroots union assemblies from January 15 to March 15, 1996 (La Riva 1996). The main objective identified was the defence of the socialist Cuban Revolution by means of strengthening the role of workers. The document opened by stating that the "essence of this 17th Congress ... will be to ... determine what we are to do, together with our people, their organizations and institutions, to guarantee under any circumstances the revolutionary power of the workers, by the workers and for the workers" (La Riva 1996).

The 18th Congress of the CTC was held in April–May 2001. This congress was preceded by seventeen months of workers' assemblies at the base level, forums, delegate elections and a thorough discussion of the unions' theses and twenty-three proposed resolutions. At the congress, the 1,675 delegates discussed defending the revolution's ideas and values, improving economic efficiency and production, and the strengthening of the union leadership at the base level (Evenson 2002b: 21–25). Workers vigorously expressed their opinions on economic and social issues, and exchanged ideas and proposed solutions with government and Communist Party leaders. Problems that were discussed and analyzed in considerable detail included, among others, employment and compensation; housing and transport shortages; the high prices in farmers' markets and recovering the previous production levels in sugar (Evenson 2000b: 24–25; author's notes 2001).

Cuban President Fidel Castro and other government ministers participated, making presentations and answering questions throughout the congress. Castro listened and spoke at length; making detailed proposals that received strong support, particularly the recommendation to extend Cuba's six-month paid maternity leave to one full year. This was adopted and took effect immediately. The congress also decided to allocate computers to the country's primary-level education. It was also resolved to endeavour to reduce unemployment to 4.1 percent by the end of 2001 (author's notes 2001). In his closing speech to the congress, President Castro focused on the nature of the Cuban State and workers' power in Cuba. He emphasized the contributions of Karl Marx, Frederick Engels, V.I. Lenin and José Martí to Cuban socialist thought and the revolutionary project. He elaborated in detail on the concept of the dictatorship of the proletariat, especially as it applied to Cuba. Castro stressed that it is the Cuban working class that holds power and runs society for the benefit of all (author's notes).

Under socialism, with the working class in power, unions advocate for workers within a framework of a cooperative relationship with the socialist government. Consequently, there is no antagonism between workers and government, a government made up of workers and others who are elected to represent particular sectors of Cuban society. In this context, the unions also work closely with the Cuban Communist Party, which is based on and represents the working class. Perhaps the simplest empirical indication of the nature of the Cuban state is the fact that the economic crisis was not resolved at the expense of workers. Invariably, within the capitalist world, the costs of economic crises are shifted onto the working and other subordinate classes. In other words, the distribution of the costs associated with the resolution of economic crises delineates the class character of the state.

THE COMMUNIST PARTY OF CUBA

While the Communist Party of Cuba (PCC) is political, it is not an electoral party. It is assigned the vanguard role of guide of the state and society. As set out in Article Five of the Cuban Constitution, the Party establishes long-range goals for society and government, promotes and facilitates the creation and development of socialist society and stimulates socialist consciousness among the population by persuading them to put the collective and society's needs above that of the individual (*Constitution of the Republic of Cuba* 1993). The PCC centres much of its work:

> towards the channelling of a plurality of points of view, interests and needs of the classes, groups and social sectors in a determined historical context on the basis of national independence, growing social emancipation and the dignity of the individual. (Fernández 1993)

Critics "decry the predominant and suffocating role of the Cuban Communist Party" (Spalding 2003: 58). By reason of its prestige, it is the most influential organization in Cuban society. But considerable efforts are made to limit its role in administration. One of the most difficult tasks has been establishing and maintaining the distinction, both in theory and practice, between the Party as guide and the Party as administrator. This demarcation "between government and the PCC has not always been clear" (Roman 1999: 91). As Fidel Castro stated, the role of the PCC is to regulate and steer "the society and state. The party doesn't administer the state" (quoted in Roman 1999: 90). Raúl Castro further laid down the parameters of PCC activity, which:

> must never meddle in the daily routine of the work of people's power … that the maximum state and administrative authority … does not rest with the party organs but with the organs of people's power. (quoted in Roman 1999: 90)

The constitutional changes, the electoral reforms and the devolution of provincial and municipal administrative power have all been parts of the process of separating the Party and government. As noted, the PCC does not participate in the nomination of candidates for the municipal, provincial or national assemblies. It is also noteworthy that the PCC does not have the power to propose legislation. The ongoing effort to avoid and remove the "overlap of Party and State" is an integral component of the goal of removing obstacles to and enhancing the citizen's political sovereignty (Bengelsdorf 1994: 172).

Approximately 1.5 million persons — 15 percent of the population — belong to the PCC and its youth body, the Union of Young Communists (UJC). Forty percent of the membership of the PCC is comprised of workers. Indeed, 13 percent of the labour force belongs to the Party; 22 percent are professional and technicians and 2.5 percent farmers (Azicri 2000: 109). The Party's congresses are preceded by massive nation-wide discussions. A comprehensive and detailed document is released as the basis for these discussions. The 1991 congress was preceded by discussions involving 3.5 million Cubans; Party and non-Party members. More than a million people in 89,000 meetings directly raised more than 500 issues and concerns (August 1999: 232; Bengelsdorf 1994: 168; Reed 1992: 17). The issues raised ranged from "the economy to the electoral process, foreign policy and the functioning of the Party itself" (Bengelsdorf 1994: 168; Reed 1992: 17). In 1997, in preparation for the Fifth Congress — held in October of that year — the PCC issued *The Party of Unity, Democracy and the Human Rights We Defend*. In defending the political system, the Party argued that Cubans "know well the multiparty formula that divided and weakened us.... We have been exceptional witnesses of what happened in the former European socialist countries and the painful political, economic and social consequences of their collapse" (Azicri 2000: 19).

The PCC further argued that it is the political system that is guarantor of the unity of the people and the social policy of universal healthcare, education, housing and employment, and racial and gender equality (Communist Party of Cuba 1997: 34). Fidel Castro has argued that the mechanical copying of the European and U.S. systems has "brought catastrophe, division, subordination and neo-colonialism" to the South. Societies have "split into thousands of pieces; societies that should be united in their efforts to develop have ended up not only with a multiparty system but with hundreds and even thousands of parties" (Castro 1996a: 23). The end result is not a multiparty system but "a crazy party system" (Castro 1996a: 89).

MASS ORGANIZATIONS AND CIVIL SOCIETY

A critical aspect of the Cuban political system is the integration of a variety of mass organizations into political activity. These organizations have very specific functions and responsibilities. In addition to the Communist Party, the Young Communist League and the Confederation of Cuban

Workers, there are the Cuban Federation of Women, the Committees to Defend the Revolution, the National Association of Small Farmers and the Federation of University Students. The mass organizations are supplemented by numerous professional and other associations that represent the specific interests of other sectors, including for example, lawyers, economists, journalists, writers and artists, the physically challenged and stamp collectors. In short, "these associations and organizations embrace practically the entire universe of activities, interests and problems of all Cubans" (Alarcón 1999: 8). Thus, Cuba has what some would term an active and vibrant civil society, despite the reality that "civil society" is invariably conceived as an entity existing against the state. For example, "political struggle in communist societies is seen as the struggle of civil society as such against a monolithic party-state" (Beverly 2002: 3). Indeed, the Cuban political process rejects "the distinction between political and civil society" (Spalding 2003: 60). It is often stereotypically asserted that civil society in Cuba can only exist and constitute itself "in opposition to the regime and goals of Cuban socialism" (Beverley 2002: 2). Yet, Cuba has a constellation of organizations and associations that reflect and represent the ambit of all social sectors in the polity. This challenges the notion "that there is only one voice in Cuba — the voice of the party, the voice of Fidel Castro… that the only ethically and intellectually honest positions in Cuba are those of the 'dissidents,' that ideological pluralism and independence of thought exist only among those who have left Cuba" (Beverly 2002: 2).

The Committees to Defend the Revolution (CDRs) are the largest and most grassroots of all the mass organizations, with a membership of more than seven million people. They were established to organize the population "to repress counter-revolutionary activity, i.e., sabotage and terrorism" (Lorimer 2000: 25). However, the CDRs' function evolved to encompass a wide range of social and community activities, for example, public security efforts, recycling drives, cultural and children's events, vaccination and blood donation campaigns. They generate community cohesion and togetherness; the CDRs "have created a social network that is critical for all sorts of activities" (Lopez Vigil 1999: 266).

The mass organizations are a key feature of the participatory culture that typifies Cuba. They are national and inclusive, augmenting the representative governmental structures by providing an organizational and institutional means by which civil society both expresses itself and intervenes in the decision-making process. Indeed, they play a key role: "no decision on matters that concern these organizations is made without their consent" (Alarcón 1999: 8). Mass organizations, unlike the Communist Party, are granted through Article 88 (c) of the Constitution the right to propose legislation in the areas that fall under their jurisdiction. Hence, these organizations have a dynamic existence, and Cuba is replete with almost daily assemblies, meetings and gatherings of various organizations to discuss and examine particular issues, in conjunction with the participation of government officials. This is part and parcel of the political process.

THE GENERATIONAL SHIFT

There is a tendency in both the western media and academia towards Fidelcentrism: the idea that everything in Cuba revolves around Fidel Castro (Kapica 1996: 218–19). This outlook leads opponents of the Cuban Revolution to conceptualize Fidel Castro

> as this one lone revolutionary in all of Cuba, their strategy is to knock him down by brute force — by assassination, by invasion, by blockading the island. By knocking down Fidel, they will knock down the Revolution. They fail to see that Fidel is not the Revolution — the Cuban people are. (Koehnlein 2001)

A generational shift is — and has been for some time — underway, in which the new generation "has moved upward in the nation's political structure" and "seems destined to be the country's next rulers" (Azicri 2000: 125). This generation is comprised of persons who were just children when the Revolution triumphed or who were born after 1959. They have moved into "the highest positions in and out of government, like ministerial posts and as members of the Communist Party's Politburo" (Azicri 2000: 125). This is particularly reflected in the administration of the economy where "a younger generation in its 30s and 40s has moved into key economic positions over the past few years" (Frank 2003a). Indeed, the day-to-day administration of the country has passed into their hands. The average age of the Politburo is less than fifty. Typifying this ongoing process of the transfer of authority and power in Cuban government are Carlos Lage Davila, in his early fifties, a vice president in charge of the economy, and Felipe Pérez Roque, in his thirties and Foreign Minister. The rise of the new generation of leaders is also reflected in the composition of the 1998 National Assembly. The average age of the 601 deputies was forty-five years, with 189 being between eighteen and forty years old; 374 were forty-one to sixty; and only 38 were over sixty.

The youngest member, at the time of the 1998 elections, was twenty (August 1999: 366–68). The transition began at the 4th Congress of the Communist Party (Fitzgerald 1994: 194). It was reaffirmed at the 5th Congress, where Castro observed:

> The number has already been mentioned of those remaining who were members of the first Central Committee. It's starting to get lower. Then comes the intermediate generations. That's grown.... The intermediate generation is important and the new generations are very important even if they are comrades who aren't very well known. (Castro 1998b: 183–84)

The political role and influence of the new generation continue to expand. They have been critical in navigating the difficulties of the economic crisis and in charting new directions. Their importance in guaranteeing the continuation of the Revolution is increasingly recognized by Cuba's fiercest critics. *Time Magazine*, for example, noted, "after Castro dies the one party system he built will remain in place for some time" (Karon 2001). As Ricardo Alarcón noted, one of the central tasks is imbuing new generations "with the responsibility of continuing the Cuban Revolution and socialism" (quoted in Tucker 2001). He further underlined the reality that the administration and running of the country is in the hands of Cubans born during the Revolution, stating:

> If you were to look through the positions of leadership in the party — the government, the provinces, every institution in Cuba — the majority of those leading the country at the moment were born after 1959. The country didn't stop 40 years ago.... This view of Fidel is linked with a completely wrong presentation of Cuba, as if Cuba were still living in the past, 40 years ago, which is not true. (quoted in Tucker 2001)

Indeed, it is this new generation, these rising figures, who will head the Revolution "in the twenty-first century... defining the ultimate nature of the country's socialist system" and taking it "out of the special period" (Azicri 2000: 126).

GOVERNMENT OPPONENTS

Considerable controversy arises in regard to the "political prisoners" and "dissidents." The arrest, trial and sentencing in March/April 2003 of seventy-eight persons on charges of treason, specifically, "working with a foreign power to undermine the government," were met with much vitriol and condemnation (Broadle 2003b; *Miami Herald* 2003). However, these "political" cases are often distorted, with the international reporting on them bearing no resemblance to the actual issues or evidence presented. These distorted cases are then used to condemn the entire Cuban political and justice system. Moreover, what is ignored is the reality that Cuba has been and continues to be the target of repeated aggressions and interference in its internal affairs by the United States (Remigio-Ferro 1999; also discussed in Chapter Five). Consequently, the Western media almost invariably portray the actions of the Cuban government as irrational and tyrannical, "arising from Castro's character flaws and having no connection with any relevant historical event," failing to acknowledge and "consider the current context or the long history of U.S. attempts to overthrow the Cuban government" (Sandels 2003).

This is the context in which the Cuban government's actions must be viewed; the censures of the Cuban Revolution "are nothing less than hypocritical if they are not framed in the context of opposition to American aggression against the island state" (McNally 2002: 186). Cuban leaders and legal experts have constantly reiterated that the Cuban Revolution does not exist or operate under normal conditions. The Cuban government asserts that any unprejudiced discussion on the situation of government opponents:

> must take as its point of departure a full understanding of the political situation in which the Cuban Revolution has developed since its accession to power in 1959. The situation is characterized by an uninterrupted series of aggressions of all types from the United States, whose resources to do not need to be emphasized. [The activists'] purported status as defenders of human rights is no more than an unusual façade for hiding the work that they do in close coordination, and under the direction of foreign enemies of Cuba, with the goal of establishing internal conditions to facilitate the United States' well-known plans to destroy the Cuban Revolution. (quoted in Schwab 1999: 150–51)

The reality of living for more than four decades under external aggression has generated a siege mentality within Cuba, especially among the leadership. However, while, as some argue, not all government opponents "can be painted with the same brush of sedition and not all of them are connected to the United States" (Schwab 1999: 151), this siege mentality — what some have called a rational paranoia — is based on a very real and constant threat. Washington's record of aggression includes sabotage, terrorist attacks, coastal raids, an invasion, assassinations, attempted assassinations against the leadership, biological warfare, an economic embargo tantamount to an economic blockade and a constant propaganda and disinformation crusade. In the 1990s, the U.S. stepped up its actions against Cuba on the economic front. The U.S. strengthened the trade embargo, which it had imposed in 1961, by passing the *American Cuban Liberty and Democratic Solidarity Act* of 1996, popularly known as the Helms-Burton Bill, which calls for a dismantling of the Cuban socialist model of development and its replacement with a free-market system and a multi-party political process.

Paralleling the economic embargo and other external measures are the active policy efforts to undermine the Revolution from within by fomenting an internal opposition in order to incite an uprising. The Cuban government views the internal opposition groups as part of a spectrum that encompasses the external aggressions against the island (Hoffmann 1998). There exists extensive relationships and linkages of government opponents to Cuban exile groups in Florida and various agencies of the U.S. government (Arboleya 2000; Calvo and Declercq 2000). Section 109 of the Helms-Burton Bill authorizes the U.S. President "to provide assistance to support efforts to establish democracy in Cuba," pledging financial aid to any "transitional government in Cuba, committed to undertaking fundamental economic and political reforms" (Alarcón 1997: 18). Thus, the Helms-Burton Bill and other U.S. measures have not only strengthened the U.S. economic embargo against Cuba but stipulate the granting of financial and material aid to individuals inside Cuba who pursue activities aimed at undermining and eventually overthrowing the Cuban government (Alarcón 1997: 14–15). Nelson Valdes, a Cuba specialist at the University of New Mexico, notes that there are several organizations and groups in Cuba that "the United States government found attractive, supported and funded" (quoted in Associated Press 2003a). The United States Agency for International Development (USAID), for example, has given more than $20 million U.S. to various groups seeking to foster an opposition in Cuba (Snow 2003). The USAID 2003 budget for Cuba activities is $6 million (Agee 2003). Here is a partial list of expenditures by the USAID, taken from their website:

Freedom House: Transitions ($500,000 — completed)

Provided 40,000 Spanish language books, pamphlets and other materials to the Cuban people on issues such as human rights, transition to democracy and free market economics.

Center for a Free Cuba ($2,249,709)
The Center gathers and disseminates information concerning the human rights situation in Cuba. Transmits the writings of Cuban human rights activists to non-governmental organizations worldwide. Sponsors travel to Cuba by representatives of democratic societies. Distributes pro-democracy literature on the island.

The Institute for Democracy in Cuba ($1,000,000 — completed)
Assisted democratic activists in Cuba, informed the Cuban people, gathered and disseminated information from inside Cuba on human rights. Provided 7,000 pounds of humanitarian assistance (food and medicine) to political prisoners, their families, and other victims of oppression.

Cuban Dissidence Task Group ($250,000 — completed)
Published and disseminated worldwide the written analysis of Cuban democratic activists on the island. Provided humanitarian assistance (food and medicine) to political prisoners and their families, and to other victims of government oppression.

International Republican Institute ($1,674,462)
Helps create and bolster international solidarity committees in Latin America and Europe in order to provide material, moral and ideological support for democratic activists in Cuba.

Freedom House: Cuban Democracy Project ($825,000)
Promotes the formation of civic and political leadership in Cuba by linking professional organizations in Cuba to one another and to those in free democracies in Europe, North America and elsewhere.

University of Miami: Developing Civil Society ($320,000)
Facilitates access to information and training for Cuban NGOs and individuals.

Sabre Foundation ($85,000 — completed)

Donated new books and other informational materials on democratic transition, free market economics and other issues to
independent Cuban NGOs and individuals in order to benefit the
Cuban people.

Rutgers University: Planning for Change ($99,000 — com-
pleted)
Supported planning for future assistance to a Cuban transition
government and, eventually, to a democratically elected government in Cuba. Transmitted planning results to the Cuban people.

International Foundation for Election Systems ($136,000 —
completed)
Analyzed assistance required to support transitional elections in
Cuba. Without discussing or considering the possible timing of
elections, the study established guidelines, costs, and options
concerning international assistance and the requirements or local
administration of comprehensive voter registration and conduct
of free and fair presidential and congressional elections in Cuba.
USAID will disseminate its findings to the Cuban people. (USAID
2002)

The impact of the Helms–Burton Bill and other U.S. measures can
only be fully understood against the backdrop of the Cuban economic
crisis of the 1990s, the context that frames Law 88 and other similar
measures taken by the Cuban government in response to the escalation of
actions against the island. It must be understood that the revenue derived
from international trade, joint ventures and economic partnerships the
Cuban state pursues with foreign capital becomes part of the social
redistribution of wealth to maintain the healthcare, education and social
systems. In numerous conversations with Cubans from all sectors of
Cuban society, the overwhelming view is that any collaboration with U.S.
legislation and policies targeted against the Cuban Revolution are a direct
assault on the well–being of the population, necessitating drastic defensive
measures. Interconnected with this consensus is the fact that the actual
changes that the opponents of the Cuban government wish to implement
in Cuba, the policies they advocate, are rarely reported on in the Western
media. Moreover, when opposition figures have attempted to use the
Cuban political process to advance their agenda, by putting forward their
own candidates at nomination meetings, they have been unable to garner

the necessary support and votes from the electors (Roman 1999: 112). As Jesús Arboleya Cervera, a professor at the University of Havana, observed in regard to the arrest, trial and sentencing of the seventy-five government opponents in March/April 2003:

> The detention and sentencing of these people has had scant repercussion within the political context in Cuba. By this I do not mean that the news was not received with interest and that some people don't share the opinion that the oppositionists deserved the sanctions they got. What I mean is that, contrary to what the U.S. media have propagated, the average Cuban does not identify with the oppositionists, what they say, what they don't say, who they are, and the manner in which they hope to achieve their objectives. The historical reality is that an inability to present a legitimate agenda and a reliable leadership are the reasons why the counter-revolution has been unable to advance in the field of Cuba's domestic politics. (Arboleya Cervera 2003)

Karen Wald, an American journalist who lived in Cuba for more than twenty years, underscores this point:

> The U.S. media often state that many men and women in prison in Cuba are "those who oppose the official line." But those journalists omit an important question: what is the official line? In Cuba, the "official line" is that food, health care, housing, education, jobs and culture are fundamental human rights to be protected at all costs. Cubans often find it puzzling that the foreign press insists on the "right" of certain individuals to attempt to take these away. Why should they let a small, individualistic, and self-serving minority try to take away the rights they struggled so hard to gain? (Wald 1999b: 86)

Internationally, the most controversial legal measure implemented by Cuban legislators has been Law 88: *Law for the Protection of National Independence and the Economy of Cuba*, approved by the National Assembly on February 16, 1999. Law 88 was adopted for a specific purpose: to establish sanctions against Cuban citizens who collaborate with the United States' economic war against Cuba. Ricardo Alarcón described Law 88 as a necessary and direct response to the Helms–Burton Bill (*Granma* 1999a). The preamble to Law 88 mentions that U.S. hostility has created a peculiar and unique situation requiring "measures against counterrevolutionaries and annexationists" (*Gaceta Oficial de la República de Cuba* 1999). Alarcón emphasized that the legislation is very clear in its objectives, being directed at those who cooperate in the application and implementation of U.S. legislation aimed at subverting Cuban internal order and reasserting U.S. domination over the country. He further reiterated that "Cuba has the obligation to use judicial and penal measures to confront the U.S. blockade" (*Granma* 1999a).

Law 88 is the enabling legislation for Law 80: *Reaffirmation of Cuba Dignity and Sovereignty Act*, passed in 1996, which had made illegal any collaboration or facilitation of the implementation of the Helms-Burton Bill (*Gaceta Oficial de la Republica de Cuba* 1996). It also augments Article 91 (Acts Against the Independence or Territorial Integrity of Cuba), Article 94 (Assistance to the Enemy) and Article 95 (Revealing of State Secrets) of the *Codigo Penal* (penal code). Specifically, the articles embodied in Law 88 define, criminalize and penalize actions directed at supporting, facilitating or collaborating with the Helms-Burton Bill, the blockade and the economic war against Cuba; as well as other actions intended to discredit, harm or endanger the independence, sovereignty and integrity of the Cuban state. Criminal activities in that context include supplying, seeking or obtaining information which would aid the U.S. government in its plans to asphyxiate and destroy the Cuban Revolution. Terms of imprisonment are established for those who collaborate with or facilitate the United States' economic war against Cuba or receive material backing in order to influence and affect Cuban politics. In serious cases of supplying subversive disinformation, collaborating with media outlets which systematically attack Cuba and receiving financial assistance from abroad to carry out Washington's aim of subverting and destroying the Cuban Revolution, offenders can receive up to twenty years in prison.

The most prominent and publicized cases prior to the March/April 2003 arrests and trials were those of Vladimiro Roca, Rene Gomez, Felix Bonne and Marta Beatriz. In June 1999, they were tried and convicted under Law 88, receiving sentences of five, four, four and three years, respectively. This provoked an outcry in the West. The Canadian media, for example, repeatedly called for a cooling of Canadian government relations with Cuba. The four dissidents were portrayed as innocents: imprisoned for merely having opinions different from that of the Cuban government. However, the facts of the case were never discussed in that same media. It is interesting to note that the facts presented by the *fiscal* (Cuban prosecutor) were never disputed or denied by the defendants.

Indeed, their defence consisted of their right to carry out these actions (*Miami Herald* 1999: 3).

The four individuals were convicted of very specific activities under Law 88:

1. Seeking to undermine the Cuban economy by issuing statements coinciding with the Helms-Burton Bill, calling on all countries including Canada to refrain from investing in Cuba, and threatening foreign businesses who negotiate with and invest in Cuba, with reprisals.
2. Having ties with organizations financed and put into motion by the Miami-based exile groups that historically have carried out illegal and terrorist actions against Cuba.
3. Issuing a document that called for the political destabilization of Cuba and aimed at disrupting the 1997–98 elections.
4. Issuing statements on Radio Martí encouraging a boycott of the elections. Radio Martí is financed by and based in the United States, with the express goal of fostering the overthrow of the Cuban government, in violation of international telecommunications treaties.
5. Receiving money, communication equipment and guidance from the United States Interests Section in Havana, in order, to further the actions mentioned above. (*Granma* 1999c, *Granma* 1999b and Roman 1999: 86).

As noted, the four "dissidents" did not dispute the charges. The Cuban government characterized them as "an organised, paid fifth column of the foreign power which pursues the policy to revert back to the situation which existed before the revolution" (*Granma* 1999c). The government further asserted that no one in Cuba is imprisoned for merely having different political opinions (*Granma* 1999c). In short, the four individuals were active and deliberate participants in the destabilization war against Cuba, willing and able accomplices to foreign intervention in Cuba's internal affairs.

The government opponents arrested and put on trial in March/April 2003 committed similar acts, i.e., receiving money and other resources to engage in activities against their nation state. Contrary to the "conventional wisdom," those who were arrested and tried were "charged not with criticizing the government, but for receiving American government funds and collaborating with U.S. diplomats" (Associated Press 2003b).

They were specifically charged with violations of Article 91 of the Cuban penal code, which establishes that anyone who "executes an action in the interest of a foreign state with the purpose of harming the independence of the Cuban state or the integrity of its territory shall incur a sentence of 10 to 20 years of denial of liberty or death." They were also charged with violating Law 88, particularly those sections relating to furthering the objectives of the Helms–Burton Act.

Under a directive of the Bush administration, U.S. officials "stepped up their contacts with dissidents in recent months, offering free Internet access inside the mission and giving them radios, pamphlets and other material" (*New York Times* 2003; see also Smith 2003a). Felipe Pérez Roque, Cuba's Foreign Minister, stated that the "U.S. Interests Section has been instructed to establish there what is practically the headquarters of internal subversion in Cuba.... The head of this section has the highest profile of anyone in its 25 years of functioning, in open violation of the laws governing diplomatic conduct, openly interfering in Cuba's internal affairs, with a tone and demeanour totally inappropriate for a diplomat." He further added that these actions reflected "the obsession of the U.S. governments to fabricate an opposition in Cuba" (Pérez Roque 2003).

The opposition figures meet frequently with James Cason, the head of the U.S. Interests Section in Havana, to receive directions (Broadle 2003a; Knox 2003). Cason "even held press conferences after some of the meetings. Such meetings might have been considered routine, had the purpose not been regime change. But given that it was, the Cubans came to see them as "subversive" in nature and as increasingly provocative (Smith 2003b). Cason traveled through out the country distributing money, equipment and other resources, with the objective of generating an opposition movement. These actions violated the 1961 *Vienna Convention on Diplomatic Relations*, which codifies the laws governing the conduct of diplomats. Article 41 (1) of the Convention declares that diplomats "have a duty not to interfere in the internal affairs of that State" (*Vienna Convention* 1961). Accordingly, the Cuban government lodged several protests asking Cason to cease such behaviour. In response, he intensified his activity and held a press conference where he stated his express objective to assist the financing, organizing and uniting of all the groups opposed to the government into one party. Alana Yu-lan Price and Jessica Leight, research associates at the Washington, D.C.-based Council on Hemispheric Affairs, noted:

In fact, James Cason and his colleagues in the U.S. Interests

Section in Havana have been actively supporting Cuban dissidents since Mr. Cason's arrival in September — actions that no self-respecting government should be expected to tolerate, especially when initiated by a hostile superpower only 90 miles away. (Yu-lan Price and Leight 2003)

Some members of government opposition groups received twenty-four-hour-access passes to the U.S. diplomatic compound. U.S. diplomats also instructed the "independent journalists" on which topics to write about and provided them with, among other things, tape recorders, computers and digital cameras and paid them "using a Canadian bank debit card called Transcard" (Broadle 2003a). Others also obtained televisions, lamps and pots (Pérez Roque 2003). For example, Espinosa Chepe had received in the course of one year $7,154 U.S. and had accumulated a further $13,000 (Associated Press 2003b). In 2002, the U.S. government handed over $8.99 million to various groups and individuals working against the Cuban government (*Prensa Latina* 2003).

On the basis of this evidence, Cuban authorities contend that the seventy-five individuals were demonstrably not independent thinkers, writers or human rights activists, but persons directly in the pay of the U.S. government, guilty of receiving directives, money, equipment and other resources from a foreign power to engage in activities against their own country. In twenty-nine separate trials, where they were represented by fifty-four lawyers (forty-four chosen by the families and ten court appointed), the seventy-five were found guilty and sentenced to six to twenty-eight years in prison. Karen Wald succinctly captures the salient issues, ignored by the press:

> What were they jailed for? What were they doing? What was their objective? What would have been the results of their gaining those objectives? Whose lives would have been damaged, lost...?
> ...these people are in fact in bed with the most unsavoury representatives of the United States, whose goal is to undo the Cuban political system so the island can be safely returned to the fold of global (U.S.) corporate capitalism. (Wald 2003)

Moreover, having witnessed the complete disregard by U.S. ruling circles for international law in connection with the war waged against Iraq, Cuba is prudent in taking measures by which to defend itself, especially given the fact that Washington continues to place Cuba on its list of rogue states. It is even included by some senior Bush officials in the "axis of evil" (*Globe and Mail* 2003a). The arrests and subsequent trials of the seventy-five individuals reflected "a justifiable fear that Mr. Cason's liaisons with dissidents indicated an intensification of U.S. aggression toward Cuba" (Yu-lan Price and Leight 2003). The stated objective of the U.S. government is the overthrow of the Cuban Revolution and a re-imposition of U.S.-dependent capitalism on the island. Toward this end, the Bush administration seeks to create an opposition movement by substantially raising the level of the support provided, with the ultimate aim of provoking an uprising. In order to thwart these efforts to manufacture a fifth column, the Cuban government took action. After all, "it is easier for a burglar to break into a house if he has an accomplice to let him in" (General Voroshilov, quoted in Davies 1943: 168).

Revealingly, Hans Hertell, U.S. Ambassador to the Dominican Republic, said: "I think what is happening in Iraq is going to send a very positive signal, and it is a very good example for Cuba," adding that "the U.S.-led invasion of Iraq is just the beginning of a campaign aimed at having all countries implement a multi-party democratic system" (*Globe and Mail* 2003a). Wayne Smith, a former head of the U.S. Interests Section in Havana, was told by a Cuban diplomat, "This new pre-emptive-strike policy of yours puts us in a new ballgame, and in that new game, we must make it clear that we can't be pushed around. Who knows? We may be next" (Smith 2003a). Moreover, U.S. Secretary of Defense Rumsfeld declared that Washington would consider military action against Cuba if "weapons of mass destruction" were determined to be on the island (*Globe and Mail* 2003a). Revealingly, Cuba was added to the U.S. list of countries that allegedly have chemical or biological weapons (*The Philippine Star* 2003). These charges against Cuba were first alleged by the Bush administration in 2002 and emphatically disputed by the Cuban govern-ment, international experts, former U.S. President Carter and other U.S. officials. Moreover, in its annual report, *Patterns of Global Terrorism*, the U.S. once again included Cuba on the list of states that Washington alleges sponsor terrorism at the international level (U.S. Department of State 2003; *Dallas Morning News* 2003).

The arrests and trials of the "dissidents" occurred against a background of a series of hijackings (discussed in greater detail in Chapter Four) involving aircraft and a ferry that the Cuban government argued were closely connected to the Florida exile organizations. Castro iterated: "We are now in a battle against provocations that are trying to move toward conflict and military aggression by the United States" (Associated Press

2003a). Wayne Smith observed:

> I think that the Cubans have looked at what is happening in Iraq and have concluded that the United States will not be restrained by international law. (Associated Press 2003a)

Cuban officials consider the West's condemnation of Law 88 and the conviction of the dissidents not only an unconscionable distortion of what actually transpired but also an exercise in hypocrisy. President Castro has stated: "For 40 years you try to strangle us. And then you criticize us, for the way we breathe" (quoted in Durand 1998). Under international law, among other things, the efforts by Washington to disrupt the Cuban economy by severing the island's trading links constitute an act of war (Bravo 1996: 54–55; D'Estefano 1989: 359). Thus, Law 88 and other similar measures are justifiable acts of self-defence. Concordantly, Cuban officials maintain that Western governments, specifically the United States and Canada, have passed and implemented legislation similar to Law 88 when they perceived their security to be threatened. As Wayne Smith mused:

> imagine the reaction of the U.S. Government if those [Cuban] diplomats were meeting with members of the Puerto Rican Independence Party to promote Puerto Rico's transition from commonwealth to independence. Perhaps the Attorney General would not have everyone involved arrested, but I wouldn't take any bets on it. (Smith 2003b)

Furthermore, the right of a people to determine their own future is a fundamental principle incorporated into Article 1 of the United Nations charter. The right of a people to self-determination is re-affirmed in Article 1.1 of both the *International Covenant on Economic, Social and Cultural Rights* and the *International Covenant on Civil and Political Rights*. The *Declaration on Principles of International Law Concerning Friendly Relations and Co-operation Among States in Accordance with the Charter of the United Nations* declares:

> All peoples have the right to freely determine, without external interference, their political status and to pursue their economic, social and cultural development, and every state has the duty to respect this right in accordance with the provisions of the

Charter. (United Nations 1971)

All governments reserve the right to defend their respective nation-states from sedition and treason. For example, the Canadian *Criminal Code* maintains sedition and treason as reasonable grounds for the limiting of a person's freedom: conspiring with an enemy of Canada can result in life imprisonment. Under U.S. law these activities are liable to "criminal prosecution and a 10-year prison sentence for anyone who agrees to operate within the United States subject to the direction or control of a foreign government or official (Title 18, section 951 of the United States Code)" (Sandels 2003). Thus, Cubans argue, Western countries claim for themselves rights that they deny Cuba. This assumes greater irony given the legislation that has been passed in the aftermath of the events of September 11, 2001, particularly in the United States and Canada. Yet, this is not the first time that both countries have constrained the political and civil liberties of their citizens, justifying these actions in the name of national security.

In 1917, during World War I, the *Espionage Act* was passed in the United States. One of its provisions established penalties of up to twenty years imprisonment for:

> Whoever, when the United States is at war, shall wilfully cause or attempt to cause insubordination, disloyalty, shall mutiny, or refusal of duty in the military or naval forces of the United States, or shall wilfully obstruct the recruiting or enlistment service of the United States. (Zinn 1995: 356)

The *Espionage Act* was used against U.S. citizens who simply expressed opposition to the war. More than nine hundred people were imprisoned under the Act (Zinn 1995: 357; Kohn 1994: 7–25; Churchhill and Vander Wall 1990: 19), including Charles Schenck, who was arrested and convicted in August 1917. He appealed to the U.S. Supreme Court on the basis that the Act violated the First Amendment of the U.S. Constitution, which guarantees freedom of speech and the press. However, the Court upheld the Act as constitutional, holding that it was an acceptable and reasonable abridgement, asserting that constitutional protection did not extend to speech that posed a "clear and present danger" to society or country (Zinn 1995: 357).

In 1940, the U.S. Congress passed the *Alien Registration Act* — widely know as the Smith Act — buttressing the *Espionage Act* (Zinn 1997: 411,

357; Churchhill and Vander Wall 1990: 29). The Smith Act made it a crime to:

> knowingly or wilfully advocate, abet, advise or teach the duty, necessity, desirability or propriety of overthrowing or destroying any government in the United States by force or violence, or by assassination of any officer of such government. (Churchhill and Vander Wall 1990: 29)

It was also illegal under the Act to belong to, organize or help create any organization or "assembly of persons" who advocated or encouraged the same. The penalties were set at ten years imprisonment and a fine of $10,000 (Fariello 1995: 18). The Smith Act also applies the prohibitions of the *Espionage Act* to peacetime (Fariella 1995: 29). In 1943, eighteen members of the Socialist Workers Party were convicted under the Smith Act and sentenced to ten years imprisonment (Zinn 1995: 411; Goldstein 1978: 252–53). In total, during World War II, under the Smith Act, 611 people were convicted with an aggregate sentence of 1,637 years and $251,709 in fines (Foster 1951: 384). Eleven members of the Communist Party of the United States were tried and imprisoned under the Smith Act in 1949. In 1951, the U.S. Supreme Court upheld that the Smith Act did not violate the U.S. Constitution (Davis 1971: 289). Several trials followed, resulting in the conviction of numerous individuals (see Caute 1978). In 1969, Geronimo Pratt and Roger Lewis, leaders of the Black Panther Party, were charged with being in violation of the Smith Act (Churchhill and Vander Wall 1990: 81).

The *Internal Security* (McCarran) *Act* was passed in 1950. It required that certain organizations register as "communist action," "communist front" or "communist infiltrated" (Carr 1979: 1–11; Caute 1978: 170–71, 563–64; Davis 1971: 358; Churchhill and Vander Wall 1990: 33). Justice Hugo Black stated that the Act was designed to make it impossible for these organizations to continue to function by stipulating crushing penalties for failure to register. The penalties were $10,000 and/or five years in prison for every day of non-registration (Fariello 1995: 454–55). Title II of the Act — not repealed until 1968 — provided for the use of concentration camps in times of national emergency, invasion or insurrection. Members of the Communist Party of the United States were to be detained and incarcerated without trial (Carr 1979: 195; Davis 1971: 358; Zinn 1995: 423–24).

The *Internal Security Act* bolsters the Logan Act, also incorporated under Title 18 in Section 951 of the United States Code, which makes it a criminal offence to operate as an undisclosed agent of a foreign government (Moore et al. 1990: 1053, 1058, Tanner 1971: 16–17 and Sandels 2003). The Logan Act establishes:

> That any United States citizen, wherever he or she may be, who without authorization from the United States, directly or indirectly establishes or enters into correspondence or any form of contact with a foreign government or official, or an agent of a foreign government, can be fined up to $5000 or serve 3 years in prison. (18 U.S.C., s 951. See also Moore et al. 1990: 1058)

Canada, which has vigorously criticized Cuba, also employed similar measures. In the 1930s, various labour and political activists were arrested and imprisoned under what was then Section 98 of the *Criminal Code,* which outlawed "subversive organizations" (MacKenzie 1972: 469–83; MacKinnon 1977: 631–32; McNaught 1974: 149–69; Communist Party of Canada 2000). Tim Buck, the general secretary of the Communist Party of Canada, and seven other party members were convicted under this section. Section 47 of the present *Criminal Code* provides for a minimum sentence of fourteen years and a maximum sentence of life imprisonment for treason. Under section 61, a maximum sentence of fourteen years is established for any person who "speaks seditious words, or publishes a seditious libel, or is a party to a seditious conspiracy."

In 1983, the Canadian government had planned, in the event of war, to round up more than a thousand "subversives" and hold them in internment camps (Beeby 2000). This was to be done under the then *War Measures Act,* upon it being invoked by the government. During World War II, the *War Measures Act* was used as the basis for the dispossession and internment of Japanese Canadians (Peppin 1993: 161–67; Sunahara 1981: 102–105). During the 1970 October Crisis in Québec, the Act was again invoked, resulting in the detention of numerous individuals (Holthuis 1991: 5), including a wide range of activists who belonged to designated "radical organizations." The Communist Party of Canada (Marxist-Leninist) asserts that more than a thousand of its members were arrested across Canada; six were deported, one of whom had been born in Canada (Seed 2000; Canada Commission 1981). In 1988, the *War Measures Act* was replaced by the *Emergencies Act.* However, the same powers are preserved, permitting the Canadian government "to take special temporary measures that may not be appropriate in normal times (Rosenthal

1991: 563–99). The Act enables Ottawa to impose terms of imprisonment from six months to five years upon the finding that an "urgent and critical situation" exists that "seriously threatens the ability of the Government of Canada to preserve the sovereignty, security and territorial integrity of Canada."

In the final analysis, it is worth quoting Carlos Fernández de Cossío, Cuba's Ambassador to Canada, at length:

> The individuals arrested, prosecuted and sentenced in Cuba in recent days were not accused, nor were they detained, tried and sentenced for being economists, journalists, human rights activists or for expressing their opinion and dissent. They have violated laws clearly known by them that are aimed to legitimately protect Cuba from the attempt by the U.S. Government to destabilize the country, undermine and destroy Cuba's Constitutional order, its Government, its independence and its Socialist society.... The U.S. does not have the right in Cuba and should not have the right anywhere to instruct their diplomats to interfere in the domestic affairs of a foreign country. It is not acceptable to Cuba for the chief U.S. diplomat in Havana to act as an organizer or agitator against the Government and to have Cuban citizens acting not only in complicity but also as instruments of the policy of hostility of the U.S. against Cuba. It is not true that the accused did not enjoy proper defense, in most cases designated by them and in the absence of such designation, assigned by the Government. It is not true that they were uninformed about the charges before the trials. It is not true that the trials were held in secret or behind closed doors. Relatives and other Cuban citizens were present in all of the trials. These were indeed summary trials, conducted in accordance with the law, with full guarantees and based on provisions for summary procedure similar to those existing in over one hundred countries, including the United States.... No action similar to the abuses of Afghans, Arabs and citizens from different countries detained in Guantánamo base has taken place in Cuba. No secret military trial like the ones established in the United States has been nor can be carried out in Cuba. There do not exist thousands of detainees still unaware of the charges against them and whose names have not been released in totality, as is happening in the United States since September 11, 2001. None of the individuals tried in Cuba has been submitted to solitary

confinement, to psychological torture or cruel separation from
their families.... The 75 Cuban individuals and their attorneys
have had full access to the information used against them by the
prosecution.... This is not an issue of human rights, liberty or
freedom of expression; it is about the right of a nation to build a
just society protected from foreign aggression. (Fernández de
Cossio 2003)

THE VARELA PROJECT

On May 10, 2002, Osvaldo Payá, a representative of the Cuban Christian
Liberation Movement, submitted a petition containing more than 11,000
signatures to the National Assembly. The petition was part of the Varela
Project, as it is commonly referred to in the Western media, which takes
its name from a nineteenth-century Cuban priest and national hero, and
was endorsed by both President George W. Bush and former President
Carter. It also continues to receive assistance from the diplomatic staff in
the U.S. Interests Section. The petition contained twenty points that
ostensibly called for broader freedom of statement and association,
amnesty for political prisoners, property rights, free enterprise and changes
in the electoral system (Evenson 2002a). In short, it solicited a dramatic
change to the political, economic and social systems.

The petitioners stated that the right to present the demands and
request a referendum was guaranteed under articles 63 and 88(g) of the
Constitution of Cuba. Article 88 of the Constitution establishes that the
right of legislative initiative, the right to present new laws to the National
Assembly for consideration, accrues to:

a)   the deputies of the National Assembly of People's Power;
b)   the Council of State;
c)   the Council of Ministers;
c)   the commissions of the National Assembly of People's Power;
d)   the National Committee of the Central Organization of Cuban
     Workers and the national boards of the other mass and social
     organizations;
e)   the Supreme Popular Court, in material related to the administration
     of justice;
f)   the Attorney General, in material within its competence;
g)   to the citizens (with the stricture that this right be exercised by at least
     ten thousand citizens who are eligible to vote) (*Constitution of the
     Republic of Cuba* 1993, Evenson 2002a and Ramy 2002).

Article 88 does not include the right to call a referendum, nor does it legally compel the National Assembly to do so in response to the exercise of the right to legislative initiative. This "would be absurd since it would mean that every one of the persons and entities listed could insist on a popular referendum on any proposal" (Evenson 2002a). A proposal presented to the National Assembly under Article 88 of the Constitution would be reviewed by a commission with

> jurisdiction over the subject matter and such commissions (committees in the U.S.) debate the proposal, suggest amendments, vote on it and determine whether and when it should be introduced to the full legislative body. (Evenson 2002a)

Likewise, Article 63 does not cover or deal with the issue of referenda. It focuses on the rights of citizens to lodge complaints and requests to the authorities and obtain, within a legally prescribed period, a reply. Article 63 commonly "applies to complaints brought to the Attorney General's Office concerning denial of rights, seeking remedies to administrative decisions perceived to be unjust or redress of harms caused by a public agency" (Evenson 2002a). Only the National Assembly, under Article 75, is authorized to call a referendum. Thus, it is necessary to "differentiate between an initiative to pass a new law and an initiative to amend the Constitution" (Ramy 2002).

The National Assembly has the power to amend particular sections of the Constitution. However, Article 137 stipulates areas that

> cannot be amended or that require a broad spectrum of approval before they can be amended. That is why the Constitution contains an article that specifically states that certain issues in the Constitution may not be amended directly by the actual members of the Assembly, that is, they are reserved as intangible aspects, as aspects that must be protected. (Ramy 2002)

In fact, the petitioners sought to bypass the legally established procedure by which the Constitution may be amended. They wished to utilize a mechanism by which ordinary laws are proposed in order to alter the Constitution. As the modification of a constitution, by definition, is an extraordinary legal act, all countries require very specific and special means and methods by which these changes can be made. In legal terms, the Varela Project was *ab initio*, that is, invalid from the beginning, because it attempted to achieve an objective through an avenue that "is not the proper way to try to amend the constitutional text" (Ramy 2002).

The Varela Project was more than just a legal exercise. It sought fundamental change in the arrangements that exist under the Cuban Revolution. At its core was the drive to dismantle the socialist state, re-install capitalism and reverse the trajectory followed since 1959. The Cuban government characterized the Varela Project as

> part of a strategy of subversion against Cuba that has been conceived, financed, and directed from abroad with the active participation of the U.S. Interests Section in Havana. It is part of the same subversive design and has no basis whatsoever in Cuban law. It is a crude manipulation of Cuba's laws and Constitution. (Pérez Roque 2003)

During the trials of the seventy-five government opponents in April 2003, it was revealed that Osvaldo Alfonso had received money from Carlos Montaner — a known operative of the U.S. Central Intelligence Agency — and instructions on how to further advance the Varela Project. In a March 22, 2001, letter to Alfonso, Montaner communicated:

> Dear Osvaldo, a friend you know has been kind enough to get these 30,000 pesetas to you.... Very soon you will receive a call from some high-level Spanish friends to talk about the Varela Project. I recommended five names to found this new idea: Payá, Alfonso, Arcos, Raúl Rivero and Tania Quintero. I'm sending you my best wishes and a copy of Encuentro magazine. Carlos Alberto Montaner. (Pérez Roque 2003)

A follow-up letter to Alfonso was sent on March 24, 2001:

> Dear Osvaldo, a common friend has been kind enough to bring you these 200 USD and a personal message that Raúl will give to you. Call me in Spain when you get this note. Sincerely, Carlos Alberto Montaner. (Pérez Roque 2003)

In June 2002, more than eight million Cubans mobilized around a petition organized by the mass organizations, to declare the socialist foundations of the Republic of Cuba "untouchable." In a special sitting lasting three days, the National Assembly discussed the petition and then voted to declare "the socialist system to be 'irrevocable,' and stated also that Cuba would not return to capitalism" (BBC 2002 and *Granma* 2002). Vice-President Carlos Lage affirmed that "a return to the past is undesirable, unthinkable and impossible for our people. The revolution is invincible" (BBC 2002). Ramy sums up the position of Cuban jurists:

> what seems clear is that, from a legal standpoint, any evolution of the system has been protected, so it may operate on the basis of socialism, of its enrichment and innovation. The Varela Project attempted to rely on the socialist Constitution to change the established system. Now, in the wake of the constitutional reforms that were approved, the system and the redefinitions of socialism that Cuban protagonists may make have been protected. Any future evolution must emerge from that reality. (Ramy 2002)

CONCLUSION

The Cuban political process is almost invariably identified as spanning the range between totalitarianism and rigid authoritarianism. Upon closer observation, it is difficult to sustain this position. The clearest refutation lies in the political response to the economic crisis. Given the scale of the economic contraction, the decline in the quality of life, the intensification of U.S. pressures and the prevailing conventional preconceptions about the Cuban Revolution, a restriction on "democratic channels and a resort to authoritarian control" (Fitzgerald 1994: 193) would have been expected. Indeed, some Cuba specialists predicted a future of "tears, sweat and perhaps bloodshed" for the island (Azicri 2000: 101). However, what transpired was the obverse: an extensive and comprehensive period of national consultation, transforming Cuba into an island–wide parliament. Poignantly, from 1989 to 1997, the Cuban military budget declined 4.7 times, reducing the size of the Armed Forces from an estimated 300,000 to 55,000 (Cuban Armed Forces Review 1997; Hernández 2002: 23) a mere fraction of its Cold War strength. Indeed, the activities of the military are now concentrated in social and economic tasks, for example, implementing its own self-sustaining food production programs (Hernández 2002: 23). The Cuban Revolution's political stability is a product "of the democratic characteristics that describe the political system and facilitate the existence of a community of mutual interests and actions" (Fernández 1993).

In a very real sense the level of Cuban popular participation in day-to-day politics exceeds that of the West, where political participation for the vast majority is limited to casting a ballot at election time: the "voting cattle phenomenon." In Cuba, the participation of the people in government, in choosing who will represent them and in having an impact on changes to legislation, is something that happens at the community or workplace level. Neither is Cuban democracy based solely on the parliamentary model. The national, provincial and municipal assemblies are supplemented and complemented by a variety of other democratic channels. Cuba's political process represents a serious challenge to the dominant model of democracy that is being imposed across the globe and is an affirmation of self-determination and national sovereignty. Cuba continues to defy "the crisis of socialism ... and dissents from the bourgeois democratic model" (Fernández 1993). The governing principles of the Cuban political system

> are radically different from the previous ones, such as the equality of all citizens without distinction to race, sex or creed, and the social conditions also created to guarantee such equality. (Fernández 1993)

At the very least, the plethora of Cuba's critics must concede that the present political system "has brought a level of democratization without precedent in the history of Cuba" (Roman 1999: 79). Cuban participatory socialist democracy can be considered a movement towards the "parliamentarization of society," a movement, as Fidel Castro stated, "not in search of a formal, alienating democracy that divides people, but rather a democracy that really unites peoples and gives viability to what is most important and essential, which is public participation in fundamental issues" (Castro 1996a: 22). As decision-making power resides with the Cuban people, it is they in whom sovereignty is vested. As Ricardo Alarcón, President of the National Assembly, emphasized, the Cuban political system is dedicated to the conviction that

> the essence of democracy is to try to realize the ideal aspiration that has accompanied civilization since antiquity: to achieve self-government, real leadership — from the bottom up — of society by the people, not only in appearance, but in actual fact, something that is only possible when government exists for the people. The people must forever cease to be spectators, and become actors, protagonists. (Alarcón 1999: 9)

The Cuban political and societal process revolves around the base of its citizenry. This is the basis of policy formation and formulation. Politics is a creative process embedded in the people. A society-wide consensus is forged, centred on reducing the distance between institutions and citizens. The objective is a political process in which authorities are compelled to accept and implement the best rational and appropriate proposals coming from the polity. Consequently, there is no special or protected prerogative of institutions, whereby they monopolize initiative, reducing politics to the static dance between the institutional order and those it is supposed to serve. Moreover, while democracy is the rule of the majority, Cuba's ultimate goal is to go beyond democracy — which is an historically specific system — in order to achieve the complete union of civil society and the state, with the long-awaited goal of the withering away and eventual disappearance of the state (Brigos Garcia 2002).

The construction of this new "politics" is, of course, occurring in an international environment that is hostile to the Cuban socialist project. Additionally, the internal changes Cuba has been forced to implement continue to have an impact throughout the society and on the political system. One of the problems is the lack resources — a continuing consequence of the economic crisis — at both the municipal and provincial levels, which complicates the regional differences that exist in the operation of the political system. The devolution of administrative powers to provinces and municipalities is part of the plan to overcome this issue, while simultaneously endeavouring to resolve the tension between democracy and centralization in order to strengthen the sovereignty of the people, specifically in the areas that affect their lives. The "new rich" — overwhelmingly from the self-employed sector — pose a particular challenge, private entrepreneurs who embody anti-socialist practice and consciousness. Nevertheless, they have not coalesced to become a political force. While in other countries, economic wherewithal is necessary for — and does lead to — political power, in Cuba this is not the case. Those who have the most money do not have political power, as they have no support among the masses and, thus, do not offer up candidates in the elections. Consequently, Cuba has escaped the tendency of internal cabals to form, which later seize control and power. Indeed, this underlies the profound importance of the political reforms of the 1990s, which strengthened the role of the masses within the political process, preventing any tendency for a new bourgeoisie to cohere, consolidate and capture the state.

3. RACE, INEQUALITY AND REVOLUTION

For many, the Cuban Revolution is, if not a model, then an example of a society built upon social justice, equality and equity. In some ways, it was an experiment upon whose success numerous hopes for a better world rested. Indeed, it can be argued that Cuba has done more than any other country to promote equality and equity, dismantle institutionalized racism and create racial harmony. However, in the wake of the economic crisis of the 1990s and changes in the economy (specifically, the introduction of "capitalist elements"), Cuba is confronting widening social inequality. Most disquieting is the resurgence of racism and racial inequality. Thus, the Cuban revolutionary process and experience offer profound and indispensable insights into the nature and reproduction of inequality and racism. The national project of social justice illustrates the successes and limitations of an enterprise based solely on structural transformation and the prism of class. Moreover, the economic crisis that began in the early 1990s — the "Special Period" — leads to the drawing of tentative, yet significant, conclusions surrounding the relationship of capitalism and socialism to racism and inequality.

While privileged strata have emerged as part of an incipient stratification, the inequality in Cuba does not approach the levels experienced elsewhere in the South, particularly in Latin America. Nevertheless, it is, by its very nature, a potent challenge to the egalitarian paradigm that has defined the Revolution, threatening to erode the material foundations upon which stand the spirit and practices of social solidarity, collectivism and socialist consciousness. While the process of the quantitative and qualitative material transformation of Cuban society had achieved tremendous progress and success during the first three decades of the Revolution, it was perforce incomplete. Thirty years is too short a time to overcome five centuries of slavery, colonialism and neo-colonialism, not to mention the impending crisis of the 1990s. The collapse of the U.S.S.R. and the Eastern Bloc, the ensuing economic crisis, the strengthening of the U.S. economic embargo and a resurgent imperialism in the mode of neoliberal globalism exerted tremendous pressures on the island. Indeed, the economic crash was spectacular, framing Cuba's entry into the Special Period.

INEQUALITY IN THE GLOBAL CONTEXT

In the midst of the crisis of the 1990s, various economic reforms and measures were implemented. However, while these measures resulted in economic recovery, they also engendered inequality. Most of the inequality centres around those who receive remittances from abroad, work in the tourist sector and for joint ventures with foreign firms, or engage in self-employment activities or private farming (Lopez Vigil 1999: 10–14). The decriminalization of the possession of foreign currency, particularly the U.S. dollar, led to a partial dollarization of the economy — or perhaps more accurately (and as a means of differentiating Cuban "dollarization" from the more complete and thorough-going "dollarization" process of some countries in Latin America) — an economy where the U.S. dollar has a significant role. Persons who have regular access to hard currency are able to purchase goods that are only available in the "dollar" stores or the underground economy. The decline in the value of the peso due to the economic contraction had an adverse impact on Cubans who are dependent on pesos as their sole or major source of income; most affected were retirees, unemployed workers, who receive part of their salary while unemployed, and those who work in the peso economy, such as teachers and doctors.

Before the Special Period, the estimated average income inequality across the nation was 4–5 to 1 (Lopez Vigil 1999: 7). As a consequence of the economic changes initiated in the 1990s, income inequality dramatically increased. In 1986, it was estimated that the top quintile of the population garnered 33.8 percent of national income, while the bottom quintile received 11.3 percent. By 1999, the uppermost quintile had increased its share of national income to 58.1 percent, with the bottom quintile's portion declining to 4.3 percent. The Gini Coefficient also deteriorated over the same period, rising from 0.22 to 0.41 (Brundenius 2002: 378). The Gini Coefficient measures equality of distribution within societies. It ranges from 0 to 1, with 0 representing perfect equality and 1 total inequality (Creedy 1998; Slottje and Baldev 1998). Most countries fall between 0.5–0.7. However, once the high social wage of free healthcare and education, subsidized housing, utilities, pensions and food is factored in, the actual level of inequality in Cuba is much lower.

Cuban patterns of inequality are revealing in contrast to world and regional patterns. From the 1960s to 1994, the gap in per capita income between the richest 20 percent of the world's population and the poorest 20 percent grew from a ratio of 30:1 to 78:1. By 1995, the gap had further expanded to 82:1. In 1997, the richest 20 percent garnered 86 percent of world income, the bottom 20 percent only 1.3 percent (UNDP 1998). In 2003, it was estimated that the richest 1 percent — 60 million persons — of the world's population had an total income equal to the total income of the poorest 57 percent — 3.42 billion people (UNDP 2003). In the South, this pattern repeats itself, where the richest 20 percent obtain on average almost two-thirds of national income (Chossudovsky 1998: 4). As a region and within individual countries, Latin America replicates this state of affairs (Veltmeyer 1999: 15–24; Coburn 2002: 82). For example, the top 20 percent in Brazil, Columbia, Guatemala, Nicaragua and Honduras "earn over 60 percent of national income, while the poorest 20 percent earn less than 3 percent" (*Latin America Weekly Report* 2001: 330). In Argentina, before the economic collapse of 2002, the top 20 percent garnered an income twenty-five times greater than the bottom 20 percent. This situation has only been exacerbated by the ongoing crisis of the Argentine economy. In Brazil, the gap between the uppermost and lowermost tenth is 44 to 1 (Petras and Veltmeyer 2001: 86). The Gini Coefficient for the world as a whole is estimated to be 0.63 (Coy 2002). For Latin America — excluding Cuba — the range is from 0.59 for Brazil to 0.43 for Uruguay (IADB 2000).

Thus, while levels of inequality have arisen, the extreme polarization that persists across the globe does not exist in Cuba. Moreover, Cuba has been identified as one of the few countries in which less than 10 percent of its population is subject to "human poverty" (UNDP 1996). In stark contrast, more than 40 to 60 percent of Latin America's population lives in poverty (*Latin American Weekly Report* 2002: 536; Veltmeyer 1999: 20; Petras and Veltmeyer 2001: 42). Moreover, as the economy has recovered, more Cubans have access to hard currency, with an estimated 60 percent of families in 2000 having access, as opposed to 40 percent in 1997 and 15 percent in 1995. In 1999, 62 percent of Cubans had U.S. dollar bank accounts, compared with 56.4 percent in 1998. The Cuba Ministry of Labour estimates that 1.1 million of the 4.3 million workforce earns an allotment in U.S. dollars (LeoGrande and Thomas 2002: 350; *Florida Today* 2001).

The institution of a tax system — targeted primarily at the self-employed and those who rent facilities to tourists — has operated to curb the growth of the gap (Turnbull 2000: 314–15). The majority of the Cuban workforce — 75 percent — is state employed and does not pay taxes, but as many people began earning incomes that considerably exceed the wages paid by the state, it became necessary to establish taxes, it was necessary to guarantee that funds would keep coming in to the state, the enterprises, the national enterprises and joint ventures, and it was necessary to create a whole taxation system in order to redistribute, in order to assure social justice, in order to guarantee funds for the budget. (Castro 1998b: 31)

A graduated and progressive tax rate has been established. For peso incomes, the annual tax rate for net profits starts at 5 percent for the first 3,000 pesos, rising to 50 percent for net profits above 60,000. For foreign currency income, the annual rate is 10 percent for the first $2,400 U.S., rising to 50 percent for the first $60,000 U.S. (Gaceta de La República de Cuba 1994; Azicri 2000: 150–52; Jatar-Hausmann 1996: 212–15). Also, workers in the tourist industry who receive tips — i.e., taxi drivers, waiters, and others who regularly provide direct services to tourists — share these monies with co-workers whose jobs do not offer similar interaction with foreigners. Additionally, regular, voluntary contributions have been made to the healthcare system. In 2000, in the City of Havana, for example, tourism workers donated more than $700,000 U.S. to a paediatric hospital (Evenson 2002b: 52; LeoGrande and Thomas 2002: 351). Also, as noted in Chapter Two, the state, together with the unions, instituted policies to ensure that workers employed by foreign companies do not become a privileged stratum in Cuban society. The management of the wages of these workers not only mitigates against inequality but contributes to the redistribution and recirculation of wealth.

As the unemployment rate declined — from 6 percent in 1998 to 5.4 percent in 2000, from 4.1 percent in 2001 to 3.3 percent in 2002 — the Cuban average monthly wage increased from 182 pesos in 1996 to 223 pesos in 1999, to 249 pesos in 2001 (*Cuba Business* 2001e: 7; Evenson 2002b : 49). The government raised the salaries of more than 80 percent of state employees, and various incentives have raised the potential annual average wage to 373 pesos. Latin America, as a whole, has experienced a steady, and at times dramatic, fall in real wages in the 1980s and 1990s. In some countries, the decline in the value of wages has been particularly steep, in the case of Mexico, dropping as much as 40 percent (Veltmeyer 1999: 18–20; Petras and Veltmeyer 2001: 86). Critical to the modest but gradual recovery in real wages in Cuba was the stabilization and increase in the purchasing capacity of the peso. While circumscribed, the buying power of the peso continues to have concrete meaning. This is ensured through a regime of price controls that cover basic items, including staple foods. To further enhance the peso, interest rates on medium-term peso bank accounts are 50 percent higher than for U.S. dollar accounts (author's notes; Castro 2002b: 5).

WOMEN IN THE REVOLUTION

In working towards gender equity, Cuba has performed well compared to other countries (Randall 1981; Harris 1983). In terms of political representation of women, Cuba ranks first in the Americas (Lopez Vigil 1999: 157). Female presence in the National Assembly — Cuba's parliament — places Cuba tenth in the world (Seager 2000: 90, 96–97). The Cuban Women's Federation is granted special status under the Cuban Constitution and, as with all mass organizations, peruses proposed, and initiates new, legislative and policy changes (*Constitution of the Republic of Cuba* 1993).

More than 60 percent of university students are female, with 47 percent of university instructors being women. Seventy percent of medical students are women. Cuba also has one of the highest rates of school enrolment of young girls (Seager 2000: 84–87; Grogg 2001). Women are guaranteed equal pay, and the Women's Commission on Employment operates to thwart discrimination in hiring and at the workplace. The government subsidizes daycare, maternity leave, abortion and family planning (United Nations 1997; Espín 1991). There has been a steady increase in the proportion of women in the labour force, rising from 13 percent in 1959 to 39 percent in 1989. During the mid-1990s, the proportion of women in the labour force plateaued and then declined slightly, eventually recovering. In the latter half of the 1990s, it began to increase again. At present, more than 40 percent of the workforce is made up of women, constituting an estimated 60 percent of the upper echelons of technicians and 67 percent of professionals. Women constitute 61 percent of prosecutors, 49 percent of professional judges, 47 percent of magistrates and 30 percent of state administrators and ministry officials (Vasallo Barrueta 2001: 83–92; Castro 2002d; Martinez Reinosa 2001: 83–92).

However, despite the revolution's ongoing efforts to overcome patriarchy, sexism — specifically in the form of *machismo* (male chauvinism) — continues to be a major factor shaping the lives of women. This situation was exacerbated by the economic crisis, which had a significant impact on women, complicating and obfuscating the issues surrounding the struggle for women's equality (Nuñez Sarmineto 2001: 41–64; Vasallo Barrueta 2001; Lopez Vigil 1999). One manifestation of the impact was the decline in women's representation in the political structures. In 1986, women comprised 38 percent of National Assembly delegates. In 1993, representation declined to 23 percent (Azicri 2000: 124). This was attributed to hardships brought on by the crisis, leading women to "concentrate their efforts on the home front" (124). In other words, in order to cope with the challenges of making ends meet, women recused themselves from participation in the political process and consideration for political office. This reflected the burden of the second shift (i.e., household work), which fell predominantly on women's shoulders. Despite the promulgation of the *Family Code*, which legislates — among many other legal provisions toward gender equality and equity — equal sharing of household chores and family tasks between both sexes, women performed thirty six hours of work in the home per week as opposed to ten hours for men. As the crisis intensified, women spent more time at home resolving the crisis in the family setting and fewer hours at their jobs.

Thus, while women without exception receive equal pay for equal work, the combined salaries of all women in the public sector represented only 85 percent of the combined total male salaries. The situation was further exacerbated by the fact that the highest paying jobs are in mining, fishery and construction. Also, many women had to augment their income with a second job. Moreover, many switched from the public sector to the non-state sector, engaging in self-employment activities or working for joint ventures,

Nevertheless, despite the dimensions of the economic crisis, women stayed in the labour force and remained active participants in society. First, this participation continued because it is entrenched legislatively: the *Family Code* establishes the legal basis on which to both defend and expand women's rights. Second, under the Revolution, there has been an intensive and ongoing educational campaign against gender inequality and discrimination. Third, the state has continued to actively promote gender equity. Fourth, the influx and predominance of women in education — the feminization of education — has generated the conditions for women's empowerment. Fifth, there has been a transformation in the way men perceive women, who they now accept as professionals, managers and leaders. Increasingly, men take on more family work than they have traditionally. Critical in the transformation of these attitudes toward women is the acknowledgement that women are not economically dependent on men and, in many cases, earn more than them. Perhaps this new outlook is most poignantly reflected in the encouragement that men give their daughters to pursue professional careers.

There has also been a concerted effort to increase women's representation in the political, state and managerial structures and bodies. In the 1998 national elections, the decline in the number of women delegates in the National Assembly was slightly reversed, with women's membership rising to 27.6 percent (August 1999: 366). The 2003 elections saw women's parliamentary representation increase to 35.9 percent (Martinez Puentes 2003: 411). In the Council of State — the highest executive body — 16.1 percent of the members are women. At the time of writing, women head five ministries: Science, Technology and the Environment; Interior Commerce; Finance and Prices; Foreign Cooperation and Investment; and Auditing and Control. Women occupy 52.5 percent of the union leadership positions and comprise more than 30 percent of the active membership of the Communist Party (Martinez Reinosa 2001: 85; Porcheron 2001). Women also constitute 31 percent of all managers in state enterprises. Thus, despite the challenges of the Special Period, the policies of the Cuban Revolution continue to embody "a clear willingness to achieve equality between men and women" (Lopez Vigil 1999: 173).

AFRO-CUBANS BEFORE THE REVOLUTION

The question of race is intimately interwoven through Cuban history. In order to feed the voracious appetite of the sugar plantations for African flesh, the black population grew steadily. From 1774 to 1841, the number of slaves increased from 39,000 to 436,000 (Franklin 1997: 2). In the nineteenth century, more than 600,000 enslaved Africans were imported into the country (Franklin 1997: 2; McManus 1989: 21). As a consequence, a variety of African nationalities and ethnicities — such as Yoruba, Bantu, Congolese, Dahoman, Mandigo — were represented in the Cuban population. In short, King Sugar was enthroned "dripping with the blood of Africans" (James 1998: 105).

Resistance to slavery took many forms: from *cimarrones* (runaways), who established independent communities in the mountains, to rebellions. One critical locus was culture, specifically religion. Africans were forbidden, sometimes upon pain of death, to practise their own religions, traditions and languages, with the aim of destroying unity among the African population. As Christianity was the only cultural space available to enslaved Africans, they used it as the shell to encapsulate African religious beliefs and spiritual frameworks, resulting in new syncretic creations binding Christian elements within an African cosmology. African-derived religions became a profound unifying influence, preserving and transmitting culture and traditions that have remained vibrant to the present, leaving a profound imprint on Cuba.

Despite the attempts to divide the slaves, there were many revolts, the first recorded revolt occurring in 1533. In order to discourage further uprisings, the captured rebels were decapitated and their heads put on display. This became "a common practice" (Franklin 1997: 1). Nevertheless, slave revolts continued. On November 5, 1843, an enslaved African woman, Carlota, led a revolt. In her honour, Cuba's 1975 military mission to Angola to repel the South African invasion was called Operation Carlota. In 1844, rumours spread that slaves, together with free blacks (those who had been able to earn their freedom or were the children of slaves and whites) and some whites, were planning to stage an uprising with the objective of creating a republic founded on the principle of equality for all. What followed was a mass arrest by the Spanish colonial authorities of more than four thousand persons — the vast majority, black. Hundreds were killed. This repression became known as *La Escalera* (the ladder) because the victims were lashed to ladders and beaten.

Connected with the physical oppression of slavery was the generation of a justifying ideology. The development of a dogma of race "not only served as a useful justification for slavery but it was used to justify both the exclusion of people of colour from political participation and the imposition of barriers to social mobility" (Pérez Jr. 1988: 90). An integral aspect of a worldview positing superior (white) and inferior (black) races was the almost paralyzing fear of slave rebellions that permeated Cuban ruling circles. This fear transmuted itself into the dread that all people of colour, both unfree and free, would revolt (Pérez Jr. 1988: 102–103).

Cuba's First War for Independence, 1868–1878, began with Carlos Manuel de Céspedes freeing and arming the slaves on his plantation, calling on them to join the struggle for Cuba's independence. This act not only signalled the beginning of the island's struggle to free itself from Spanish control but led to "a greater political role for black people" (Jorquera 1998). The rebel forces were "comprised of rural and urban whites, mulattos, free blacks and slaves" (McManus 1989: 24). The most prominent among the black participants was Antonio Maceo y Grajales, the military commander referred to as the Bronze Titan, who refused to accept the Zanjon Pact that brought the First War for Independence to an end. The pact offered a general amnesty in exchange for the laying down of arms by the rebels. While the majority acceded to the pact, Maceo rejected it in what became known as the Cry or Protest of Baraguá. Indeed, this seminal event, an example of fealty to principles, was invoked by the Cuban Revolution in the face of the collapse of the U.S.S.R. and

Eastern Bloc and the intense pressures on Cuba to abandon its socialist project.

With the abolition of slavery in 1886, Afro-Cubans had an ever-increasing role in the struggle for Cuban independence. José Martí, the intellectual author of the Second War for Independence, attacked the racial antipathy that pervaded Cuba, aiming to "unite all Cubans regardless of class or race" (McManus 1989: 27). He rejected the concept of race as "divisive and a sin against humanity" (Liss 1987: 49). Martí held that only through the mobilization of all sectors of Cuban society could the cause of independence prevail. He famously asserted that Cubans were more than black or white, that above all they were Cubans (James 1998: 246; Kirk 1983: 111–12). Martí emphatically stated:

> Must we be afraid of the Cuban who has suffered the most from being deprived of his freedom in the country where the blood he shed for it has made him love it too much to be a threat to it? Will we fear the Negro — the noble black man, our black brother — who for the sake of the Cubans who died for him has granted eternal pardon to the Cubans who are still mistreating him? Well, I know of black hands that are plunged further into virtue than those of any white man I have ever met. From the Negro's love for a reasonable freedom, I know that only in a greater natural and useful intensity does his differ from the white Cuban's love of freedom. I know that the black Cuban has drawn his noble body to its full height and is becoming a solid column for his native liberties. Others may fear him. Anyone who speaks ill of him I disown, and I say to him openly: "You lie!" (Martí 1977: 259)

For Martí, a *Cuba Libre* (free Cuba) "signified a Cuba free from racism and oppression, a republic responsive to the needs of all Cubans" (Pérez Jr. 1988: 145). This

> consistent denunciation of racism and the articulation of his vision of a liberated Cuba free of bigotry had an enormously important effect on dispelling doubts that some Cubans of colour had about the nationalist leadership. (James 1998: 243)

During the Second War for Independence, 1895–98, blacks were represented in all sectors of the movement. More than half the fighters were black. Indeed, Afro-Cubans, from the wars for independence to the triumph of the Cuban Revolution were "prominent and distinguished fighters in the anti-colonial struggle" (James 1998: 107). Participation in the war firmly established their claims on citizenship. This raised black "hopes of social justice, political freedom and racial equality" (Pérez Jr. 1988: 211).

However, the U.S. intervention forestalled Martí's dream of a united and just Cuba. The U.S. occupations, 1898–1902 and 1906–1908, strengthened racist mind-sets and practices, and the position of blacks deteriorated. The dismantling of the rebel provisional government and army at the end of the Second War eliminated "the institutional structures in which Afro-Cubans had achieved the most copious success" (Pérez Jr. 1988: 211). Policies and practices were put in place that heavily restricted black participation in all spheres of Cuban society. In the U.S. controlled 1901 elections, Afro-Cubans — as well as women and those with less than $250 U.S. — were not allowed to vote (Franklin 1997: 9). Blacks were "excluded from elective and appointment government posts and from all kinds of privately owned businesses" (McManus 1989: 30). As a visitor to the island at the time observed:

> Negroes were welcome in the time of oppression, in the time of hardship, during the days of the revolution, but in the days of peace... they are deprived of position, ostracized and made political outcasts. The Negro has done much for Cuba, Cuba has done nothing for the Negro. (quoted in Pérez Jr. 1988: 211–12)

The equitable society envisioned by Martí was not realized. A racially stratified society was once again reinforced, and as elsewhere throughout the Americas, a "multi-layered pigmentocracy" emerged (James 1998: 108). However, Afro-Cubans did not remain passive in the face of this situation. They were politically active, ultimately forming the *Partido Independiente de Color* (Independent Party of Colour, PIC). Its platform declared:

> Freedom is not asked or begged for, it is won; and rights are not handed out anywhere, rights are fought for and belong to all. If we go on asking for our rights, we will die waiting because we will have lost them. (Jorquera 1998; see also Helg 1995)

In 1911, to suppress this growing political activity and challenge, the government promulgated the *Morua Law*, banning parties formed on the basis of racial or class affiliation. The legislative objective was the dissolution of the PIC. Party leaders were incarcerated and publications banned (Pérez Jr. 1988: 222). As a consequence of this repression, the PIC became more militant and in 1912 organized a rebellion that was centred in the east of the island. The Cuban government, assisted by U.S. troops, ruthlessly crushed the rebellion, hunting down and slaughtering more than three thousand blacks.

The PIC rebellion and its immediate aftermath signalled the marginalization of the black population as a whole. The discrimination and segregation that persisted in the social, political and economic spheres set the pattern for the first half of the twentieth century. This systematic discrimination was pervasive, encompassing, among other things, differential access to occupations, education, beaches, recreational facilities, professional clubs, restaurants and public parks. More than 30 percent of black Cubans were illiterate. Their unemployment rates, health conditions and housing conditions were much lower than the rest of the Cuban population. In short, blacks "occupied the lower end of the socioeconomic order" (Pérez Jr. 1988: 307; Zeitlin 1967: 69–70), a state of affairs that continued unchallenged until 1959.

AFRO-CUBANS AND THE REVOLUTION

That the Cuban Revolution was — and is — a fundamental watershed for Afro-Cubans is indisputable (Brock and Cunningham 1991; de la Fuente 2001; Godfried 2000; Pérez-Sarduy and Stubbs 1997; Pérez-Sarduy 1995). A 1962 survey found that 80 percent of Afro-Cubans and the mixed population "were wholly in favour of the revolution." The corresponding figure for whites was 67 percent (Zeitlin 1967: 77; de la Fuente 2001: 276). The Revolution challenged entrenched segregation, with Fidel Castro publicly raising the issue of racial discrimination in several speeches. On March 21, 1959, he said:

> In all fairness, I must say that it is not only the aristocracy who practice discrimination. There are very humble people who also discriminate. There are workers who hold the same prejudices as any wealthy person, and this is what is most absurd and sad ... and should compel people to meditate on the problem. (quoted in Serviat 1997: 87)

In another speech, he added:

Why do we not tackle this problem radically and with love, not in a spirit of division and hate? Why not educate and destroy the prejudice of centuries, the prejudice handed down to us from such an odious institution as slavery? We know that in the war of independence the *integristas* came and said that no revolution should take place because if we achieved independence it would be a republic ruled by blacks. Now they stir up the same fears today, fear of the black. Why? It was unfounded and false then. Why does anyone need to be alarmed when justice is sought through persuasion and reason, not force? It is a struggle we all wage together, all Cubans, against prejudice. (quoted in Fernández Robaina 2000: 103)

Castro stated that racism was anti-nation and singled out discrimination in employment and at the workplace as the worst manifestations. In a December 28, 1959, speech, Che Guevara discussed the role of universities:

I have to say it should paint itself black, it should paint itself mulatto, not only its students but also its professors; that it paint itself worker and peasant, that it paint itself people, because the university is the heritage of none, it belongs to the Cuban people … and the people that have triumphed, that have been spoiled with triumph, that know their own strength and that they can overcome, that are here today at the doors of the university, the university must be flexible and paint itself black, mulatto, worker and peasant, or it will have no doors, the people will break them down and paint the university the colours they want. (quoted in Serviat 1997: 87)

The massive literacy campaign of 1961, the establishment of universal and free education and healthcare, the redistribution of land by the agrarian reforms of 1959 and 1963, the dramatic reduction of rents under urban reform and the building of new housing and recreational facilities, all of these, among others, radically and positively transformed the lives of the black population. The revolution's commitment to promoting equity and providing equal access to society's resources was further demonstrated by the outlawing of racial discrimination, later enshrined in the Constitution: Article 42 declares: "discrimination because of race, colour, sex or national origin is forbidden and is punished by law" (*Constitution of the*

Republic of Cuba 1993). Article 295 of the Cuban criminal code establishes fines and sanctions of between six months and two years for discrimination and incitement of hatred on the basis of gender, race or national origin (Ley 87: 1999). Thus, equal rights are mandated for all citizens. A black worker at a nickel refinery remarked:

> I am most proud of what the revolution has done for the workers and the *campesinos* — and not only at work. For example, Negroes couldn't go to a beach or to a good hotel, or be *jefes* (bosses) in industry, or work on the railroads or in public transportation in Santiago. This was because of their color! They couldn't go to school or be in the political office, or have a good position in the economy either. They would wander in the streets without bread. They went out to look for work and couldn't get it. But now, no — all of us — we're equal: the white, the Negro, the mulatto. (Zeitlin 1967: 85)

In the 1960s, an intense national discussion and debate on Cuban culture and history paralleled the revolutionary transformations. The contributions of Afro-Cubans were increasingly outlined and popularized (de la Fuente 2001: 286). The non-racist reconstruction of Cuban culture and historiography was seen as essential to the creation of the New Cuba and was reflected in film and cultural institutions (de la Fuente 2001: 288–89). It was considered a necessary break with the bourgeois stage of the island's history, an indispensable and inevitable step on the road to socialism. Cuba's national poet, the late Nicolas Guillén, an Afro-Cuban, summed up the significance of the Revolution for blacks in the 1967 poem "Tengo" (I Have):

> I have, let's see:
> that being Black
> I can be stopped by no one at
> the door of a dancing hall or bar.
> I have, let's see:
> that I have learned to read,
> to count
> I have that I have learned to write,
> and to think
> and to laugh.
> I have that now I have

a place to work
and earn
what I have to eat.
I have let's see:
I have what was coming to me. (Guillén 1995: 89)

Before the onset of the Special Period, Cuba "had achieved relatively high levels of equality and racial integration" (de la Fuente 2001: 318; Dzidzienyo and Casal 1979). Castro declared that Cubans were a Latin-African people, acknowledging the critical African role in Cuban history and culture. This ran counter to dominant Cuban historiography and challenged the conceptions that prevailed in the Cuban exile community, which was predominantly upper class, white and comprised of those who had fled the island in the wake of the Revolution. Increasingly, this valorization of Black Cuba was — and is — an "anathema in the ethno-specific Cuban diaspora" (Harney 1996: 21).

The estimates — from both internal and external sources — of the proportion of the Cuban population that is black have ranged from the ridiculously low figure of 11 percent to the more realistic 75 percent. This wide and confusing range is based on, one, a conscious or unconscious obfuscation aimed at downplaying the role of blacks in Cuban history and in the contemporary period, and two, the elasticity of defining who is black. In North America the "one drop" thesis prevails: if a person has one black ancestor, he or she is black. In other parts of the world, a strict phenotypic standard is used, based on the various shades and hues of skin colour, hair texture, etc. Thus, there are some who would be classified as black in one country or region but be placed in the non-black category in other parts of the globe (Davis 1991). Of course, this reflects the historically, socially and ideologically constructed nature of race (Watson 2001: 465). This is not to deny that the concept of race is a material force in the lives of the vast majority of humanity, a force that impacts deleteriously on their options. It is a fair estimate to say that at least 70–80 percent of the Cuban population is of African descent (Pérez-Sarduy and Stubbs 1997: 6; Proenza 2000: 75–85; Lussane 2000: 85–99).

It can be argued that Cuba has done more than any other country to dismantle insitutionalized racism and generate racial harmony. As discussed in Chapter Six, there is also an international dimension to this effort. Cuba has repeatedly supported Third World liberation struggles and development. Of particular note is Cuba's singular and unparalleled contribution to ending apartheid. Cuba was the only country to send troops to combat South African aggression. The decisive defeat of the South African Defence Forces at Cuito Cuanavale, Angola, in 1988, was a critical factor in accelerating the dismantling of the apartheid regime.

In comparison with the United States, before 1959, "the racial stratification was also similar, with whites monopolizing positions in the economic and political structures and blacks generally consigned to the lowest class positions" (Sweezy 1990: 18). The revolution's policies dramatically altered this social reality, leading to a considerable Afro-Cuban presence and participation in various professions, such as medicine, law, teaching, etc. In the political arena, blacks "moved into positions of responsibility and influence throughout the state structure right up to the top levels" (Sweezy 1990: 18; de la Fuente 2001: 310-311). As black Cubans were

> at the bottom of the social and class hierarchy before the revolution, they have gained the most from the vast societal changes which have occurred. A quarter-century after the revolution, employment, infant mortality, and life expectancy rates were better off for Blacks in Cuba than for Blacks anywhere in the world, even in the United States. (Marable 2000)

Because blacks "were disproportionately poor and the poor benefited disproportionately from the change in political system," the advent of the Castro government represented a sea change for Afro-Cubans (Knight 1996: 107). Moreover, the socialist revolution "fundamentally altered the social dynamics, liberating both black and white from their previously fixed positions of racial stereotyping" (Knight 1996: 107). One of the key measures was the elimination of unemployment, which had a very immediate and significant impact as "it removed competition between black and white workers" (Cole 1986: 28). The following anecdote is revealing:

> I was travelling on a very crowded bus. At a bus stop, where many people got off, a black man got a seat. A middle-aged woman said in a very loud and irritated voice: "And it had to be a black who gets the seat." The response of the people on the bus was incredible. People began to criticize the woman, telling her that a revolution was fought to get rid of those stupid ideas; that the black man should be viewed as having the same rights as she had — including a seat on a crowded bus. The discussion and the

criticism became loud and animated. The bus driver was asked to stop the bus because the people engaging in the criticism had decided that the woman expressing racist attitudes must get off the bus. For the rest of my trip the people apologized to the black comrade and talked about where such racist ideas come from and what must be done to get rid of them. (Cole 1986: 28)

While the government had "altered the dynamics," it had not eliminated the problem (Knight 1996: 107); it "subordinated considerations of race to other, more explicitly articulated goals of the socialist society" (115). The equality of all citizens was accepted and understood as immanent, natural and inevitable in the social order of the New Cuba. This new order was being established under a project of social justice based on the elimination of classes. Nevertheless, the Cuban government was unable to completely remove race — and for that matter gender and class considerations — from the daily life of the country (116). Indeed, "the weight of the racist superstructure of the past, conscious and subconscious ideological assumptions, and cultural patterns and social relations transcend the particular social formation which gave it life" (Marable 1996: 175). While a persuasive case can be made that "racism in its institutionalized forms had been eliminated in Cuba" (Cole 1986: 15), the state was, of course, unable to regulate relations at the personal level (Knight 1996: 116–17).

Despite the reality that Afro-Cubans overwhelmingly benefited from the revolutionary changes, racism was not eliminated from Cuban society. While the formal barriers to equality had been removed, the underlying social relations and cultural modalities had not been totally transformed. Moreover, until the mid-1980s, this disjuncture was not addressed or acknowledged in official discourse. Thus, while the state had altered the institutional order, racism — while not predominating, as profound changes had occurred in the relationships between blacks and whites and the views each held of each other — continued to exist in the cultural sphere and realm of consciousness, particularly in the form of racist attitudes and stereotypes of blacks. Thus, while it is

superficial to say racism is institutionalized in Cuba… at the same time, people have their personal prejudices. Obviously these people, with these personal prejudices, must work somewhere, and must have some influence on the institutions they work in. (Shakur 2003)

Likewise, although the quantitative and qualitative changes in the material conditions of life for Cuban blacks had been immense, the process was — and is — incomplete. Enormous strides had been made in the transformation of the social and economic conditions that generated and sustained inequality, but complete equality and equity had not been achieved. For example, blacks continued to predominate in poorer neighbourhoods. Overall, this was reflective not only of the reality that a few decades is a very short time in which to alter social phenomena, structures and ideations which are the product of nearly five centuries of slavery, colonialism and imperialist domination, but also of the failing of government policy to comprehend the complexity of the situation facing Afro-Cubans and to appreciate that dealing with this inheritance required the active participation and intervention of the state in all spheres of society.

In 1986, the revolutionary government introduced new policies to directly address the issue of race and racial inequality. This represented a deviation from the orthodox or dogmatic Marxist position that understands race and racism as phenomena that are totally subordinate to class and class oppression. In the orthodox or dogmatic approach, racism is viewed as a problem that resolves itself naturally as society transforms its socio-economic and political structures; racism and racial discrimination were conceptualized as "remnants of the past that would disappear in due time" (de la Fuente 2001: 276; see also Serviat 1986). In short, they would automatically wither away under socialism.

At the Third Congress of the Communist Party, in 1986, it was acknowledged that racial discrimination and racism had not been eliminated. Castro challenged the political structures and the entire society to address the issue, declaring:

> The hypocritical societies that promote racial discrimination are afraid to talk about this, but revolutionary societies are not. (quoted in de la Fuente 2001: 312)

A race, gender and youth affirmative action program was adopted, with the aim of bringing more Afro-Cubans, women and youth into the decision-making bodies of the Party and the government. Fidel Castro stated that it was necessary that leadership structures "duly reflect the ethnic composition of our people" and that the process of promotion of blacks "must not be left to chance" (Castro 1986: 80). He further observed:

> The correction of historic injustice cannot be left to spontaneity. It is not enough to establish laws on equality and expect total equality. It has to be promoted in mass organizations, in party youth.... We cannot expect women, blacks, mixed-race people to be promoted spontaneously.... We need to straighten out what history has twisted. (de la Fuente: 313)

This new direction was a recognition of not only the successes but also the limitations of a program based solely on structural transformations. The significance of this new policy cannot be overstated as it initiated a society-wide discussion:

> They talked about race, they talked about gender, and they also talked about young people. And there were changes made in terms of people being promoted to vice ministers. There were a lot of black vice ministers and when I say that I'm not saying it in a sarcastic way. I'm saying that the old guard, those who fought in the mountains, you don't get rid of those people easy. So it was a big shift, moving [black] people into positions [of power]. (Shakur 1999)

This policy was reaffirmed at the Fourth Party Congress in 1991 and again in 1997 at the Fifth Congress:

> At this time we must continue consolidating the just policy of promoting blacks and women in particular as cadres.... The Party must insist on the application of this policy in all spheres of society. (Communist Party of Cuba 1997: 32)

As a consequence of this policy, black representation in the uppermost political structures and organs has notably risen. At the time of writing, there are six Afro-Cubans on the Politburo of the Communist Party: one quarter of the total. More precisely, these six individuals fit the "extreme" phenotypic definition of who would be indisputably classified as black. Provincial party leaders in several of the provinces are black, most notably in the provinces of Havana and Santiago. The Afro-Cuban presence on the Council of State, a major arm of the executive branch of Cuban government, has also expanded.

However, it must be stressed, as discussed in Chapter Two, that political power in Cuba does not revolve solely around the Cuban leadership. Indeed, the Cuban political process, as previously noted, institutionalizes extensive popular participation and consultation, which exercises considerable influence on national policy and planning. Cuba's unique and viable alternative form of governance has an active and vibrant polity and civil society, and blacks actively participate in these arenas. There is significant Afro-Cuban representation in all three levels of government: the national, provincial and municipal assemblies (de la Fuente 2001: 311). This was readily apparent in the televised deliberations and delegate interventions of the June 2002 Extraordinary Session of the National Assembly. According to one official estimate, in 1993, blacks and *mestizos* (individuals of mixed ancestry) comprised 28.36 percent of the deputies; in 1998, 28.29 percent and in 2003, 32.84 percent (Mesa Redonda 2003). Of course, these figures are dependent to a certain extent on a phenotypic definition of "black." Afro-Cubans also play a substantial role in the leadership of mass organizations, and the numerous professional and other associations that cover the entire range of activity within Cuban society.

> The problem is that the bourgeoisie teaches us that power derives from leadership, rather than from the masses, and so therefore we look for "leadership" rather than where the power really resides, which is in the masses.... So while the Cubans do not have a black president, I do feel that black people in Cuba are better repre- sented that black people are in the U.S. (Cole 1986: 45)

AFRO-CUBANS AND THE SPECIAL PERIOD

Clearly, within a relatively short time frame — from the end of the 1950s to the beginning of the 1990s — the Cuban Revolution "had a profound effect on racism" (Cole 1986: 14). However, the economic crisis of the 1990s has, after an interregnum of thirty years, reintroduced into Cuban society forces that generate inequity and inequality in their wake, and the most disturbing development of the Special Period is the racial dimension of the inequality. The U.S. economic embargo has had a disproportionate impact on blacks given that they were more economically vulnerable (TransAfrica Forum 1999).

One of the central measures taken to combat the economic crisis was the decriminalization of the possession of foreign currency, especially the U.S. dollar, creating an economy of both dollar and peso sectors. This duality introduced considerable space for "a competitive economical market-place in which access to foreign currencies" has created new privileged social layers (Knight 1996: 117).

Central to the negative impact on blacks have been the critical role of remittances from abroad, particularly from the United States, the reliance on tourism and joint ventures with foreign capital. Since the beginning of the 1990s, remittances have become an important source of national revenue for Cuba (Azicri 2000: 139). In 1999, for example, remittances to Cuba amounted to an estimated $725 million U.S. (*Financial Times of London* 2001). For comparison purposes, it is interesting to note that in Latin America as a whole, remittances amount to $15 billion U.S. annually (*Financial Times of London* 2001) and El Salvador, for example, receives $1 billion U.S. in remittances, which exceeds the earnings of coffee, the country's main export (Coburn 2002: 123).

The central problem stems from the fact that the bulk of those sending money from abroad and those receiving money on the island are white. This is the product of the historical intersection of class and race. The vast majority of those who left Cuba in the early 1960s — in protest and rejection of revolutionary policies — were from the rich, upper-middle classes and professional strata, and were overwhelmingly white. It is ironic to note that the exercise of U.S. hegemony and power "depended on their presence inside Cuba, those who shared U.S. values and identified with U.S. ways, and who, in defense of their own interests, could be relied on to defend U.S. interests" (Pérez Jr. 1999: 501). While this exodus opened up opportunities for Afro-Cubans in the 1960s, it also resulted in a situation whereby, in the 1990s, very few blacks had relatives living abroad to send them money when the economic crisis struck. A study by the Cuban *Centro de Antropologia* (Centre of Anthropological Research) estimates that 30–40 percent of white Cubans receive remittances, as opposed to 5–10 percent of black Cubans (Rodriguez 2002).

Large-scale tourism operations and joint ventures with foreign companies generate many contradictions and serve as both a source of material inequality and conduits through which racist ideas, attitudes, values and practices of imperialism are inevitably transplanted. Jobs in the tourist sector and joint ventures provide much greater and easier access to foreign currency and other goods. Furthermore, the European firms managing many of the Cuban hotels and tourist resorts bring (and, in many cases, impose) their corporate policies and cultures, which are often infused with racist ideas, outlooks and practices. These firms hire persons they consider to be "appropriate" employees; in most cases, these "appropriate" employees are white. Foreign companies confine Afro-Cubans, for the most part, to menial work, while white Cubans predominate in the managerial positions. Moreover, it became an increasingly enforced policy for black Cubans to be discouraged, if not outright prevented, from entering hotels.

The very nature of the pattern of global wealth distribution and the nature of the tourist industry dictate that vast majority of tourists are white, "many of whom are racists and expect to be waited on subserviently" (Shakur 2003). Tourism reinforces racist attitudes by attracting visitors with

> racist ideas and the racist attitudes about the natives.... People come down here with big money, with big money attitudes, and no respect for the people, no respect for the revolution.... So the tourism industry makes a kind of attitude that does not do anything but reinforce white supremacist values, mentality, relations, and power relations. You don't see a lot of black tourists come into Cuba. It's economic, so that power is associated with white people. (Shakur 2003)

A resurgence of racist ideas and stereotypes within Cuban society has paralleled these practices. While the Cuban government promotes an egalitarian society, the changes in the economy have generated inequalities that have proved to be fertile ground for the revival of attitudes that had been significantly circumscribed before the crisis. Perceptions of black laziness and criminogenic behaviour rest on the concrete foundations of the concessions to capitalism and the impact on the incomplete material and cultural transformation of Cuban society. Blacks are perceived to have a greater preponderance in and predilection for hustling, crime and prostitution. Since statistically blacks are the majority of the population, it is hardly unusual that this demographic reality is reflected in the numbers of those involved in criminal activities. It should not be surprising that in the "race for dollars," those who are precluded from "legitimate" avenues choose "illegitimate" means by which to acquire foreign money. Undoubtedly the differential access to hard currency has created significant pressures for black Cubans. However, the mindset that accepts stereotypes and caricatures of Afro-Cubans as true reflections of reality has found new fertile soil within the economic changes. Ideas that had become muted during the period of socialist construction have found new life.

This complex subject has provoked intense debate within Cuba. In numerous discussions with Cubans, especially with Afro-Cubans, while it is acknowledged that the economic crisis has had the greatest impact on blacks, many state that the old misconceptions and stereotypes that had been kept in check and diminished during the period of socialist construction have re-emerged with new vigour. There have been no detailed studies on the social distribution of crime, but these attitudes reflect not only the objective material circumstances but also the fact that not all racist ideas and stereotypes had been erased in Cuba during the 1959–1989 period.

Before the crisis of the 1990s, Afro-Cubans seldom encountered "overt discrimination publicly or privately in their daily lives," and "individual ethnicity, while certainly not abolished, assumed less importance in their daily interpersonal relations" (Knight 1996: 117). However, with the advent of the economic crisis and the introduction of capitalist elements into the society, racism and racial discrimination, together with race, ethnicity and colour, have re-emerged as decisive components of Cuban social reality. Therefore, while the assault on class hierarchy and privileges in the pre-Special Period overwhelmingly benefited Afro-Cubans, the reappearance of social stratification has had a disproportionate impact on them.

The revolutionary leadership has not remained passive in the face of these changes and increasingly addresses racial discrimination and marginalization within Cuba. The problems associated with the activities of various foreign firms that manage hotels were recognized by the Cuban government and declared unacceptable violations of Cuba's anti-discrimination laws. Raúl Castro, First Vice-President of Cuba, declared

> that if a person is denied entry to a hotel because he or she is black, then that establishment should be closed, thus applying our laws, even if the installation concerned is a joint venture. (Pages 2000)

Under the Cuban *Foreign Investment Act*, Cubans employed by a foreign business have the same benefits and protection as other Cuban workers. The same social legislation that covers Cuban enterprises applies to foreign companies. Discrimination on the basis of race, sex and ethnicity are prohibited under Article 30, Law 77: *Foreign Investment Act*. Under Article 33 (1) and 34 (2), a worker can challenge a dismissal as unfair or discriminatory. In the mid-nineties, a contract with the Spanish firm Guitart Hotels S.A. was voided. The firm was administering the famous Habana Libre Hotel, when in the course of its management it fired eight hundred workers, almost all black (author's notes 1997; Puma 1996: 104; *Cuba Business* 1993: 2; Smith 1996: 102). A successful grievance was brought through the Cuban Confederation of Workers against Guitart for discriminatory practices (author's notes 1997). A similar complaint of discrimination was brought against the management of Parque Central Hotel, resulting in the replacement of the individuals responsible (Evenson 2002b: 91). Moreover, in the personal observations of this author, based on visits to various hotels, there has been a marked and substantial increase in the number of black Cubans "behind the desks" (i.e., in managerial positions).

Raúl Castro has also expressed dissatisfaction "with the results of the drive to promote not only women but also blacks and mixed race Cubans to leadership positions within the government and Party" (Pages 2000). Likewise, President Fidel Castro has discussed the immense task involved in transforming material and cultural conditions:

> We thought that to decree absolute equality and civil rights would have been sufficient to wipe out these traces. However, today we still observe that the poorest sectors are still those descendants of slaves. Before the triumph of the revolution, there existed on the island a culture of poverty and wealth, where the middle class was fundamentally white and were better prepared and had better material conditions. People with a better educational level influenced their children because they taught them, they looked over their homework, and they demanded of them. In the same way, poverty was transmitted. For all that everyone was made equal under the law, for all that assistance was rendered, the best grades came from those families headed by professionals. This does not mean there were no advances in these years, but that despite the equality in opportunities for all, it is difficult to carry out a revolution because it implies a change of the society. (1999)

In a September 8, 2000, speech in Harlem, New York, he further addressed the issue of social transformation:

> I am not claiming that our country is a perfect model of equality and justice. We believed at the beginning that when we established the fullest equality before the law and complete intolerance for any demonstration of sexual discrimination in the case of women, or racial discrimination in the case of ethnic minorities, these phenomena would vanish from our society. It was some time before we discovered that marginality and racial discrimina-

tion with it are not something that one gets rid of with a law or even with ten laws, and we have not managed to eliminate them completely in 40 years. (2000a: 58)

In relation to crime, President Castro commented on continuing inequality in Cuban society, noting that there is a "connection between education, culture and crime" and that the criminal element is the product of "imperfections in socialism, by the fact that there is still not a real equality of opportunity for all children" (Castro 2002b). At the Pedagogy 2003 Conference, he made his most detailed and sharpest critique:

One of the cruellest sufferings to afflict human society — and I mention it intentionally, for reasons that will become clear later — is racial discrimination. Slavery, imposed by bloodshed and the gun on men and women uprooted from Africa, lasted for centuries in many countries of this hemisphere, including Cuba. Millions of Native Indians were likewise forced to endure it. While science incontestably demonstrates the real equality of human beings, discrimination persists. Even in societies such as the Cuban one, which emerged from a radical social revolution in which people were able to attain full and complete legal equality and a revolutionary level of education that cast out the subjective component of discrimination, this continues to exist in another form. I would describe it as objective discrimination, a phenomenon associated with poverty and the historic monopoly of knowledge. Due to its characteristics, objective discrimination affects black people, those of mixed race and whites; in other words, those who historically made up the poorest and most marginalized sectors of the population. Although slavery was formally abolished in our homeland 117 years ago, men and women subjected to that abominable system continued living for close to 75 years (up until the revolution triumphed) as apparently free workers in huts and shacks in rural areas and the cities, where large families shared one bedroom, without schools or teachers, in the worst-paid jobs. Many very poor white families who migrated from the rural areas to the cities experienced a similar fate. The sad thing is to observe how poverty, associated with a lack of knowledge, tends to reproduce itself. Other sectors, mostly from very humble backgrounds, but with better living and working conditions, were able to take advantage of study possibilities created by the revolution, and now make up the bulk of university graduates, and who likewise tend to reproduce their improved social conditions derived from education.

Put more bluntly and the fruit of my own observations and reflections: having radically changed our society to a degree that women, who previously experienced terrible discrimination and for whom only the most humiliating jobs were available, are today a decisive and prestigious segment of society constituting 65 percent of the country's technical and scientific, well beyond the rights and guarantees attained by all citizens of any ethnic origin, the revolution has not achieved the same success in the struggle to eradicate differences in the social and economic status of the country's black population, even though this sector has an important role in many highly significant areas, including education and health. On the other hand, in our search for full justice and for a much more humane society, we have observed something that would appear to constitute a social law: the inversely proportional relation between knowledge and culture and crime.

Without going any deeper into this phenomenon, it has been noted that the sectors of the population still living in the marginal neighbourhoods of our urban communities, and those with less knowledge and culture are the ones who swell the ranks of the great majority of young prisoners, whatever their ethnic origin. From this it can be deduced that even in a society that is characterized as being the most just and egalitarian in the world, certain sectors are called on to occupy the places most in demand in the best educational institutions, to which entry is through one's personal file and examinations, where the influence of the knowledge attained by the family nucleus is reflected, and later to take on the most important responsibilities. But children in other sectors with a lower index of knowledge, for the reasons already outlined, generally drift to educational centers that are less in demand and less attractive, constitute the largest percentage of those who abandon their studies at intermediate secondary level, gain a lower number of university places and have a high profile in the ranks of young people imprisoned for common crimes. (2003c)

Thus, the impact of the Special Period on Afro-Cubans is also marked by a renewed and vibrant debate on race and ethnicity — within the leadership and the society as a whole. A new commission, Cuban Culture and Race, has been formed within the Communist Party as a result of extensive consultation with the population. This is paralleled by the high profile given Afro-Cuban culture, religion, history and traditions. For example, in the early days of the Revolution, Santeria, an African derived religion — along with other religions — was viewed as a holdover from the past that would be replaced by more "scientific" worldviews as socialism was established. Santeria is now the dominant religion in Cuba, encompassing whites and blacks, and is supported by the Cuban government. In contrast, the Catholic Church discourages the practice of Santeria and other Afro-Cuban religions.

Nancy Morejón, one of the country's foremost poets, won the prestigious 2002 National Prize for Literature. Rogelio Martínez Fure, the noted Afro-Cuban folklore specialist, singer, composer and choreographer won the National Prize for Dance. There have been various appearances and representations of blacks in the media and the numerous conferences and expositions on aspects of Afro-Cuban history, culture and experience. A central issue under scrutiny, in the wake of the growth of and heavy investment in tourism, is the commodification and commercialization of Afro-Cuban culture and black women, in order to avoid the reduction of music, art and religion — indeed, a people — to exotic artifacts paraded for the enjoyment of foreigners. The role of culture and education is a major focus, as negative conceptions and representations of blackness continue to pervade Cuban language and conventional wisdom. For example:

> Some people still talk about "good hair" and "bad hair." Some people think light skin is good, that if you marry a light person you're advancing the race. There are a lot of contradictions in peoples' consciousness. There still needs to be de-eurocentrizing of the schools, though Cuba is further along with that than most places in the world. (Shakur 2003)

At the heart of this exploration and examination is an analysis of the ways in which the positive difference the Cuban Revolution has made for blacks is being affected by the Special Period and how to reverse the negative trend. The discourse on the black role in Cuban society reflects the growing historiography and research into the African component of the Cuban identity. It is also an outgrowth of the development and deepening of experience since 1959. The new awareness surrounding race, racism and identity underscores that a major shaping force of

> ideas about race in Cuba is that the revolution happened in 1959, when the world had a very limited understanding of what racism was.... Over the years, the revolution accomplished so much that most people thought that meant the end of racism. For example, I'd say that more than 90 percent of black people with college degrees were able to do so because of the revolution. They were in a different historical place. The emphasis, for very good reasons, was on black-white unity and the survival of the revolution. So it's only now that people in the universities are looking into the politics of identity. (Shakur 2003)

The revolution's goals of equality, equity and social justice have always resonated with Afro-Cubans, who are, it is often argued, among its staunchest supporters. While the Revolution has not been able to remove the historical burden of racism, racial discrimination and racial inequality, it has made substantial inroads and laid a solid foundation upon which further advances can be consolidated. Assata Shakur, the long-time African-American political exile in Cuba, observed:

> The first lesson I learned was that a revolution is a process, so I was not that shocked to find sexism had not totally disappeared in Cuba, nor had racism, but that although they had not totally disappeared, the revolution was totally committed to struggling against racism and sexism in all their forms.... It would be pure fantasy to think all the ills, such as racism, classism and sexism, could be dealt with in 30 years. But what is realistic is that it is much easier and much more possible to struggle against those ills in a country which is dedicated to social justice and to eliminating injustice. (1996: 9)

The distinction must be made between the resurgence of racism within Cuba and the anti-racist role of the state. Indeed, the role and nature of the state are critical variables in the Afro-Cuban experience. As a much larger percentage of black Cubans than white stayed in Cuba, supported the Revolution and benefited from its policies, it is clear that "their personal situation remains closely aligned with that of the government" (Knight 1996: 117). Indeed, the restoration of capitalism "may again return [Cuba] to the situation where the majority of the least competitive sector of that society are distinguished by race and colour" (Knight 1996: 117). Thus, there is great opposition to those who fled — primarily the white upper-class elite — and who seek to overthrow the Revolution and reinstate the Cuba of pre-1959, together with the "values against which the revolution had fought officially for more than three decades" (Knight 1996: 118; see also Smith 1996: 108). This position is almost invariably representative of the numerous — formal and informal, structured and unstructured, in official settings and "in the street" — discussions and interviews the author has had with Afro-Cubans. Perhaps, this is best captured by a black professional who asserted: "We are too educated and politically aware to let go what we have gained. We are not going back" (de la Fuente 2001: 339).

CONCLUSION

The concessions to capitalism and the introduction of market elements have challenged the material basis for equality and equity in Cuban society, forcing Cubans "to walk back on a stretch of the road we had travelled. Painful inequalities emerged" (Castro 2001d: 22). However, these inequalities are not to be compared with the ones that prevail globally. While the emergence of privileged strata has posed a serious challenge to the revolution's values and goals, the government has not stood still. It has taken up the challenge of combating the significant problems that have been posed by the Special Period. Despite the travails of the 1990s, Cuban society continues to be characterized as having the least inequality and inequity and the most equality and equity. Indisputably, the Cuban Revolution provides the following valuable and poignant lessons regarding the promise of and the constraints on radical programs of social transformation, particularly concerning race, race relations and racism.

First, the Cuban Revolution is a veritable laboratory, particularly for an empirical study of the relationship between racism and capitalism. It provides a concrete test case for evaluating — however incompletely — the validity of various Marxist postulates. While the debates on race, racism and race relations are wide and nuanced, they can perhaps be divided roughly into three camps. The first camp reduces racism to a set of ideas, values and attitudes held by people. Consequently, the individual psyche is the locus of reference, with racism — its practice and reproduction — centred on various "personality types" (Moore 1995: 6). Hence, as racism is rooted in the minds of individuals, the solution is merely to educate individuals "out of" these mindsets — through educational campaigns and anti-racist workshops. Accordingly, inequality between social groups is understood not as a product of the system *per se* but a result of culture, attitude and aptitude. Adherents of this outlook, such as the well-known authors Glen Loury, Thomas Sowell and Dinesh D'Souza, argue that the key to comprehending social inequality is analyzing "why certain groups are intimidated by obstacles, while others persisted and often prevailed in spite of the so-called 'obstacles'" (Ryan et al. 1997: 45).

The second camp — intimately related to the first — argues that these ideas, values and attitudes are operationalized through the institutional framework. Thus, the proposed solution is active government involvement in transforming the institutional culture, policies and practices. These two camps — both of which can be termed accommodationist — complement each other as they view race and racism, their generation and reproduction, as independent of and divorced from historical and material conditions, making it possible to eradicate racism within the prevailing socio-economic relations and structures. Moreover, the state — the capitalist state to be precise — becomes the ultimate ally in fighting racism and creating an anti-racist society. It is viewed as a neutral arbiter whose power can be deployed in the project of eliminating racism (Aylward 1999; Dei and Calliste 2000; Dei 1996; Driedger and Halli 2000; Fleras and Elliott 1990; Kivel 2002; Loury 2002; Mensah 2002).

The third camp — the radical transformationists — directly links either the origins and/or the reproduction of racism to the existing socioeconomic order: capitalism, particularly in its imperialist form. Racism is a social relation that is inextricably bound up with existing social structures, the underlying order upon which arises the institutional framework. Inequality between groups is the result of their historical position within society, specifically the relationship to the state and the axis of economic ownership and power. Race and racism do not exist in a vacuum but "acquire meaning within capitalist social relations of production, ideologically, politically, culturally and materially, through slavery, indenture, share-cropping and wage labour, under colonialism and imperialism" (Watson 2001: 449).

The radical transformationists fundamentally disagree with the primordialism that pervades the accommodationist position, which treats racism as an inevitable and, even, permanent feature in human relations. This "stranger hypothesis" argues that racism is a natural result when two different groups interact (Moore 1995: 6). Racism is viewed as an instinctive and inescapable product of human interactions and societies, akin to a bio-psychical coding in our genes and unconscious. Entwined with the belief that racial antipathy and ethnocentrism are primordial is the assumption that racism is a normal and inexorable characteristic of European heritage. The historicism of racism is denied, ignoring the mass of evidence that racism had a definite origin in a particular historical period and juncture, linked to very specific circumstances — namely, the trans-Atlantic slave trade — and with the rise of a particular socio-economic system — capitalism (Allen 1994; Rodney 1972; Pieterse 1992; Snowden 1983; Williams 1983).

Before the trans-Atlantic commerce in African humanity, which serviced the burgeoning European capitalist economies, racism as a global historical phenomenon, universalized and pervasive — inherent at all levels of society — did not exist. The development of the biological concept of race — the division of humanity into "biologically" distinct categories where phenotypic characteristics (especially skin colour) are identifiers — is a construct originally generated to justify African bondage and exploitation and, later, extended to rationalize the colonial and imperialist projects. The idea of whiteness and white people, separate and apart from blackness and black people, was a direct product of the historical elaboration of racist ideology. It operated not only to justify slavery, colonialism and imperialism, but also to drive a wedge between black and white workers, carefully crafted in order to prevent acts of labour solidarity. By instituting a system of racial privileges for white workers it was possible to generate, define and establish the idea of the white race, which then operated as an instrument of social control (Allen 1994; Bennett Jr. 1988; Fields 1990; Morgan 1979; Zinn 1995).

The construction of racist ideology and implementation of racist practices encompass a pervasive set of social relations deeply rooted in the functioning and material reproduction of capitalism. By moving the discussion of racism from the level of racial prejudice and the modality of the individual, the understanding of the origins and reproduction of racism is raised to the social order — particularly the state — where racist ideology and practice is continually generated and re-generated. Thus, while racial prejudice and stereotypes are "widespread in popular attitudes and beliefs," it is "the entire social structure" that must be implicated (Moore 1995: 11). The reality that racism is endemic — ideologically and in state practice — is not an accidental outcome. As a smokescreen, it hides the real dynamics and control of productive forces and finance capital. Racism facilitates the super-exploitation of non-white peoples as cheap labour, operating as a mechanism to drive wages down for all workers and maximize capitalist profit; justifies the characterization of people of colour as expendable surplus populations; and deflects the struggles of white workers into the *cul-de-sac* of national chauvinism, thus dividing and splintering the working class, splitting the polity and polarizing society. In other words, racism — by undermining the power of workers and depreciating labour — is integral to capitalist accumulation.

While there are, of course, important differing distinctions within the radical transformationist camp, it is united in the conclusion that only the far-reaching transformation of society will generate the necessary conditions to eliminate racism. It rejects the position that reduces the problem of racism to racist beliefs and practices held and carried out by individuals and/or dominant institutions. Within this conceptualization, the solution is merely to target the individual racists or attenuate the institutions: racism, thus, has no real material basis and is simply sustained by retrogressive worldviews. The radical transformationists understand racism as a systemic phenomenon, embedded in the very fabric of the operation, assumptions, laws and rules of capitalism. Consequently, the radical transformationists, while not ignoring other factors, give primacy to the underlying socio-economic arrangements. Accordingly, racism is not seen as a function of prejudice, which, while an important component of racism, is secondary to the capitalist imperative of profit. Racist ideology and practices are erected upon and nourished by the underlying structures that define society. Accomodationists, on the other hand — in theory and practice — focus on the analysis of and engagement with the reflections and representations of power relations, rather than the power relations themselves.

Therefore, the eradication of racism requires systemic change, a fundamental shift in economic, political and social organization: an end to capitalism. The state is seen not as a neutral arbiter, standing over and above society, but as a condensation of the existing political and economic power relations. State policies give "particular meanings to race and racism" (Watson 2001; 449). Thus, an anti-racist state will be the product of a society constituted on an anti-capitalist basis.

The Cuban revolutionary experience offers profound insights into the validity of the radical transformationist versus the accomodationist camps. The impact of the revolutionary socialist process on the material, cultural and ideational forms and manifestations — particularly, the positive and decisive role of the state — on racism cannot be understated. With the turn in the 1990s from active socialist construction to the project of survival and preservation of the revolution's achievements, necessitating a retreat and reintroduction of "capitalist elements" — though in limited and controlled ways — we have witnessed the racial divide grow materially. The gap, which had narrowed dramatically from 1959 to 1989, began to widen again. Also, in the sphere of ideas and images, racist conceptions resurfaced openly and have assumed a material force in the ways they affect Afro-Cubans. Thus, the Cuban experience offers a persuasive case for an integral link between capitalism and racism, and, further, for the abolishment of the capitalist order as an indispensable step towards the elimination of racism.

Second, the Cuban Revolution demonstrates that, while the elimination of capitalism and the creation of a socialist society are necessary conditions for the elimination of racism, they are not sufficient in and of themselves. Revolution and socialism do not constitute a magic wand "that you wave and everything is transformed" (Shakur 1996). While great progress was made, inequality and racist imagery persisted, demonstrating the limitations of an approach based wholly on structural transformation and exclusively located in the matrix of class. Active and direct state intervention on the question of racism in the political, economic, social and cultural spheres is imperative. There must be persistent activity on the educational front. The struggle "against racism always has two levels; the level of politics and policy but also the level of individual consciousness" (Shakur 2003). Race and racism cannot be reduced to an epiphenomena. Above all, the transition from one political–social–economic system to another — especially from capitalism to socialism — is not a mechanical process. It requires continual, organic and conscious activity on behalf of the leadership and the people.

Third, the Cuban experience underlines the global character of racism. Racism can either be conceived as a critical component of the world capitalist order, or it can be considered an interconnected parallel world system in its own right. The problems that beset Cuba, on one level, reflect the incomplete material and cultural transformation of the society. The ongoing and determined transformation, with its twists and turns, was halted by events and factors external to and beyond the island's control. In short, the locus of the crisis is exogenous, leading to the unavoidable implementation of measures that erode the national project of social justice based on the extension of equality and equity. Cuba is caught in the international cauldron that has trapped the South. Hence, while it is possible to make great advances and inroads into racism within a national setting and framework, in the final analysis, the ultimate elimination of racism can only occur on the global scale.

4. CRIME AND CRIMINAL JUSTICE

So ingrained are the prejudices against Cuba that the very idea of a Cuban criminal justice system that functions according to internationally established norms provokes derision from the majority of Western — particularly North American — legal scholars. The Cuban criminal justice system is frequently condemned for "alleged violations of international standards" (Montanaro 1999). It is quite surprising that, while off the cuff and knee-jerk condemnations are frequent, there is a paucity of Western legal scholarship on this topic. The few specialized works on the Cuban legal system are marginalized and given scant attention in Western academic circles. Nevertheless, Cuba has arguably the fairest and most efficient criminal justice system in Latin America and the Caribbean (Evenson 1994: 170). This chapter provides a general overview of Cuban criminal law, both substantive and procedural, elucidating the thinking and historical conditions that have shaped — and continue to shape — its role in Cuban society.

Cuban criminal law and its application have been extremely controversial and the target of sustained criticism from many legal circles, governments and international organizations. One has only to read the annual reports from organizations such as Amnesty International, the U.S. State Department and the Americas Human Rights Watch. These reports invariably focus on the issue of "political prisoners" and "dissidents," condemning the overall criminal justice system as arbitrary and devoid of any of the basic elements of fairness, impartiality and due process. The Cuban response has been to assert that the these reports distort, falsify and decontextualize the situation, while ignoring the most salient features of Cuban reality: the unrelenting U.S. economic war, acts of aggression and subversion, and Cuba's right to enact measures of self-defence. However, the central problem and lacunae of these critiques have been their inability — or unwillingness — to locate Cuban criminal law in its proper historical context: the Cuban Revolution's explicit goal of promoting social justice and the preservation of Cuban independence in the midst of continued U.S. hostility. These are the imperatives that underpin Cuban criminal law.

Many of the criticisms of Cuba that originate in North American legal circles are criticisms that would be — and are — leveled at other civil law jurisdictions, particularly regarding the use of the inquisitorial model. However, because of the controversial nature and politicization of Cuba, these critiques are subsumed within the accusations of human rights abuses on the island. The Cuban criminal legal system utilizes the inquisitorial model that is employed in several European countries, e.g., Spain and France (Michalowski 1997). This model differs from the one that typifies Anglo-American derived legal systems in that considerable time is devoted to an extensive pre-trial investigation (i.e., before any charges are laid). In this system, unlike those based on the British common-law tradition (e.g., Canada and the U.S.), charges are not laid unless the investigation establishes that there exists overwhelming evidence of the person's guilt. As a consequence, on one hand, the majority of investigations do not lead to charges and trials and on the other, most charges and trials result in convictions. Moreover, the role of lawyers — prosecution and defence — as will be discussed later, are quite different; their roles and functions are much more specifically defined and delimited. This varies markedly from the adversarial model that exists in Britain, most of the British Commonwealth and the United States. In these countries, the prosecutors and the defence attorneys are part of a process from the very beginning.

HISTORICAL BACKGROUND

As noted in Chapter One, the initial process of transformation of Cuban society involved a remarkable amount of experimentation. A radical innovation was the peoples' courts (*tribunales de base*), which eschewed the strictures of formal legal proceedings, rules and practices by opening the process to ordinary citizens. Thus, lay persons served as prosecutors, defence and other advocates, and judges (Baerg 1993: 249–50; D'Zurrilla 1981: 1275–76; Michalowski 1997). The existing judicial system was supplemented by and subordinated to the new institutional order. The new regulatory frameworks did not eliminate the "old" system, they merely bypassed it. This process of renovation eventually led to a new Cuban Constitution (proclaimed in 1976 in a national plebiscite), which was paralleled by a restructuring of the entire administrative and legal apparatus (Evenson 1994: 13–14; Michalowski 1997).

In 1973, the new *Law of Judicial Organization* was promulgated (Evenson 1994: 13; Baerg 1993: 252; Michalowski 1997). A hierarchical and more formal court system was instituted, superseding the private practice of law. Law collectives known as *bufetes colectivos* were established.

The goal of this thorough-going change was to implant concepts and practices of socialist legality more firmly in the Cuban legal system (Evenson 1994: 47; Michallowski 1997). An important part of the mid-1980s period of "rectification" was dealing with the problems in the legal sphere that were generated by the emulation of policies and practices from the U.S.S.R. and other Eastern European countries (Fitzgerald 1994: 153–69). One component of this era was the passage, in 1987, of a new penal code (*Codigo Penal*) — the equivalent of a criminal code — which removed a variety of political acts and other activities from the ambit of criminal justice. It also embodied new rehabilitative approaches to crime by creating a series of alterntives to imprisonment (Evenson 1994: 150; Michalowski 1997; Zatz 1994: 69).

As detailed in Chapter One, in the 1990s, with the collapse of the island's main trading partners, Cuba entered the Special Period. This crisis was exacerbated by the intensification of U.S. economic pressures. Faced with the challenge of preserving both the island's independence and the extensive social gains of the Revolution, new development paths were pursued. This necessitated various modifications to existing Cuban law, such as the legalization of the use of foreign currency by citizens, liberalization of laws governing foreign investment, authorization of self-employment options and the transference of state farms *in usufruct* to workers. Particular emphasis was placed on the development of tourism, which dramatically increased the number of tourists travelling to the island.

The economic crisis and the influx of foreign visitors introduced challenges and problems that had either been eliminated by or were unknown to the Revolution. Prostitution, while not approaching the levels of pre-1959, reappeared. This was accompanied by a rise in the number of other crimes, most notably robberies. The aspect that causes the Cuban government the greatest anxiety is the use of the island as a drug transhipment point by foreigners who pose as investors or tourists, as well as the emergence of a small domestic drug market. In 1999, to meet these new challenges, the *Codigo Penal* was substantially modified. The express goal was to protect Cuban society from these phenomena (Remigio-Ferro 1999).

However, this situation must be placed in context, as Cuba is overwhelmingly considered the safest country in the Americas. This is the opinion of travel agencies and travel writers, and also reflects this author's experience. (Frank 1998: 156; Baker 2000: 326–27; Cramer 1998: 187–88; McAuslan and Norman 2000: 55; Ullyssses1999: 51; Fodor 1998: 188;

APA 1999: 330). While Cubans, especially residents of Havana, believe that crime has escalated, this perception must be balanced against the very low crime level that existed before the economic crisis. Thus, despite the dramatic — for Cubans — increase in criminal activity, the crime rate is still very low compared to the rest of Latin America and the Caribbean. Indeed, apart from visiting "one of the last bastions of communism," this has been a very attractive feature to tourists.

THE COURT AND LEGAL STRUCTURE

The Cuban state is organized along democratic-centralist principles stemming from Marxist-Leninist theory and practice. However, as discussed in Chapter Two, Cuba defies the stereotypical classification of a regimented society in which decision-making and initiative is concentrated at the centre of a rigid, inflexible and unchanging political and legal structure. Thus, while the Communist Party of Cuba is the only official political party, its role in policy and lawmaking is considerably constrained. The Cuban national government is arranged into three distinct and separate branches: executive, legislative and judicial. The executive level is comprised of the Council of State and Council of Ministers. The President of the Council of State also presides as the President of Cuba. The National Assembly of Peoples' Power, as noted in Chapter Two, is the sole legislative body (Azicri 1988: 99–101; Zatz 1994: 55–58). The Supreme Court of Cuba is the country's highest judicial level and functions as "the court of last resort for all appeals from convictions in provincial courts" (Michalowski 1997). It is divided into different sections of specialization (*salas*) that handle 1) penal, 2) civil and administrative, 3) labour and 4) state security and military matters. (Azicri 1988: 109; Evenson 1994: 72; Michalowski 1997).

Cuba is administratively comprised of 14 provinces and 169 municipalities (August 1999: 257; Michalowski 1999; Zatz 1994: 57). In addition to an elected assembly, every province and municipality has its own court system (Azicri 1988: 108; Evenson 1994: 75–76). Provincial courts have a similar structure as the Supreme Court, with the exception of a military *sala*. The jurisdiction of provincial courts encompasses felony-equivalent crimes and various types of civil affairs, including divorce. Provincial courts also hear and adjudicate appeals from the municipal court level. The work of municipal courts centres on less serious crimes and civil concerns (Michalowski 1997). There is no formal division of municipal courts into jurisdictional areas, although larger municipal courts may subdivide into sections with specific responsibilities (Azicri 1988: 109; Evenson 1994: 74).

Judges in the Cuban court system are elected for fixed terms by legislative bodies at various levels. The Supreme Court has twenty-six full-time professional judges, who are elected by the National Assembly for five-year terms. In addition, 156 laypersons are elected by the National Assembly to serve as co-judges in the Supreme Court. Lay judges are "a central feature of the Cuban judicial system" (Zatz 1994: 165). They serve two months a year for two-and-a-half years and continue to work their regular jobs when they are not serving the court

Lay judges serve only in cases where the Supreme Court has original jurisdiction; in those cases, two lay judges sit with three professional judges on a bench of five (Evenson 1994: 76; Remigio-Ferro 1999). In criminal cases, lay judges vote on the issue of guilt or innocence but not on the sentence. Lay judges sit in the lower courts as well, where they also vote only on innocence or guilt. In the lower courts, however, the court sits in benches of three judges, two of whom are lay judges, who may outvote the professional judge (Remigio-Ferro 1999; Zatz 1994: 165). As Cuba uses lay judges at all levels of the judicial system, they have a considerable degree of input in ascertaining guilt or innocence.

Lay judges are chosen from all strata of Cuban society: among others, peasants, workers, professionals, homemakers and university students (Remigio-Ferro 1999; Zatz 1994: 167–73). They are elected by neighbours, by trade unions and by other mass organizations (Remigio-Ferro 1999; Zatz 1994: 168). Their presence is to ensure that justice is not just administered technically, but that it reflects popular will and sentiment (Remigio-Ferro 1999). Thus, great discretion has been given to the grassroots organizations and social formations to "devise both the substance and the means of application" of the law (Tigar 2000: 250). Dr. Ruben Remigio-Ferro, President of the Supreme Court of Cuba, emphasizes that "in revolutionary Cuba, justice is administered by the people. This is not just a slogan" (Remigio-Ferro and Goite 2000: 32). He further elaborated: "this system guarantees that justice reflects popular will. That's the reason a person like me, a son of humble peasants, and as you can see, black, can be elected to serve" (quoted in Montanaro 1999).

PHILOSOPHICAL AND IDEOLOGICAL BASIS OF THE LEGAL SYSTEM

The Cuban legal system reflects three main phases of Cuban history. It is a dynamic amalgam of its Spanish colonial past, the influence of the United States, and the advent and consolidation of the socialist project. In the civil law system — a direct product of Spanish colonization — written codes, rather than case precedent, are the main source of legal principles (Berman and Whiting 1980: 482; Michalowski 1997). The pre-eminence of codes, as opposed to case law, together with the use of the inquisitorial model, differentiates the Cuban legal system from the U.S. and other British-derived and influenced legal arrangements. Combined with the civil law tradition are various aspects of Anglo-American law, such as *habeas corpus*. Additionally, the overlap between the courts and the state — especially in regards to the role of prosecutors — is considerably less than is typical of countries that are (and have) been classified as "Marxist-Leninist." In these countries, the legal system is viewed as an extension of the state (Bernstein 1993: 191; Evenson 1994: 17; Michalowski 1997).

While the form of the legal system reflects the Spanish and U.S. imprint, the most critical and pervasive contemporary influence has been Marxism. The Cuban legal system has a distinct and overriding socialist quality. Within the interrelation between law, ideology and socio-historical context, law is viewed as inevitably reflecting the beliefs of the ruling class: under capitalism, the capitalist class, and under socialism, the labouring classes (Bernstein 1993: 213; Evenson 1994: 148; Zatz 1994: 32–49). The primary purpose of law within Marxist legal theory is to further the construction and consolidation of the socialist project (Bernstein 1993: 206; Evenson 1994: 14; Zatz 1994: 96–97). The underlying features of the Cuban legal system are: 1) a focus on substantive approaches and definitions of justices as opposed to juridical ones; 2) the integral role of law in the construction of socialism; 3) the eschewing of formalized methods and rules to settle non-criminal private conflicts between individuals; 4) the resolution of social issues (e.g., housing and work questions) in non-formalized settings; 5) the extensive engagement of the citizenry in the functioning of the judiciary; 6) the participation of the community in crime prevention; and 7) the provision of universal access to legal services and representation through government sponsored law collectives that ensure affordable fees (Michalowski 1997; Azicri 1988: 109; Evenson 1994: 14).

One overarching objective must be added: Cuban law operates to protect Cuban sovereignty and independence, defending the country against annexationist pressures and U.S. aggression (Bernstein 1993: 213–14; Remigio-Ferro 1999). This unique situation (examined in greater detail in Chapter Five) has confronted the Cuban Revolution from its inception.

Cuban criminal law reflects these objectives (Remigio-Ferro 1999;

Frank 1993: 92–94). In accord with these goals, the effort to provide all citizens with education, healthcare, housing and employment is a pillar of crime policy in Cuba (Bogdan 1989: 327; Evenson 1994: 48; Remigio-Ferro 1999; Frank 1993: 93). Social justice is considered far more effective in preventing crime than punishment and the removal of the individual from society through imprisonment (Remigio-Ferro 1999; Frank 1993: 95). The Committees to Defend the Revolution, neighbourhood organizations comprised mainly of lay people, are an example of this approach. They play an important role in the municipal courts, which serve as primary courts and hear cases of minor crimes (Michalowski 1997; Remigio-Ferro 1999; Frank 1993: 96). While concerned with the dispensation of justice and the deterrence of crime, the courts also focus on the eventual reconciliation of offenders with their victims, the victims' families, the community and society as a whole (Frank 1993: 96). The roots of criminal behaviour are perceived not only to reside within the domain of individual responsibility but also to encompass a social and structural dimension. This view is opposed to the classical criminological approach, which holds individuals as wholly accountable for the consequences of their crimes and, therefore, fully deserving of punishment. In this traditional view, in order to prevent crime, it necessary to increase the cost of crime (i.e., the outcome of any cost/benefit analysis must be made to be prohibitively negative). Severity is not only vital; it is the main means by which to reduce the level of crime.

Within Cuban criminology, social science and social work are the chief means by which to reduce the likelihood of crime being considered a rational option by individuals. In concord with this approach, a massive nation-wide study of crime—its causes and sources — is underway:

> We are now studying crime and the things that cause it. We are carrying out all kinds of studies. There are cases of such horrible crimes that they seem to be the work of mentally disturbed people. Anyone who has studied law knows that there is a principle in law that says that a mentally disturbed person is unfit to plead. Much research has been done in the world on the psychological reasons, which could well have a genetic or accidental origin, that cause people problems and make them violent. What are the genetic or accidental agents that affect the way the human mind works, which more or less turns these people into monsters? We are studying those factors. (Castro 2003b)

DEVELOPMENT OF THE PENAL CODE

The source of Cuban criminal law is statutory and is enumerated in the *Codigo Penal*. In 1979, the *Social Defense Code* (the penal code adopted in 1936) — which had remained in operation, being modified by various decree-laws — was replaced (Evenson 1994: 147; Zatz 1994: 65). As noted, the pre-1959 criminal justice system was viewed as having operated to the benefit of the privileged classes and to the detriment of workers, peasants, the poor and unemployed. The 1979 code was constituted as a final break with that past and was designed to represent the interests of these previously subordinated classes (Evenson 1994: 148).

As discussed in Chapter Two, the initiation, elaboration and adoption of legislation, as well as the development of and changes to the legal system, occur against a backdrop of intense popular involvement and continual consultation with the polity, a process that continues until a society-wide consensus emerges (Evenson 1994: 157–59; Zatz 1994: 68–69). The development of the 1979 *Penal Code* reflected the numerous discussions and considered opinions of Cuban jurists as they wrestled with the legal needs of the Cuban social, economic and political reality (Evenson: 147; Bernstein 1993: 199). The imperative to develop penal law corresponding to the new Cuba was recognized early in the revolutionary process. In 1969, the first efforts at a new code commenced; the proposed legislation was not presented until 1973 and was only adopted after a seven-year consultative process (Evenson 1994: 148).

While the code was designed to reflect the socialist reality of Cuban society, it was not a copy of codes that existed in other socialist countries (Evenson 1994: 147; Zatz 1994: 69–71). The enumerated fundamental precepts that guide Cuban criminal law were: 1) the protection of society, individuals and the social, economic and political order; 2) the protection of socialist, collective and personal property; 3) the promotion of the observance of both the rights and duties of citizens; and 4) the re-enforcement of socialist legality (Evenson 1994: 148). These continue to be the foundational tenets of Cuban penal law.

The 1987 code, while not a rupture with the 1979 code, grew out its perceived weaknesses. As with the 1979 code, there was considerable deliberation, involving the active participation of the Cuban population. Various codes, from both socialist and capitalist countries were studied, as were United Nations documents, such as the 1985 General Assembly Declaration "Basic Principles on Independence of Judiciary" (Evenson 1994: 151; Remigio-Ferro 1999; Zatz 1994: 139–59). The central thrust of the 1987 code was the attenuation of the sentencing procedures available to judges. The objective was to move further from an approach to crime prevention based on punishment — particularly the deprivation of liberty — to one in which alternatives to imprisonment were established. Criminal sanction became the last option, and within criminal sanction, incarceration was "the last resort, to be used only when alternative sanctions would not be adequate or appropriate" (Zatz 1994: 68). Mandated sentences were reduced, and judges were empowered to explore a variety of alternative measures (Evenson 1994: 151). This new approach to sentencing, coupled with the decriminalization of a series of minor offences, resulted in a significant decrease in the prison population. In 1985, ahead of the adoption of the 1987 code, a judicial review of all previous sentences, with the specific goal of reducing most sentences, was established under *Decree-law 87*. Thirty-five thousand cases were reviewed, resulting in 15,000 prisoners being conditionally released, while others were released unconditionally (Zatz 1994: 69). At the enactment of the new code, the number of prisoners was estimated at 30,000–40,000. By the early 1990s, it had fallen to less than 19,000 (Remigio-Ferro 1999; Evenson 1994: 151–52; Michalowski 1997).

Several articles of the *Codigo Penal* are devoted to the protection of internal order and state security. Sanctions encompass acts aimed at overthrowing the government, undermining Cuban independence and sovereignty, and working in collusion with a foreign power to affect Cuban domestic affairs, including the dissemination of enemy propaganda and sedition: Article 92 (Acts against the Independence and the Territorial Integrity of the State); Article 93 (Promotion of Armed Attack against Cuba); Article 94 (Assistance to the Enemy); Article 95 (Revealing State Secrets); Article 96 (Espionage); Article 97 (Sedition) and Article 103 (Enemy Propaganda) (*Ley 87/99*: 1999). Vietnam also has the same provisions in its criminal code (Bernstein 1993: 214). Also, as discussed in Chapter Two, the promulgation of *Law 88: Law for the Protection of National Independence and the Economy of Cuba* further strengthened these provisions.

Under Cuban criminal law, persons less than sixteen years of age are held not to be criminally responsible; they cannot be subject to any charge, let alone criminal sanction. From the age of sixteen, individuals can be tried, although depending on their age, they may receive special care with the aim of rehabilitation, instilling respect for law and order, and/or training for an occupation or trade (Frank 1993: 97; Salas: 1979: 15–36). Those under the age of twenty may not only receive substantial reductions in their sentences but also serve them in special facilities.

In Cuban jurisprudence, an act is a crime only if it is prohibited under the *Penal Code*, an act deemed socially dangerous or harmful (*socialimente peligrosa*). Acts that do not result in a social harm are categorized as less serious offences and are designated as infractions (*contravenciones*), non-criminal breaches. Crimes are divided into two categories, similar to the felony and misdemeanour offence distinctions in the U.S. (Salas 1979: 44–45; Michalowski 1997).

Felony crimes are acts that violate the *Penal Code* and carry a possible prison sentence longer than one year or a corresponding fine in excess of 300 *cuotas*.[1] Violations in this category, where the potential sentences are one to eight years, are referred to provincial courts for prosecution. If the potential sentence is over eight years, the trial is conducted in the criminal chamber of the Supreme Court. The municipal courts handle misdemeanour offences. The maximum penalty applied in these cases is a sentence of less than one-year imprisonment and a fine below 300 *cuotas* (Azicri 1988: 110; Evenson 1994: 74; Michalowski 1997).

Felonies consist of "the standard array of offences against persons or property, including murder, rape, assault, death or injury by vehicle, robbery, burglary, larceny, vehicle theft, arson and drug trafficking" (Michalowski 1997). With the exceptions of murder, rape and robbery, all felonies have a corresponding lesser misdemeanour (Michalowski 1997 and Bogdan 1989: 329). Specific acts that are deemed to be harmful to the socialist society, particularly the economy, are also penalized (Bernstein 1993: 213; Evenson 1994: 149). Actions that are subject to criminal sanction include: selling of goods from a state enterprise for illegal personal gain (*malversación*); illicitly receiving and/or diverting money or resources from a state enterprise (*receptación*); the illegal slaughter and sale of livestock (*sacrificio ilegal*); and illegal emigration (*salida ilegal*) (Michalowski 1997; *Ley 87/99*: 1999). The prosecution and defence of charges arising from these offences "constitute a regular part of the case load" dealt with by the courts (Michalowski 1997; see also Remigio-Ferro 1999).

THE STATE OF DANGEROUSNESS PROVISIONS

The "state of dangerousness" provisions in the *Codigo* have been the target of sustained criticism by various human rights organizations. Notably, other countries, for example, Italy, contain similar provisions in their criminal law. The Cuban provision predates the Revolution, being part of the 1936 *Social Defence Code* (Evenson 1994: 156). The 1979 code reduced the list of categories of proscribed offences under this provision from twelve to seven, and in the 1987 reformulation, the number of categories was further reduced to three (Evenson 1994: 157). Article 73 of the *Penal Code* defines the state of dangerousness as "a person's special proclivity to commit offences as demonstrated by conduct that is manifestly contrary to the norms of socialist morality." Article 74 establishes that "a dangerous state" exists when the subject displays any of the following three indicators of "dangerousness": (a) habitual inebriation and dipsomania; (b) drug addiction; (c) antisocial behaviour." Furthermore:

> Any person who, through antisocial behaviour, habitually transgresses the norms of social coexistence by committing acts of violence, or other acts of provocation, or who violates the rights of others, or whose general behaviour imperils the rules of coexistence or disturbs the order of the community, or who lives as a social parasite off the work of others or exploits or practices socially reprehensible vices, shall be considered to be in a dangerous state.

Under Article 75:

> Anyone who, while not falling under any of the dangerous states referred to in article 73, might develop a proclivity to commit offences, because of connections or relations with persons who are potentially dangerous to society, other persons, or the social, economic and political order of the socialist State, shall be given a warning by the competent police authorities to avert involvement in socially dangerous or criminal activities.

Both pre-crime and post-crime measures can be applied. In the case of pre-crime measures, Article 78 sets out that anyone found to be in a "dangerous state" may be subject to security measures encompassing therapy, re-education or police surveillance. Re-education measures are applied to antisocial individuals and consist of internment in a specialized labour or study institute and delivery to a labour collective for monitoring and modification of their behaviour (Evenson 1994: 158).

In 1991, as a direct response to criticisms by Cuban jurists that more precise legislation was required, given the severity of the sanction imposed upon a finding of dangerousness, the National Assembly enacted *Decree-Law 128*. It instituted a new procedure governing the determination of a pre-crime indicator of "dangerousness" entailing antisocial behaviour. To accelerate the process, the law established that the finding of a state of dangerousness should be done within summary proceedings. Under the procedure, the National Revolutionary Police opens a case file, which contains a police officer's report or account, the testimony of persons in the neighbourhood attesting to the suspect's "dangerous" conduct and any official warnings. Upon completion, the file is submitted to the judge of the district court, who then makes a further determination on whether the case should be referred to the people's municipal court. Once a case is sent to the people's municipal court, a two-working-day deadline is imposed. Within this time period, the court must decide whether additional investigation of the matter is required to ascertain if a state of dangerousness exists. A five-working-day deadline applies to this activity. When the review of the file is concluded, a formal arraignment date is established. The court is then constrained to render its decision within one day of arraignment (Evenson 1994: 158).

Cuban jurists have defended the "state of dangerousness" provisions on the basis that they are important crime prevention measures. They argue that, as the provisions are not interpreted broadly, they do not sweep in every activity and that the narrow construction enables proof. Additionally, defenders of the provisions emphasize that similar provisions exist in other countries (Evenson 1994: 158).

CUBAN CRIMINAL PROCEDURE: RIGHTS OF THE ACCUSED

Incorporated into Cuban criminal jurisprudence are many of the recognized international norms protecting the rights of the accused, including, among other things, the presumption of innocence, the right to counsel, the right of non-self-incrimination, rules of evidence and strictures governing search and seizure. These rights are enumerated under articles 59, 61, and 63 of the Cuban Constitution and enabled within Cuban criminal procedure law (LCP) through articles 3, 125–99, 215–27, 281, and 312 (*Ley 5/77: Ley de Procedimiento Penal (Actualizada)* 1977). Under Article 59 of the Cuban Constitution, a person can only be tried or convicted by a competent court, under the laws prior to the offence and with the rights and formalities enumerated in articles 60, 61 and 63. Six rights in respect to due process and the right to justice are established: 1) trial under a regular jurisdiction, 2) assistance of counsel, 3) the inviolability and protection of personal integrity while in the custody of the authorities, 4) non-self-incrimination and the right not to testify during trial, which is linked to the guarantee against statements made under torture, 5) application of provisions of criminal law enacted prior to when the offence was alleged and 6) the right to recur freely to the courts to seek justice (Berman 1980: 482; Evenson 1994: 158).

There has been controversy around whether these rights exist in practice and can be exercised by Cuban citizens (Amnesty International 1998: 86). The criticism centres on Article 62 of the Constitution, which states that none of the enumerated rights can be exercised "against the existence and aims of the socialist state." It is contended that Article 62 stringently regulates the exercise of these rights and completely subordinates the citizen to the state, rendering the rights meaningless. The controversy arises in regard to the "political prisoners" and "dissidents," who receive disproportionate attention given their very small numbers. As argued in Chapter Two, these "political" cases are often distorted, with the international reporting on them bearing no resemblance to the actual issues and evidence. These distortions of a very small number of cases are then extrapolated to condemn the entire Cuban justice system. Moreover, it must be noted that many of the criticisms of Cuba's legal system — especially criminal law — that originate in North American legal circles are criticisms that would be — and are — levelled at other jurisdictions (e.g., European nations). However, because of the controversial nature and politicization of Cuba, these critiques are elevated to and subsumed within accusations of human rights abuses.

Cuban criminal procedure law was reformulated in 1973 and again in 1977. As noted, it covers, among other things, the right to counsel, the right to silence, rules of evidence, search and seizure, and presumption of innocence. The evidence indicates that for the vast majority of Cubans, these rights do exist and are operational. Many convictions have been overturned on appeal on the basis that the convictions were obtained in violation of the law (Baerg 1993: 264). Indeed, on several occasions, the police have been castigated for the commission of errors in the carrying out of their investigations (D'Zurrilla 1981: 1261). In 1977, when the LCP was revised for the second time, 43 percent of all cases filed were dismissed as a result of findings of police error. At trial, more than 34 percent of the accused were acquitted because of police error. Furthermore, the appellant level voided 33 percent of convictions at lower court levels (Evenson 1994: 162; Salas 1983: 60).

THE RIGHT TO COUNSEL

Every defendant has the right to legal representation. The law collectives (*bufetes colectivos*) guarantee that this representation is affordable. All defence attorneys have the right to consult with their clients in privacy. They also have the right of access to all the evidence, investigation reports and documents. If within forty-eight hours, the accused has not retained a lawyer, the court will designate one. However, the exercise of this right reflects the inquisitorial nature of Cuba's judicial system, a central juridical assumption of which is that no criminal case exists until an initial investigation (*fase preparatoria*) has demonstrated that a crime has been committed and that a particular person is the probable offender (Evenson 1994: 161–62). Evidence is gathered and witnesses interviewed by the police and prosecutors (*fiscals*). When the *fase preparatoria* is complete and the accumulated evidence is considered to be compelling enough to proceed, an indictment (*conclusiones provisionales*) is issued by the prosecutor (Evenson 1994: 162; Michalowski 1997). The indictment is delivered to the court in which the case will be tried and to the defendant or his/ her defence attorney (*Ley 5/77*: 1977; Michalowski 1997). In the Cuba criminal justice system, there exists no equivalent to plea-bargaining; all cases and the attendant charges must be resolved in a trial (Michalowski 1997).

Under, Cuban criminal procedure law, a suspect in a crime cannot be held longer than twenty-four hours. Within that period, the police must send the case to an investigator. A time limit of three working days is then imposed on the investigator, who then refers the case to a prosecutor. Another time constraint of three working days is applied to the prosecutor's work. At the end of this time period, the suspect must either be released or judicial assent obtained to further the detention (*Ley 5/77*: 1977; Michalowski 1997).

In determining whether pre-trial detention (*prision provisional*) is appropriate and necessary, the court assesses the seriousness of the crime and its harm to society, the number of crimes committed and whether the suspect(s) are flight risks (Zatz 1994: 69). Pre-trial detention is most often used for crimes such as murder, rape, armed robbery and drug trafficking (Michalowski 1997). If bail is granted, individuals are released under their own recognizance or under the supervision of their place of work, their union or one of the various mass organizations (Michalowski 1997).

In 1988, a study of pre-trial detention was conducted. The study centred on one law collective in the city of Havana. Of the 982 defendants served by the law collective, 35 percent of those indicted had been detained. The detention rates were: 61 percent for felonies against property; 40 percent for crimes against the economy; 33 percent for felonies against state security; and 19 percent for traffic offences resulting in fatalities or injuries (Michalowski 1997 and Evenson 1994: 163).

Pre-trial detention has been an area of sustained criticism, both from without and within Cuba. The power to detain a person for weeks, even months, while the investigation proceeds is seen by many jurists, Cuban and foreign, to be at odds with the presumption of innocence (Berman 1993: 483; Evenson 1994: 163). Of course, it is important to note that the same criticism can be levelled at other countries, such as France, Germany or Italy, whose criminal law incorporates similar "investigation prior to indictment" models (Berman and Whiting 1980: 483).

It is important to note that in Canada for example, the right to counsel under section 10(b) of the *Canadian Charter of Rights and Freedoms* is not absolute, and evidence obtained when the accused has not been instructed of their right to counsel, or counsel is not available, is not necessarily inadmissible. Indeed, police officers do not have to explicate to accused persons the virtues of retaining counsel, nor in every instance is an accused person entitled to counsel (see the case *R. v. Bartle* 1994: 173). The right to counsel is subject to "reasonable limitations," and in exigent circumstances the rights under section 10 (b) of the Charter may be ignored (see the case *R. v. Feeny* 1997: 13).

Some Cuban jurists emphasize that as a formal legal case against a person does not exist until the investigative stage is complete, there is no need for a defence layer to become engaged in the process (Berman and Whiting 1980: 483; Evenson 1994: 162; Michalowski 1997). While defence attorneys formally become part of the process only when the accused is charged, they begin their preparations once they have been contacted by the arrested person or a member of their family. Thus, their role in defence of their client quite often precedes their official involvement in the case. However, there continues to be serious discussion by Cuban jurists and government officials about revising Cuban criminal procedure law in order to create the space for attorneys to intervene as soon as someone is charged and an investigation initiated (Berman 1993: 483; Evenson 1994: 163–64; Michalowski 1997; Zatz 1994: 84). The introduction of structures establishing an earlier formal role for defence lawyers would be a substantial attenuation of Cuban criminal procedure law (Michalowski 1997; Zatz 1994: 84–85).

THE RIGHT TO SILENCE AND CONFESSIONS

Under Cuban criminal procedure law (LCP) Cuban citizens have the right of non-self-incrimination. In Canada, the U.S. and Britain, this is considered a fundamental tenet of the legal system. It is seen as an essential protection of the accused from having police investigations proceed in ways contrary to human dignity (see the case *R. v. Wooley* 1998: 539). However, under Cuban law, this right is further strengthened by Article

3 of the LCP, which requires that all criminal charges be proven at trial by evidence other than a statement proffered by the accused. Moreover, the evidence adduced for conviction must be independent of any statement of the accused. Thus, while criminal suspects may confess guilt, they cannot be convicted solely on the basis of a confession (Michalowski 1997). This contrasts with other jurisdictions, such as Canada and the U.S., where convictions could occur solely on the basis of confessions.

The requirement that independent evidence beyond the accused's statement of guilt be adduced gives the Cuban right to silence greater force than in other countries. Indeed, it is rendered an absolute right by effectively making all evidence obtained solely through self-incrimination inadmissible. This strikingly contrasts with the contortions that must be performed in Canada and the U.S. In the United States, the "poisonous tree" doctrine is applied. In Canada, the "conscriptive," "non-conscriptive," "derivative" and "discoverability" guidelines govern the admissibility of evidence (see the case *R. v. Stillman* 1997: 607). In the process of negotiating these intricate tests, evidence that should be excluded may be ruled admissible.

In Canada the right to silence is broader than the rule governing confessions (see the case *R. v. Herbert* 1990: 151). However, intrusion on the right to silence is permissible as long as it is consistent with the principles of fundamental justice enunciated in Section 7 of the Charter (see the cases regarding Section 94(2) of the *Motor Vehicle Act* 1985: 486 and *R. v. Boyles* 1991: 595). Thus, the Canadian construction of the right to silence does not provide absolute protection from police abuses. The police are quite adept at persuading individuals to forgo asserting their right to counsel or silence. Consequently, there are a series of cases setting out the framework for the inquiry to determine whether the right to silence was infringed. While the police are not allowed to use trickery to obtain a confession, they can use more subtle forms of deception (see the case *R. v. Jones* 1994). For example, they can use an agent of the state to passively obtain information from an accused (see the case *R. v. Herbert* 1990: 151 and *R. v. Oickle* 2000: 147: 321). Of course, there is no violation of the right to silence where an individual chooses to make a voluntary statement or where they have chosen to make a statement or answer questions after they have spoken to counsel (see the case *R. v. Van Haarlem* 1992: 982.).

SEARCH AND SEIZURE

The Cuban Constitution specifies that a court must issue a warrant (*resolución*) before a private dwelling can be searched. The warrant must also have the approval of the attorney general (*fiscal*). The warrant must specify the location, reasons for the search and the type of the evidence that may be found. It is required that the resident or his/her representative and two neighbours attend a search, and, except in urgent and exigent circumstances, a search cannot occur between 10 p.m. and 5 a.m. This is similar to the corresponding sections of the Canadian *Criminal Code* (CCC), which require judicial assent to obtain a warrant and that the warrant specify the offence, items sought and the particular premises to be searched. The warrant must be executed during the day, unless the court is satisfied that there are reasonable and probable grounds for it to be executed at night. The CCC authorizes the seizure of items mentioned in the warrant and anything obtained by, used in or affording any evidence of an offence.

The LCP sets down a two-step test that must be satisfied in order for a warrant to be issued. First, there must be indications that the accused and objects and other material related to the crime and relevant to the investigation are at the location for which the warrant is sought. Second, there is the requirement of urgency, designed to ensure that only essential searches will occur (D'Zurrilla 1981: 1259). This test has been character-ized as simpler and easier to satisfy than the "probable cause" benchmark in the United States (D'Zurrilla 1981: 1259). Under the Canadian *Criminal Code*, there must be reasonable grounds to believe the specified item(s) is at the location and that a search will afford evidence of the offence. Thus, the threshold appears to be higher than in the Cuban test, which *prima facie* would seem to be satisfied by mere suspicion. However, there appears to be no literature that clearly defines what constitutes acceptable "indications" and "urgency" (D'Zurrilla 1981: 1260)

The Canadian *Criminal Code* also permits a police officer to use any device, investigative technique or procedure, including video surveil-lance, which otherwise would constitute an unreasonable search or seizure. In the LCP there exists no similar provisions governing the utilization of electronic surveillance. However, the opening of private correspondence may be authorized "if sufficient indications exist that the discovery or proof of any criminal act or important circumstances relating to the same will be obtained."

Under the LCP, a warrant is not required if a house is also the scene of the crime and if the police are in hot pursuit of an offender. In this case, procedural law permits investigators to search the premises and to remove any items deemed as evidence. The Canadian *Criminal Code* excludes several offences from the requirement of a search warrant, including weapon-related offences and counterfeiting of money. In Canada, police may enter a dwelling without a warrant in order to prevent bodily harm, death or loss of evidence. Similar powers can be exercised in other circumstances where it may be impracticable to obtain a warrant by virtue of exigent conditions.

In Canada, the *Criminal Code* establishes the legal basis for taking body samples and blood from a suspect. It also authorizes the search of computers, covering data, copying and the seizure of printouts. At present, the LCP does not incorporate provisions to address the issue of forensic DNA evidence. Nor do provisions exist for the search of computer systems. This reflects the Cuba's Third World status. DNA-testing technology is expensive and generally not available to police forces and other investigative branches in the South. The use of computers as an everyday feature is a phenomenon overwhelmingly concentrated in the developed world.

TRIAL AND SENTENCING

Accused persons have the right to a trial by a judicial panel. For felony-equivalent cases heard in provincial courts, these panels consist of five judges, three of whom are trained jurists with law degrees and two of whom are citizens chosen to serve as lay judges (D'Zurrilla 1981:1278). Municipal court panels consisting of one jurist and two lay judges adjudicate less serious criminal offences (Evenson 1994: 76). A member of the attorney general's provincial office prosecutes felonies, with police investigators prosecuting misdemeanours (Evenson 1994: 163; Michalowski 1997). Under Cuban law, a time limit of six months is set for the completion of cases once the indictment is laid (Michalowski 1997). While this requirement is not strictly fulfilled, one study found that more than 90 percent of cases were finished within eight months of the issuance of the indictment (Michalowski 1997). Also, as noted, defendants may be released on bail before their trials.

All evidence is considered relevant and admissible (Bernstein 1993: 195; Zatz 1994: 181–82). The accused's character is part of the evidence that can be adduced in court. Thus, the defendant's behaviour, attitudes, character, criminal past and work record may all be factored into the court's rulings on both verdict and — if the accused is convicted — sentence (Michalowski 1997; Zatz 1994: 182). There is no formal separation between trial and sentencing procedures. The judges who adjudicate the trial proceedings and hand down the verdict also decide upon the sentence. Municipal courts, in their adjudication of misdemeanours, establish the sentence at trial. The sentences handed down for felony offences are usually issued several weeks after the completion of the trial (Michalowski 1997).

The 1987 *Penal Code* established specific punishments: execution, imprisonment, labour at a specific workplace with restrictions, labour at a workplace without restrictions, probationary terms, monetary penalties and public censure (*la amonestacion*). A person may also be sentenced to work on a particular social project. In 1999, life imprisonment was added to the list of possible criminal sanctions. However, while crimes and ranges of punishment are defined in the code, neither the *Penal Code* nor the criminal procedure law indicate which of the enumerated attributes of a crime will mitigate or aggravate the punishment. Also, no special role is assigned to victims during prosecution or sentencing, other than providing evidence and testifying at trial. However, this is quite distinct from the active social role given to victims by organizations such as the Committees to Defend the Revolution.

THE DEATH PENALTY

The death penalty may be applied in cases where the crime involved multiple murders, murder of a minor, murder involving torture, certain forms of drug trafficking or treason. Execution is carried out by a firing squad. Those under the age of twenty or who were pregnant at the commission of the crime cannot be sentenced to death. In December 2001, in the wake of the events of September 11th, the National Assembly passed the *Law against Acts of Terrorism*, which in the most serious instances, stipulated the death penalty for various terrorist activities, including hijackings involving armed force and violence and the planning of terrorists attacks (*Granma* 2001).

From 1959 to 1987 — a twenty-eight-year period — there were 212 executions (Durand 1998). Most of these executions took place in the early 1960s, when the sabotage campaigns aimed at weakening the government were at their peak. Globally, in 2002, there were 1,560 judicially sanctioned executions. Not one was in Cuba. Eighty-one percent of these executions occurred in China, Iran and the United States. In the U.S., 71 persons were put to death (Amnesty International 2003). The rate of executions in Cuba is therefore much lower than that in the United States (Durand 1998). Until the executions of three hijackers in Cuba on April 11, 2003, the government had instituted a moratorium —

initiated in May 2000 — on the use of the death penalty.

Cuban government officials have stated their opposition to the death penalty on principle. They argue, however, that the occasional resort to capital punishment is an unfortunate necessity imposed by the unceasing efforts of the United States to destroy the Cuban Revolution (Remigio-Ferro 1999). They further assert that, in spite of this circumstance and because of the abhorrence of the death penalty, this extreme measure has only been used sparingly. Still, the death penalty generates considerable debate in Cuba (Remigio-Ferro 1999; Durand 1998). At the February 1999 meeting of the National Assembly of People's Power, three members voiced their opposition and voted against the expansion of the death penalty (*Granma* 1999e). The President of Cuba's Supreme Court, Ruben Remigio-Ferro, commented that eventually the death penalty would be

> condemned to death in Cuba. The problem is when this will be possible. The imposition of the death penalty in Cuba is very exceptional. Even more exceptional is for it to be actually carried out. It's always related to crimes that are very, very serious — serial murders, or recidivism with crimes of extreme violence or acts of extreme aggression against the Cuban state.... When a prosecutor seeks the death penalty, there are many safeguards. Immediately following the imposition of such a sentence, a new trial before the Supreme Court is automatically convened. Even their ruling has to be reviewed by the Council of State. However, this doesn't justify our continuing to have the death penalty, in my opinion. It is very much a contradiction with the humanistic goals of the revolution. (quoted in Montanaro 1999)

The April 11, 2003, executions of three of the participants in an April 2, 2003, ferry hijacking generated a maelstrom of international condemnation. The executions were the first applications of capital punishment in almost three years. The eleven hijackers used force and violence to commander a passenger ferry. Their objective was to reach the United States. They held the passengers hostage — tying up one pregnant woman — and threatened to kill them to achieve their objective. They held knives to people's throats, a gun to one person's head and indicated their willingness to throw others overboard. In short, they terrorized the women, children and men on the ferry.

At trial, the hijackers were convicted under the *Law against Acts of*

Terrorism, which included the sanction of the death penalty for hijackings involving the use of armed force and violence. Three were sentenced to death, while the others received prison sentences. The decision to sentence and then apply the death penalty was not taken lightly. The death sentences were automatically appealed to the Cuban Supreme Court, which decided not to commute the sentences. This triggered another automatic appeal of the death sentences to the Cuban government, specifically, the Council of State. Following several hours of deliberation, the Council of State upheld the sentences. The crucial factors influencing this decision included the seriousness of the crime, the escalation of efforts by Florida-based groups to incite further acts of terror and attempts by the U.S. military to instigate an incident, which could be used as an excuse for direct acts of aggression against the island.

The April 2nd ferry hijacking was one of seven similar acts involving violence and weapons. Four of these hijackings were successful in reaching Florida, where U.S. courts did not prosecute the hijackers but instead released them. Moreover, Cuban authorities discovered and foiled another twenty-nine hijacking plans. After investigation, the Cuban government concluded that this wave of hijackings and planned hijackings were part a deliberate plan to generate a series of incidents aimed at destabilizing the island and justifying U.S. intervention. Furthermore, the Cuban government stated that on April 25, 2003, the Bush administration directly communicated to Cuban diplomats that the series of hijackings was regarded as "a serious threat to the national security of the United States" (Castro 2003b: 5). Foreign Minister Felipe Pérez Roque underscored Cuba's predicament:

> We would like not to have it [the death penalty] one day. It is not in accord with our philosophy of life. For us today, it is no more than an exceptional resort to which we only have recourse to for reasons of *cause majeur*, with which we have had to defend a country under attack for more than 40 years. It is true that we have had to do it now, to avert the creation of a situation in Cuba, a crisis, a migratory incident aspired to by the sectors in the United States that want a war. It has been applied to avert that war, to save lives. We have had to make a painful decision, which we did not enjoy, quite the opposite, because we have on our shoulders the lives of millions of Cubans and tens of thousands of U.S. citizens who would lose their lives in a confrontation between the two countries. (quoted in *Granma International* 2003a)

In an April 28, 2003, television appearance, President Castro expressed the sentiment that "we are moving towards a future in our country when we might be able to abolish the death penalty, not simply on philosophical grounds, but out of profound feelings of justice and humanism." However, he further accentuated the particular context of the Cuban Revolution;

> Political movements have had to defend themselves, both revolutions and counterrevolutions have defended themselves through procedures of one sort or another. For us the most important thing was to defend ourselves with rules, legal procedures, to avoid injustices and above all to avoid anything that was not legal and that was not judicial, which we avoid and have avoided at all costs. Not that we were happy to apply the death penalty. We looked at it as a matter of life or death. On the whole, those who are involved in these struggles start out from the principle that it is a life or death struggle. If revolutionaries do not defend themselves, their cause is defeated, and they pay with their lives. In this case we could say the lives of millions of people in this country would die, either fighting or murdered later on. For us that was very clear. (2003a: 7)

In his 2003 May Day address, Castro once again discussed the inherent tension surrounding capital punishment within the context of the Cuban Revolution:

> We fully respect the opinions of those who oppose capital punishment for religious, philosophical and humanitarian reasons. We Cuban revolutionaries also abhor capital punishment, for much more profound reasons than those addressed by the social sciences with regard to crime, currently under study in our country. The day will come when we can accede to the wishes for the abolition of such a penalty.... The Cuban Revolution was placed in the dilemma of either protecting the lives of millions of Cubans by using the legally established death penalty to punish the three main hijackers of a passenger ferry or sitting back and doing nothing. The U.S. government, which incites common criminals to assault boats or airplanes with passengers on board, encourages these people, gravely endangering the lives of innocents and creating the ideal conditions for an attack on Cuba. A

wave of hijackings had been unleashed and was already in full development; it had to be stopped. We cannot ever hesitate when it is a question of protecting the lives of the sons and daughters of a people determined to fight until the end, arresting the mercenaries who serve the aggressors and applying the most severe sanctions against terrorists who hijack passenger boats or planes or commit similarly serious acts, who will be punished by the courts in accordance with the laws in force. (2003b: 5)

IMPRISONMENT

Cuban prisons are administered through the Penal Directorate of the Ministry of Justice (Salas 1979: 287). The penal system consists of traditional prisons and *granjas* (farming facilities). The prisons are surrounded by fences or walls and house the most serious felony offenders. The *granjas,* modelled on farms, are not fenced and are primarily reserved for those individuals who have committed misdemeanours (Evenson1994: 166; Michalowski 1997).

Rehabilitation and re-education, as opposed to retribution and punishment, are the central organizational principles of the Cuban penal system. In discussing the role of incarceration in Cuba, Rueben Remigio-Ferro observed:

> Prisons are a necessary evil. In the best of all worlds, there would be no prisons. But no human society has yet been capable of finding a successful alternative. In Cuba, people are sent to prison only for the most serious crimes. Whenever it is possible to avoid incarceration, the court tries to find another way. We do not view the prisons as warehouses for people being shunned by society. The people being punished are human beings. Since prisons are organized on the principle of rehabilitating those who have lost their way, prisoners work and study to learn skills that will prepare them for their reincorporation into society. They receive a salary for their work, so they can help their families and save for future needs. Ours is a progressive system. At first the rules are very rigid, but little by little the person is given more flexibility to have contact with society and with his family, which plays a key role in the rehabilitation. I am not trying to present the prisons of Cuba as a paradise. These people have committed crimes for which they need to receive punishment. Our enemies attempt to persuade the rest of the world that Cuba itself is practically a prison and that

> Cuban prisoners are starving and tortured. This propaganda has nothing to do with reality. Starting with the 1990s our country went through a very difficult economic period when it was hard to guarantee the basic necessities of life to our people. Even then, the government made sure that prisoners got the basic items they needed to live. (quoted in Montanaro 1999)

The aim of the Cuban rehabilitation and re-education process is to return, as rapidly as is feasible, inmates to society as productive citizens (Elijah 2000). To abet this process, prisoners are incarcerated in the province in which they live, facilitating regular contact between the prisoner and family members. Prison staff, in concert with families, actively aid in preparing the prisoner for re-entry into society (Elijah 2000). An average of six conjugal visits is allowed per year. (Elijah 2000; Evenson 1994: 164–77; Michalowski 1997). In addition, inmates can be granted conditional liberty passes to visit family members who have become ill. At the halfway point of their sentences, prisoners can apply for a conditional release. After serving two-thirds of their sentences, prisoners are released (Elijah 2000).

Another crucial component of the rehabilitation process are programs of work and study, designed to insure that prisoners acquire skills for use once they are reintegrated into their communities. Inmates who have not completed high school are given the opportunity to do so. Those without a trade are provided with the necessary training to acquire one. Those not involved in an educational or trade program can work, and they are paid on the same wage scale as other workers. They do not have to pay for room and board, education, medical or dental care. Those prisoners that choose to work also pay into and receive social security and pension benefits (Elijah 2000; Frank 1993: 96). In China, for example, "re-education and reform through labour" have been mainstays of the criminal justice system. Chinese justice officials stress that in their a network of "re-education through labour camps" there is much heavier emphasis on education than on labour. Previous reports conclude that work conditions in the penal system's light-manufacturing facilities are similar to those in ordinary factories (Brady 1982: 346).

In the 1980s, several international delegations visited and inspected prisons in Cuba. Among these delegations were lawyers and researchers from the U.S. and from Amnesty International. Both delegations "found no widespread complaints from common prisoners about their treatment in the prisons" (Evenson 1994: 168). Additionally, the Cuban authorities, in response to recommendations from the delegations, refurbished buildings and instituted changes in administrative structure and practice (Evenson 1994: 168). Prisons in Cuba are overseen by the Attorney General's office. The work of Mayda Goite, a former provincial vice attorney-general, focused on ensuring

> that the rights of citizens, including prisoners, are protected. There are specialists working within the prisons, whose job is to ensure this protection to those fulfilling their sentences. These specialists can interview any prisoner at any time to find out if there are complaints or signs of abuse. If they detect a violation, they have the authority to correct the situation. In addition, throughout Cuba there are departments of government set up to attend to the rights of citizens, [and] through which citizens can submit complaints when they believe their rights have been violated. If a family member goes to this department and complains that the rights of a member of his family in prison have been violated, the authority has the power to investigate the situation and to issue an order to re-establish justice. (quoted in Montanaro 1999)

Accusations of mistreatment, abuse and even torture in Cuban prisons emanate predominantly from those who "were convicted of crimes against the security of the state, particularly those who fought against the regime in the 1960s and who refused to work or accept other prison programs" (Evenson 1994: 169). However, none of these charges have been corroborated by independent sources. The Amnesty International team that visited Cuba "found no evidence to substantiate torture" (Evenson 1994: 169). Probably the most publicized case was that of Armando Valladares, a police officer under the Batista regime. In 1960, he was convicted of several acts of terrorist bombings (Calvo and Declercq 2000: 90; Franklin 1997: 33; Otero 1987: 84). He became a *cause célèbre* and was fashioned as a persecuted poet. In the 1970s, a campaign seeking his release was launched. Prison authorities were accused of abusing and maltreating Valladares, causing him to become paralyzed. The Cuban government stated emphatically that Valladares was not being mistreated, that he was in good health and that all the charges of abuse were fabrications. On October 21, 1982, he was released and left Havana for Paris, where an expectant crowd of journalists and representatives of nongovernmental organizations were left with their mouths open, seeing the poet-martyr skip down the boarding ramp while his wheelchair was discreetly removed. The next day, Valladares was strolling though the streets of Paris in perfect health. (Calvo and Declercq 2000: 90–91)

Valladares embarked on a European speaking tour that was heavily financed by various U.S. organizations (Calvo and Declercq 2000: 91). Eventually, he was expeditiously granted U.S. citizenship and became a high profile representative of the U.S. government in Geneva, sitting on the U.N. Human Rights Commission (Franklin 1997: 230). On October 13, 1988, U.S. Vice President George Bush declared that Valladares was an American hero. On January 18, 1989, as one of his last acts before leaving office, President Ronald Reagan awarded the presidential medal to Valladares. On August 31, 1994, Valladares supported the call for a military blockade of Cuba and the right for Cuban exile groups "to launch military attacks from U.S. soil" against the island (Franklin 1997: 349). In summing-up the entire Valladares affair, Regis Debray, one of the many prominent individuals who had been part of the campaign to win his release, stated: "The man wasn't a poet, the poet wasn't paralyzed, and the Cuban is now a U.S. citizen" (Calvo and Declercq 2000: 91).

THE 1999 MODIFICATIONS TO THE CUBAN PENAL CODE

At a Special Session of the National Assembly of People's Power, *Law 87: The Modification of the Penal Code of Cuba* was discussed and approved. This constitutes the most recent major change of Cuban criminal law. The thrust of the modifications were toughened penalties for a series of offences, the addition of a new offence (trafficking in persons) and alteration of twenty-five articles of the code. As mentioned, the sentence of life imprisonment was introduced. However, *Law 87* did not alter any fundamental propositions of the code.

The introduction of the new law followed a January 5, 1999, speech by President Fidel Castro on the fortieth anniversary of Cuba's National Revolutionary Police. President Castro called on authorities to get tough in the fight against crime. He stated that criminal activities had increased in last few years as the island opened up to foreign business and tourism. He further emphasized that the rise in crime was a threat to the social order, which would be exploited by the United States in its efforts to overthrow the Revolution (*Granma* 1999f). Echoing this theme, Ricardo

Alarcón, President of the National Assembly, stated that the modifications "establish a commitment to fight crime and will demonstrate the Cuban people's capacity to defeat Washington's destabilising campaign against the island" (*Granma* 1999e). Indeed, the new legislation described crime as "a social phenomenon that poses the greatest danger to the stability of the nation" (*Ley 87/99* 1999: 1).

Drug trafficking was a specific area singled out for harsher sentencing. The Cuban government has consistently expressed concerns about the use of its airspace and coastal waters by international drug traffickers. Even since the passage of the 1999 modifications, the concerns have been growing about the development of an "incipient drug market," stemming "from increased foreign trade and tourism," leading to drug traffickers "attempting to use the country not only as a transit route but as a center of operations" (*Granma* 2003a). The United Nations Office on Drugs and Crime reports that the amount of cocaine seized by Cuban authorities has been steadily increasing. In 1994, 238 kilograms were seized. From 1995 to 2001, the average annual seizure jumped to slightly more than 2,500 kilograms (UNODC 2003).

The sanctions against drug trafficking were substantially increased. Life imprisonment was established for drug trafficking. However, where government officials or officers are involved in the production, sale, trafficking, distribution and illegal possession of drugs, the death penalty has been enacted. The potential sentence was increased to ten to twenty years, or if violence is involved, a twenty- to thirty-year prison sentence or capital punishment is imposed. Offenders who involve persons under sixteen years of age in drug activities face life imprisonment but also may be punished, if violence was committed, with the death penalty. The penalty for money laundering was also increased, spurred by the case of Spanish business executives who used a joint venture with the Cuban Government to transport drugs and launder the profits (Castro 2000b: 244; *Granma* 1998). In July 2003, fourteen persons were sentenced to prison terms of thirteen years to life for drug trafficking. Seven were foreign nationals (Arias Fernández 2003).

The emergence of prostitution in the 1990s, against the backdrop of the island's extensive development of tourism, has elicited much discussion. President Castro has outlined the associated problems on several occasions:

> Our country is already being visited by nearly two million tourists [annually]. In general, these are respectable people, mostly Cana-

dians and Europeans with exemplary behaviour. But there are always visitors, from various places, who travel for sex. Our people, particularly our children and teenagers must be protected, all the more so since the outbreak of diseases such as AIDS has led unscrupulous people seeking safe pleasure to believe that eleven, ten, eight- or seven-year-old boys or girls pose a lower threat than an adult. And there is always someone willing to push such services. We have also hardened our sentences against procuring, particularly against the corruption of minors. All the gold in the world is worth less than the purity and dignity of a Cuban boy or girl. (2000b: 243–44)

Cuban lawmakers have opted to not criminalize prostitution but, rather, to focus on sexual procurement (i.e., pimping) by increasing the penalties. The sentence for pimping was increased to four to ten years, increasing to seven to fifteen years if minors are involved. Prison sentences were increased for the corruption of minors in an effort to stop the activities of sex offenders and paedophiles. The penalty for paedophilia was set at fifteen to thirty years. Several foreigners are serving prison sentences for sex offences with minors. For example, a Canadian from the city of Edmonton was sentenced to twenty-five years for sexual corruption of a fourteen-year-old girl (Reuters 2003). It should be noted that Cuban criminal law confers special protection on minors. It not only identifies specific offences (corruption of minors) but also establishes heavier penalties for other offences (against property, drug trafficking, sexual abuse, etc.) involving or directed against minors. Additionally, the provisions in the code are augmented by a children's and juveniles' code (Salas 1979: 14–41).

Violent robberies using firearms or involving attacks on police or security officers are now punishable by death. Life imprisonment — a new penalty in the Cuban criminal code, where the maximum term was previously thirty years — was introduced for violent robberies or assault. Simple robbery without violence carries a sentence of one to three years and/or a fine of 300 pesos; seven to fifteen years for robbery with violence or the intimidation of persons not involving the use of firearms; and it is twenty to thirty years for robbery involving the use of firearms. As noted, the new crime of trafficking of persons was added to the penal code, in response to vessels based in Florida that have been picking up from the coasts of Cuba emigrants hoping to enter the U.S. illegally. Life imprisonment was also established for smugglers of illegal emigrants in cases where violence is used or where people's lives are put at risk. The sentences stipulated for those penetrating Cuban territory illegally to take people out are: ten to twenty years if violence is not involved; twenty to thirty years when weapons, violence or intimidation are used; and life imprisonment where there is loss of life or lives are placed in danger, especially the lives of children.

CONCLUSION

The vicissitudes of socialist construction have shaped Cuban criminal law, necessitating the dialectical and dynamic balance between social justice and explicit legal measures of self-defence required to preserve national independence and the social and political gains of the Cuban Revolution. This, perhaps, is the underlying, historical logic that guides all facets of the Cuban social project, including Cuban criminal law discourse and creation. Cuba has attempted to build a new society while living under a *de facto* state of war. Ruben Remigio, President of the Supreme Court of Cuba, while pondering the objectives underlying the Helms–Burton Bill, commented:

> The U.S. government has determined that when there is a democratic government in Cuba — which means to them when there is no revolution — the U.S. will have to teach the Cuban justices how to administer justice U.S. style. In a way, they are right. They will have to teach us, because in Cuba, judges don't know how to administer a system of justice that tends to favor the rich against the powerless.... I don't know when they are going to teach us these lessons because they've been announcing the end of the revolution for forty years and we're still here! (quoted in Montanaro 1999)

NOTE

1. A cuota's value, determined at sentencing, varies on a case by case basis. Hence, one individual may be fined 100 *cuotas*, where each *cuota* is equal to one peso. However, another person may be assessed a fine of 100 *cuotas*, where each *cuota* is worth two pesos (Michalowski 1997; Remigio-Ferro 1999: 22).

5. THE UNITED STATES AND CUBA

It is, perhaps, axiomatic in Cuba studies that the United States holds a central place in the history of the Cuban Revolution. U.S. actions and policies impact on all spheres of Cuban life. Indeed, some Cuba specialists assert that the future of the Cuban Revolution revolves around the axis of its relations with Washington. Thus, those who are most violently opposed to the Revolution constantly demand an escalation of economic, diplomatic and — in some cases — military pressures against the island, hoping to administer the *coup de grace*. There are, of course, those who — while opposed to the Cuban socialist project — argue that the U.S. should lower its more than forty-year-old wall of hostility and flood the island with tourists and investment. In this way, they hope to undermine from within and finally demolish the Revolution by "the allure of U.S. goods, tourists and investment dollars," which would "pull Cuba back into the economic orbit of the United States ... the quickest and surest way for Washington to reassert its hegemony over Havana" (LeoGrande 2000: 35). On the other side, there are supporters of the Revolution, who consistently work to eliminate the U.S. economic embargo and normalize relations between the two countries. A significant portion of this group also sees the revolution's ultimate survival as utterly dependent on a change in Washington's policy.

However, the central lacuna of these analyses is the assumption that U.S. hostility to the island stems solely from and begins with the triumph of the Cuban Revolution in 1959. The peculiarity of the present U.S. relationship with Cuba must be seen in its fullest historical context. The geographical fact that the island exists only 160 kilometres from U.S. territory is a reality that has had profound consequences for Cuba, consequences that predate the Revolution. In the most essential ways, the contemporary U.S.–Cuba relations are a continuation and projection of this past. Cuban scholar Carlos Alzugaray Treto contends that the U.S. constitutes the overriding threat "to the existence ... of the Cuban nation" and that throughout the nineteenth century, the U.S. government was one of the main obstacles to all Cuban attempts to join the concert of American nations as a free and independent state" (Alzugaray Treto 1989: 90).

THE PRELUDE TO THE CUBAN REVOLUTION

President John Adams was the first to articulate what was to become Washington's eighteenth- and nineteenth-century policy toward Cuba. The objective of this policy was two-fold: 1) Cuba should remain a Spanish possession only until that time when the U.S. could acquire it and 2) the island should not be allowed to attain independence. In a 1783 letter, Adams expressed the notion "that the Caribbean island was a natural extension of the American continent, and, therefore, it was impossible to resist the conviction that the annexation of Cuba to the Federal Republic was indispensable to the continuation of the Union" (quoted in Ricardo 1994: 10). In 1808, Thomas Jefferson sent General James Wilkinson to Cuba with the task of demanding that the Spanish relinquish the island to the United States (Franklin 1997: 2). In 1809, Jefferson wrote to James Madison, his successor as President: "I candidly confess that I have ever looked upon Cuba as the most interesting addition that can be made to our system of states" (quoted in Franklin 1997: 2–3). However, Madison employed a variation of Adams's policy, allowing Cuba to continue under the dominion of Spain, a declining power, "while guarding against its seizure by any mightier power" (Franklin 1997: 3). Accordingly, the British government was notified that the U.S. would not countenance a British seizure of Cuba.

In 1823, the U.S. government pronounced the Monroe and *La Fruta Madura* (the ripe fruit) doctrines. The Monroe Doctrine established the Americas as an exclusive sphere of U.S. influence and control. *La Fruta Madura*, an ineluctable complement to the Monroe Doctrine, set in place "nearly a century of national policy, one based on the inevitability of the annexation of Cuba" (Pérez Jr. 1988: 185). Secretary of State John Quincy Adams best summarized this policy:

> But there are laws of political as well as of physical gravitation, and if an apple severed by the tempest from its native tree cannot choose but fall to the ground, Cuba forcibly disjoined from its own unnatural connection to Spain, and incapable of self-support, can gravitate only towards the North American Union, which by the same law of nature cannot cast her off from its bosom. (quoted in Franklin 1997: 3; see also Ricardo 1994: 11)

In 1848, another attempt was made to purchase the island from Spain. In 1854, the government of President Franklin Pierce formulated the Ostend Mainfesto, urging the acquisition of Cuba. The manifesto argued that Cuba should not be allowed to become "Africanized and become a second St. Domingo [a reference to the independent Black republic of Haiti created by the successful slave revolt], with all its attendant horrors for the white race" (quoted in Franklin 1997: 5). The very idea of an independent Cuba "raised the spectre of another black republic in the Caribbean" (Pérez Jr. 1988: 109). The goal of preventing the emergence of other Haitis — echoed in the 1960s and beyond in the call of "no more Cubas" — was a central plank of Western policy. The consequences of an independent Cuba:

> Would be the sudden emancipation of a numerous slave population, the result of which could not but be very sensibly felt upon the adjacent shores of the United States. (Pérez Jr. 1988: 109)

Interwoven with the fear of black liberation was the racist notion that Cubans were incapable of governing themselves and, therefore, were fated to come under U.S. dominion (Pérez Jr. 1988: 109). The Virginian, Edward A. Pollard, who advocated the extension of institutions of the U.S. south to all of Latin America, epitomized this thinking:

> What a splendid vision of empire! How sublime in its associations! How noble and inspiriting the idea, that upon the strange theatre of tropical America, once, if we may believe the dimmer facts of history, crowned with magnificent empires and flashing cities and great temples, now covered with mute ruins, and trampled over by half-savages, the destiny of Southern civilization is to be consummated in a glory brighter even than that of old, the glory of an empire, controlling the commerce of the world, impregnable in its position, and representing in its internal structure the most harmonious of all the systems of modern civilization. (quoted in Mannix 1977: 270)

It was also recommended that Cuba be seized if the Spanish were unwilling to cede the island. However, the U.S. government settled on the long-term plan of leaving Cuba in the hands of a weak Spain, until the opportune moment arose to assert Washington's control. In any case, the U.S. had become Cuba's main commercial partner. By the 1880s, such was this economic dominance that 83 percent of Cuban exports went to the U.S. (Franklin 1997: 7). By the 1890s, the U.S. was dependent on Cuba for more than 70 percent of its sugar (Scheer and Zeitlin 1964: 35).

U.S. capital further augmented the island's character as one huge sugar factory (Williams 1983: 26). At the time of the outbreak of the Second War for Independence, U.S. investment in Cuba was approximately $50 million, with annual trade with Cuba worth $100 million (Augier et al. 1971: 248).

The looming threat of the U.S. to Cuba was a central concern of the vanguard of Cuba's independence struggle. Foremost among its leaders and thinkers was José Martí, who saw Cuba's fight for national liberation encompassing independence from both Spain and the United States. Thus, it was imperative "to win Cuba's independence in time to stop the United States from expanding through the Antilles and falling with even greater force on the lands of our America" (Martí, quoted in Alzugaray Treto 1989: 90 and Franklin 1997: 7). This foreboding was encapsulated in the infamous Breckenridge Memorandum. Written in preparation for U.S. intervention in Cuba's Second War for Independence from Spain, this missive has its echo in the present. On December 24, 1897, Undersecretary of War J.C. Breckenridge wrote to General Nelson A. Miles, detailing Washington's policy and attitudes in regards to the Hawaiian Islands, Puerto Rico and Cuba. Regarding Cuba, Breckenridge expressed these sentiments:

> The island of Cuba, a larger territory, has a greater population density than Puerto Rico, although it is unevenly distributed. This population is made up of whites, blacks, Asians and people who are a mixture of these races. The inhabitants are generally indolent and apathetic. As for their learning, they range from the most refined to the most vulgar and abject. Its people are indifferent to religion, and the majority are therefore immoral and simultaneously they have strong passions and are very sensual. Since they only possess a vague notion of what is right and wrong, the people tend to seek pleasure not through work, but through violence. As a logical consequence of this lack of morality, there is a great disregard for life. It is obvious that the immediate annexation of these disturbing elements into our federation in such large numbers would be sheer madness, so before we do that we must clean up the country, even if this means using the methods Divine Providence used on the cities of Sodom and Gomorrah. We must destroy everything within our cannon's range of fire. We must impose a harsh blockade so that hunger and its constant companion, disease, undermine the peaceful popula-

tion and decimate the Cuban army. (quoted in Bains 1993b: 60)

Martí's fears for Cuba were realized when the United States intervened in 1898 and occupied the island until 1902. In 1901, by threatening not to end its military occupation, the U.S. congress forced the incorporation of the Platt Amendment into the Cuban Constitution. The imposition of this measure severely restricted Cuba's capacity to direct its foreign policy and manage its economic affairs (Augier et al. 1971: 252; Pérez Jr. 1988: 186–87). The Platt Amendment stipulated:

> The government of Cuba consents that the United States may exercise the right to intervene for the preservation of Cuban independence, the maintenance of a government adequate for the protection of life, property, and individual liberty, and for discharging the obligations with respect to Cuba imposed by the Treaty of Paris on the United States, now to be assumed and undertaken by the Government of Cuba. To enable the United States to maintain the independence of Cuba, and to protect the people thereof, as well as for its own defence, the Cuban government will sell or lease to the United States the land necessary for coaling or naval stations, at certain specified points, to be agreed upon with the President of the United States. (quoted in Scheer and Zeitlin 1964: 37)

In other words, the U.S. could intervene militarily any time it saw fit to do so. In August 1906, in order to put down an insurrection, Washington exercised this right and militarily occupied the island until January 1909. In 1903, the Cuban government leased Guantánamo Bay to the United States. Cuba became a U.S. protectorate, economically and politically dominated by its northern neighbour.

The Cuban ruling circles became tied to the interests of Washington and benefited from the concentration of land-ownership, the monoculture economy and the relationship of dependency on the U.S. metropolis. Until 1959, succeeding Cuban governments "acted as faithful servants of their U.S. master and the domestic oligarchy" (Alzugaray Treto 1989: 90). The sole exception was the short-lived government that emerged in 1933, an upshot of the uprising against the Machado dictatorship. The aims of the revolutionary groups leading the uprising were not only "to destroy the evils of the traditional political system, but also to do away with United States 'economical imperialism'" (Scheer and Zeitlin 1964: 48). The U.S.

refused to recognize this government and through its ambassador, Summer Welles, orchestrated the government's overthrow (Pérez Jr. 1988: 267–75; Scheer and Zeitlin 1964: 49–52). While as a tactical decision, the U.S. government formally abrogated the Platt Amendment (although maintaining control of Guantánamo Bay), it continued to dominate Cuba (Augier et al. 1971: 255). A central figure in these manoeuvres was Fulgencio Batista. He was to play a dominant — publicly and behind-the-scenes — role in Cuban politics until the late 1950s, acting as "the most faithful servant of U.S. interests" (Alzugaray Treto 1989: 90; Franklin 1997: 12–13). After seizing power for a second time, through a coup in 1952, Batista had the

> unequivocal support of the U.S. government. Arthur Gardener, the United States Ambassador in Havana from 1953 to 1957, was especially concerned with the interests of the Cuban Telephone Company (owned by U.S. capital), and succeeded in raising the rates. In gratitude, the company gave Batista a solid gold telephone (now on display in Havana) and other tokens of appreciation. (Scheer and Zeitlin 1964: 55)

Indeed, "Gardener was so effusive in his praise that he embarrassed even the dictator: 'I am glad Ambassador Gardener approves of my government,' Batista remarked, 'but I wish he wouldn't talk about it so much'" (quoted in Scheer and Zeitlin 1964: 55). Gardener's successor, Earl Smith, was appointed as a result of the intercession of John Hay Whitney, who was both the treasurer of the Republican National Campaign and a major stockholder in Freeport Sulphur, a subsidiary of Moa Bay Mining Company. In return, Smith as "one of his first political acts," obtained for Moa Bay Mining "a substantial tax reduction" (Scheer and Zeitlin 1964: 56).

Under Batista's rule in the 1950s, Cuba's national debt quadrupled to $300 million U.S. The national reserves declined to $120 million U.S. from $410 million U.S. The U.S. dollar reserves plummeted, as well, to approximately $80 million from $500 million, with "much of it flown overseas by Batista and his cronies" (Scheer and Zeitlin 1964: 55). Other calculations put the island's total debt more pessimistically at $1.35 billion U.S. and the amount purloined at $2 billion U.S. (Canton Navarro 2000: 212). The human cost of Batista's rule was just as stark, with an estimated twenty thousand people killed by his forces during the revolutionary struggle of the fifties (Scheer and Zeitlin 1964: 54–55). Immediately after the collapse of the Batista regime, many of the key figures in the government, police and armed forces sought and received sanctuary and protection from extradition in the U.S.

As detailed in Chapter One, before the advent of the Revolution, the U.S. domination and control of the Cuban economy was extensive. U.S. companies garnered 40 percent of the profits from the sugar sector, a sector that accounted for 89 percent of Cuban exports. By 1926, 61 percent of imports were supplied by the U.S. (Deere et al. 1990: 122). In 1933, more than $1.5 billion U.S. in property was in the hands of U.S. companies (Scheer and Zeitlin 1964: 48). By 1958, U.S. direct investment amounted to $956 million (Woodis 1971: 48). Enormous benefits accrued to U.S. firms. For example, "in 1957, total U.S. earnings amounted to $77 million" (Greene 1970: 139). In 1950–1960, the trade surplus with Cuba was $1 billion. However, U.S. economic activity only employed approximately 1 percent of Cubans (Greene 1970: 139). Cuba "operated almost entirely within the framework of the economic system of the United States" (Pérez Jr. 1988: 13).

Since the end of the Second War for Independence to the victory of the Revolution in 1959, Cuba had "lived more as an appendage of the United States than as a sovereign nation" (Scheer and Zeitlin 1964: 34). In his address before the fifteenth session of the United Nations General Assembly on September 26, 1960, Fidel Castro outlined the condition of U.S. dominion:

> But in our country the land was not the only thing in the hands of the U.S. monopolies. The principal mines were also in the hands of the monopolies. For example, Cuba produces large amounts of nickel, and all the nickel was controlled by U.S. interests. Under the Batista dictatorship, a U.S. company called Moa Bay had obtained such a juicy concession that in a mere five years — mark my words, in a mere five years — it sought to amortize an investment of $120 million. A $120 million investment amortized in five years! Who had given the Moa Bay company this concession through the intercession of the U.S. Ambassador? Quite simply, the dictatorship of Fulgencio Batista, the government that was there to defend the interests of the monopolies. And what is more — and this is an indisputable fact — it was completely tax-free. What were the enterprises going to leave for the Cubans? The empty used-up mines, the impoverished land — all without having contributed in the slightest to the

economic development of our country. (1992a: 47)

It was this imperial domination, together with the attendant social polarization and underdevelopment, that generated the conditions that "produced the revolutionary process of 1953 through 1959" (Alzugaray 1989: 90). Ironically, John F. Kennedy, in a 1960 U.S. presidential campaign speech, summed up the situation:

> We refused to help Cuba meet its desperate need for economic progress.... We used the influence of our government to advance the interests and increase the profits of the private American companies which dominated the island's economy.... Administration spokesmen publicly hailed Batista, hailing him as a staunch ally and a good friend at a time when Batista was murdering thousands, destroying the last vestiges of freedom and stealing hundreds of millions of dollars from the Cuban people.... Thus it was our own policies, not those of Castro, that first began to turn our former neighbour against us. (quoted in Greene 1970: 140)

THE REVOLUTION

It has often been argued that it was the actions of the Cuban government that precipitated the confrontation that now characterizes Cuba–U.S. relations (e.g., Treverton 1989). Yet, as early as 1957, Arthur Gardener, the ambassador under President Eisenhower, advised that Castro should be assassinated (Franklin 1997: 16). On March 10, 1959 — before any nationalizations of American property had occurred — the U.S. National Security Council discussed the means by which to place "another government in power" (Blum 2000: 140). Two main considerations shaped this hostility and desire to overthrow the Castro government. The first was evident in the losses sustained by U.S. financial and commercial interests once the Cuban Revolution had embarked on a thoroughgoing social transformation (Greene 1970: 139). A *Wall Street Journal* article of June 24, 1959 captured the prevailing sentiment:

> "The Revolution may be like a watermelon. The more they slice it, the redder it gets." So says an American businessman, one of a growing number of American residents here who are becoming increasingly disenchanted with the policies of Fidel Castro's revolutionary government. Cuba's controversial new Agrarian Reform Law, which will expropriate large landholdings and

divide them up among landless Cuban country folk, has crystal-
ized American opposition here [Cuba] to Prime Minister [sic]
Castro.... The harsh American appraisal here of Mr. Castro may
be clouded by self-interest, it can be argued. But even though it
is difficult to ascertain the truth or falsity of American charges that
Mr. Castro flirts with communism, the very fact that the accusations are being made is important. For the accusers are men who
help manage $800 million of American investments in Cuba.
(quoted in Scheer and Zeitlin 1964: 99)

The nationalizations of U.S. property were in accord with international
law (Bravo 1996: 28–39). Perhaps the most decisive of the nationalizations
were the seizure of the oil refineries of Texaco, Standard Company —
both U.S. companies — and the British Royal Shell Group. Cuba had
signed the first major trade deal with the U.S.S.R. in February 1960,
which included a supply of Soviet oil, vital to Cuban industry. Moreover,
the Soviet oil was cheaper and provided in exchange for sugar. The U.S.
companies, at the instigation of the U.S. government, refused to refine the
Soviet oil. As these refineries were the only ones on the island, the Cuban
government nationalized the refineries (Franklin 1997: 26; Scheer and
Zeitlin 1964: 184–85).

These nationalizations of U.S. companies were undertaken, as were
all the other nationalizations, within the context of offers of compensation. However, these offers were refused by their owners since, during the
era of Batista, it was the common practice for corporations to deliberately
undervalue their assets and earnings in order to reduce their taxes. The
records therefore represented only a fraction of the true worth of the
businesses. The Cuban government used the official company records as
the basis for assessing compensation packages, and they were deemed
unacceptable by the owners and executives of these companies. Even
when the government "requested the American owners to reassess their
property for taxes ... they gave the same low figures. As a result it is difficult
for these owners to publicly protest too much, since this would be an
admission of past tax evasion" (Scheer and Zeitlin 1964: 97).

As Cuba was a poor, underdeveloped country, which was in the midst
of undertaking and funding an unprecedented socio–economic restructuring, the method of compensation offered was in bonds issued in Cuban
currency, which would be refunded at an annual interest rate of 4.5
percent at the end of twenty years (Scheer and Zeitlin 1964: 97, 136–37;
Bravo 1996: 45–47). Castro emphasized that while the Cuban govern-

ment desired amicable relations with the U.S., it was not going to halt the ongoing social and economic transformations, as there was "no alternative; and we are going to pay for the land with the means we have" (Scheer and Zeitlin 1964: 103). Nevertheless, the U.S. demanded immediate and "adequate" compensation based on the real (i.e., the undisclosed) value of the properties. The Cuban government responded that if compensation was to occur on this basis, there should be payment of the taxes owed based on the new valuations, fines for tax evasion and interest. They also offered to place money from the sale of Cuban sugar to the U.S. in a special compensation fund. However, once the sugar quota was eliminated this proposal was rendered moot. In the end, the U.S. companies designated the nationalized properties as losses (based on the real values) and deducted them from their taxes (Bravo 1996: 45–47).

In his 1960 address to the United Nations, Castro elucidated the consequences of attempting to gain control of Cuba's wealth and resources:

> So the revolutionary government passed a mining law that obliged these monopolies to pay 25 per cent tax on the export of minerals. The attitude of the revolutionary government had already been too bold. It had clashed with the interests of the international electricity trust; it had clashed with the interests of the United Fruit Company; it had clashed, in short, with the most powerful interests of the United States, which, as you know, are closely linked with one another. This was more than the U.S. government — that is, the representatives of the U.S. monopolies could tolerate. (1992a: 47–48)

The second — and overriding — factor conditioning the U.S. determination to topple the Cuban government was Cuba's resolve to pursue an independent course, a resolve that might prove infectious throughout the region. Consequently, an example had to made out of Cuba, as a lesson to other Latin American and Caribbean countries that might dare to challenge U.S. hegemony (LeoGrande 2000: 35). Arthur Schlesinger, a key advisor to President Kennedy, fulminated about "the spread of the Castro idea of taking matters into one's own hands" (quoted in McNally 2002: 159). It was further argued by the Kennedy administration that "the very existence of his regime [Castro's government] … represented a successful defiance of the U.S., a negation of our whole hemispheric policy of almost half a century" (quoted in Chomsky 2002:

26). The Kennedy administration ultimately concluded:

> The distribution of land and other forms of national wealth greatly favour the propertied classes.... The poor and underprivileged, stimulated by the example of the Cuban Revolution, are now demanding opportunities for a decent living. (quoted in Chomsky 2002: 26)

Castro observed:

> Then the stage of harassing our revolution began. I will pose a question to anyone who objectively analyzes the facts.... Are the things done by the revolutionary government grounds to decree the destruction of the Cuban revolution? No, they are not. But the interests that were adversely affected by the Cuban revolution were not concerned about Cuba; they were not being ruined by the measures of the Cuban revolutionary government. That was not the problem. The problem was that these same interests own the wealth and natural resources of the majority of the peoples of the world. So the Cuban revolution had to be punished for its stance. Punitive actions of every type — including the destruction of those insolent Cubans — had to be carried out against the revolutionary government. (1992a: 48)

In 1961, to counter the Cuban example, President Kennedy launched the Alliance for Progress, an aid program aimed at achieving by the end of the decade "economic growth, more equitable distribution of national income, reduced unemployment, agrarian reform, education, housing, health, etc." (Blum 1998: 19; Deere et al. 1990: 127–28; Harrison 1983: 117). Kennedy declared: "Let us transform the American continents into a vast crucible of revolutionary ideas and efforts, an example to the world that liberty and progress walk hand in hand" (quoted in Greene 1970: 141). That the Alliance for Progress was aimed at forging an alliance against Cuba was underscored by the reality that the U.S. government informed all countries throughout the region that there would be "no aid for any country that allows its ships or aircraft to carry any equipment, materials, or commodities to Cuba so long as it is governed by the Castro regime" (Morray 1968: 114). In 1970, a major U.S. study was undertaken to ascertain how close the Alliance for Progress had come to meeting its goals. Ironically, it concluded that Cuba, which had been excluded from the program, came:

> closer to some of the Alliance's objectives than most Alliance members. In education and public health, no country in Latin America has carried out such ambitious and nationally compre-hensive programs. Cuba's centrally planned economy has done more to integrate the rural and urban sectors (through national income distribution policy) than the market economies of the other Latin American countries. (quoted in Blum 1998: 191)

THE UNDECLARED WAR

Successive U.S. administrations have been united in the proclamation that there will "be no more Cubas in Latin America." President Johnson declared that "the American nations cannot, must not, and will not permit the establishment of another Communist government in the Western Hemisphere" (quoted in Morray 1968: 114). With the consolidation of the Cuban revolutionary process and the beginning of the socialist transformation, it was clear that the prospects of internally demolishing the Revolution were remote. Therefore, "a consensus favouring an aggres-sive, confrontationist policy" developed within U.S. ruling circles (Morley 1987: 304). At the centre of this consensus was agreement on the necessity to take military action against Cuba. This approach "culminated in the Bay of Pigs invasion of April 1961" (Morley 1987: 304). A crucial component of the invasion plan

> was "Operation Forty," which included the assassination, by a hand-picked taskforce of professional killers, of political leaders who stood in the way of the proposed new regime, and any other obdurate elements that might oppose a return to the good old days. It was hoped that in the confusion of battle, such killings would go unnoticed. (Lerner 1973: 60).

The invasion force of Cuban exiles — trained, financed and outfitted by the U.S. Central Intelligence Agency — was defeated in less than seventy-two hours, a fact that contributed to the consolidation of the Cuban Revolution. On April 16, 1961, at an immense funeral gathering for seven Cuban citizens who were killed in the bombings preceding the invasion, Fidel Castro proclaimed the socialist nature of the Cuban Revolution, stating that Washington would not forgive Cuba for having "made a revolution, a socialist revolution, right here under the very nose of the United States" (quoted Franklin 1997: 40).

In the early 1960s, the U.S. Joint Chiefs of Staff proposed staging a series of attacks on U.S. citizens, territory and interests, attacks which would be blamed on Cuba and used to justify waging a war. They proposed to launch

> a secret and bloody war of terrorism against their own country in order to trick the American public into supporting an ill-conceived war they intended to launch against Cuba. Code named Operation Northwoods, the plans which had the approval of the Chairman and every member of the Joint Chiefs of Staff, called for innocent Americans to be shot on American streets; for boats carrying refugees from Cuba to be sunk in the high seas; for a wave of violent terrorism to be launched in Washington D.C., Miami, and elsewhere. People would be blamed for the bombings they did not commit; planes would be hijacked. Using phoney evidence, all of it would be blamed on Castro, thus giving ... the excuse, as well as the public and international backing they needed to launch their war. (Bamford 2001: 70–91; see also Robinson 1998)

Other proposals were to:

> Fake an attack on the U.S. naval base in Guantánamo, Cuba, with friendly Cubans masquerading as attackers.... Arrange for an unmanned vessel to be blown up near a major Cuban city.... Stage a "Communist Cuban terror campaign in the Miami area...." Plant arms in a Caribbean country and send jets painted to look like Cuban Migs, creating the appearance of a "Cuban based, Castro supported" subversion.... Blow up an unmanned U.S. plane that would surreptitiously replace a charter flight of civilians. (Robinson 1998)

While none of these plans were implemented, the U.S. government waged — and wages — an unceasing campaign of aggression against Cuba. During the Kennedy presidency, the island was targeted with a "systematic military, political and economic offensive" (Walton 1972: 41; see also Escalante 1995). The Bay of Pigs invasion was the most visible of these assaults, demonstrating that the U.S. government was ever "prepared to violate the territorial integrity of a sovereign state ... [against] a cardinal tenet of international law" to preserve Washington's hegemony (Walton 1972: 42). Indeed, "the Bay of Pigs invasion was the major cause of the Cuban missile crisis," as it confirmed to both Cuba and the Soviet Union that the island was in imminent danger from the U.S. (Walton 1972: 104). The positioning of Soviet missiles in Cuba was a defensive response to that aggression and ultimately resulted in the 1962 crisis, which brought the world to the brink of a nuclear war.

The "covert warfare, political-diplomatic pressures, and economic sanctions on a regional and global scale" that were unleashed in the 1960s by the Kennedy and Johnson administrations against Cuba became the guiding framework of successive U.S. governments (Morley 1987: 304; Elliston 1999; Hickle and Turner 1981). There were — and are — repeated attempts — by the CIA and through its surrogates — to assassinate Fidel Castro and other Cuban leaders (Escalante 1994; Senate Select Committee 1975: 71–180). These efforts continue. In November 1997, the U.S. Coast Guard intercepted a boat that was adrift off the coast of Puerto Rico. On boarding it, they found sniper rifles and ammunition, and one of the four men on the boat admitted "that their purpose was to kill Fidel Castro when he landed on Venezuela's Margarita Island for the Ibero American Summit" (Franklin 1998: 30). All four men were either directly linked to the CIA or part of groups that were supported and funded by the agency (Franklin 1998: 31). A plan to blow up a university auditorium in Panama City, while President Castro was delivering a speech to students, was uncovered and foiled in November 2000 (Associated Press 2002; Canton Navarro 2000: 283).[1]

Various terrorist actions have been organized against Cuba, including attacks on Cuban diplomats (in which one diplomat was killed); repeated bombings of the Cuban United Nations Mission in New York and the Cuban Interests Section in Washington D.C.; and efforts to terrorize Cuba solidarity groups in the U.S. (Blum 1998: 190). On October 6, 1976, a Cuban exile group blew up a Cubana Airlines flight enroute from Barbados to Havana, killing all of the seventy-three passengers, "including the entire Cuban championship fencing team" (Blum 1998: 190; see also Cotayo 1978). It was later revealed the CIA had foreknowledge of the bombing (Blum 1998: 190; Cotayo 1978: 32–37). In 1997, a series of bombings occurred in several hotels in Havana, injuring three and killing one person (Franklin 1998: 28–29). These acts where organized and planned by Luis Clemente Posada Carrilles, who — in an interview with the *New York Times* — stated that the Cuban American National Foundation (CANF) had financed the entire operation (*New York Times*

1998; Alvarado Godoy 2003). The CANF is the dominant Cuban exile group. It was founded in the 1980s under the auspices and with the extensive support of the Reagan presidency and receives the vast majority of its operating funds indirectly from the U.S. government (Calvo and Declercq 2000: 60–61). This money is funnelled through various institutes: for example, between 1990 and 1992, the National Endowment for Democracy — a Reagan era creation — gave the CANF $250,000 (Blum 2000: 183).

This undeclared war on Cuba also encompasses the deployment of biological terrorism. In the 1960s, the U.S. military developed war plans that entailed combining a conventional invasion of the island with a pre-emptive "biological strike against Cuba's soldiers and civilians" (Miller et al. 2001: 53). An estimated 70,000 Cubans were expected to be killed by the deployment of a variety of biological weapons (Miller 2001: 56–57). While the invasion by U.S. troops never occurred, the use of biological agents was (is) a significant feature of the destabilization campaign waged against Cuba. Cane fields were infected with various fungal agents in efforts to hamper, if not destroy, the sugar sector. Other crops, such as tobacco and rice, were also targeted (Franklin 1998: 32; National Information Service 1988: 34–35). In 1996, potato, corn, beans, squash, cucumbers and other crops were infected and devastated by the *thrips palmi* insect, after a U.S. crop-duster, enroute to Columbia, released a liquid substance over Cuba. Within six weeks, *thrips palmi* began to infest fields. Up to that point, this particular insect had never been detected on the island (Franklin 1998: 33). At one point in the 1970s, the CIA:

> deployed futuristic weather modification technology to ravage Cuba's sugar crop and undermine the economy. Planes from the China Lake Naval Weapons Center in the California desert, where hi tech was developed, overflew the island, seeding rain clouds with crystals that precipitated torrential rains over non-agricultural areas and left the cane fields arid (the downpours caused killer flash floods in some areas). (Blum 1998: 188)

In 1971, African swine fever, which had never before appeared in the Western Hemisphere, ravaged Cuba's pig farms. To prevent the disease spreading, more than half a million pigs were destroyed. The United Nations Food and Agricultural Organization described this outbreak as the most alarming event of the year (Blum 1998: 188). In 1977, it was revealed by a U.S. intelligence source that the virus was introduced into Cuba when he was instructed to transfer it form Fort Gulick, a U.S. Army base and CIA training center in the Panama Canal Zone, to a group of Cuban exiles, who took it to operatives inside Cuba in March 1971. (Franklin 1998: 32; see also Blum 1998: 188)

Cuba's population has also been a target. In 1981, a dengue epidemic "swept Cuba, of a speed and virulence previously unknown in Latin America" (Franklin 1998: 32). More than 300,000 thousand Cubans were infected, with 158 deaths, 101 of whom were children under the age of fifteen (Schapp 1982). In the 1950s, the U.S. Army had

specially-bred mosquitoes in Georgia and Florida to see whether disease-carrying insects could be weapons in a biological war. The mosquitoes bred for the tests were the *Aedes Aegypti* type, the precise carrier of dengue fever as well as other diseases. In 1967 it was reported by Science magazine that at the U.S. government center in Fort Derrick, Maryland, dengue fever was amongst those "diseases that are at least the objects of considerable research and that appear to be among those regarded as potential BW [biological warfare] agents. (Blum 1998: 188–89; see also Franklin 1998: 32)

In 1984, Eduardo Arocena, leader of the Cuban exile group Omega 7, while on trial in New York on another matter, testified that in 1980 a mission was organized

to carry some germs to introduce them in Cuba to be used against the Soviets and against the Cuban economy, to begin what was called chemical war, which later on produced results that were not what we had expected, because we thought that it was going to be used against the Soviet forces, and it was used against our own people, and with that we did not agree. (quoted in Blum 1998: 189; see also Franklin 1998: 32)

ECONOMIC STRANGULATION

An integral feature of the U.S. onslaught on Cuba has been the constant drive to undermine the Cuban economy. While numerous acts of economic sabotage were carried out, the central stratagem was the imposition of an economic embargo, which later assumed the dimensions of a blockade. The objective was to asphyxiate the Cuban economy. In 1959, the Eisenhower administration "began to make economic reprisals" (Walton 1972: 39). When in 1959 the Cuban government, having failed to secure financial assistance from the U.S., sought a loan from the International Monetary Fund (IMF), Washington exerted their immense influence to ensure the IMF "insisted on conditions that would have prevented ... any serious reforms of the Cuban economy" (Lerner 1973: 59). In March 1960, the U.S. successfully pressured a consortium of Western European banks to cancel a $100 million loan to Cuba (Franklin 1997: 25). On July 6, 1960, the U.S. government eliminated the sugar quota, thus depriving Cuba of the major market for its main export. Eisenhower stated that the elimination of the sugar quota "amounts to economic sanctions against Cuba. Now we must look ahead to other moves — economic, diplomatic and strategic" (quoted in Franklin 1997: 26). The *Wall Street Journal*, in a July 7, 1960, article, equated the slashing of the sugar quota as a declaration of "economic war on Fidel Castro's Cuba" (quoted in Scheer and Zeitlin 1964: 192). In 1961, diplomatic relations were severed, and President Kennedy imposed a total trade embargo — with the exemption of some medical material — in 1962. In July 1963, under the *Trading with the Enemy Act*, Kennedy prohibited all

> unlicensed commercial or financial transactions between Cuba and U.S. citizens, unlicensed import of or dealing abroad in merchandise of Cuban origin by U.S. citizens, and import of goods made in Third countries with Cuban materials. All Cuban owned assets are frozen.... Nobody may participate in unlicensed transactions in U.S. dollars. This prohibits the spending of money for travel expenses in Cuba or for Cuban airline tickets. (quoted in Franklin 1997: 66)

In 1964, the Johnson administration "initiated a policy of denying requests for the export of all medicines and medical supplies to Cuba" (Schwab 1999: 54). As one U.S. official commented: "Once the decision was made to isolate Cuba ... all the rest, such as economic sanctions, was detail" (Morley 1987: 304).

The U.S. economic actions against Cuba do not fall within the accepted legal definition of an embargo, which is a bilateral affair, i.e., an action that involves one country severing diplomatic and/or commercial relations with another country. The U.S. has made great efforts to disrupt Cuba's relationship with other countries. The U.S. measures are predicated

> on Cuba's isolation, Cuba's suffocation, and Cuba's immobiliza-
> tion to force it to submit. All these are precisely cardinal elements
> included in the concept of "blockade," which means to cut, to
> close, to sever communications with outside sources, to put
> pressure on the besieged, to make them surrender by force or
> starvation. (Bravo 1996: 54)

Cuba exists under a stringent siege, imposed by the most powerful nation in the world. The sanctions imposed on the island continue to be "the harshest in the world" (Chomsky 2000: 82). In 1992, the *Cuban Democracy Act* (CDA) — popularly known as the Torricelli Act — was enacted, banning "trade with Cuba from U.S.-owned subsidiaries in third countries" (Franklin 1997: 289). This trade had become an important part of Cuba's strategy of circumventing the economic sanctions. From 1980 to 1991, this trade had risen from $292 million to $718 million, with 75 percent of it being in food and medicines (Franklin 1997: 291). Furthermore, the CDA prohibited any vessel "that entered Cuban ports from loading or unloading any freight in the United States for a period of six months after departure from Cuba, and prohibiting ships with an interest [i.e., engaged in business] from entering a U.S. port" (Schwab 1999: 81). This dramatically increased the transportation costs incurred by the Cuban government.

The sanctions are aimed at "the health and, thus, the very lives of Cubans" (Schwab 1999: 55). As a consequence and because of the U.S. domination of the world pharmaceutical industry, Cuba suffers shortages of major medicines. For example, Cuba is unable to obtain most antibiotics "because most antibiotics are produced under U.S. patents" and "cannot be exported to Cuba under the terms of the embargo" (Schwab 1999: 72). U.S. law disallows "the re-export of U.S. products from a third country, while products even developed through the use of U.S. technology or design cannot be sold to Cuba" (Schwab 1999: 72). Companies and countries that violate these strictures face serious legal repercussions. These prohibitions have a significant international reach and impact. Examples of these bans include:

> A sale by the Japanese company Toshiba of medical equipment
> used to detect cardiovascular diseases and blood analysis labora-
> tory equipment from the Swedish firm LKB. U.S. commerce

officials also forbade the Argentine supplier Medix from shipping spare parts needed by Cuban hospitals to maintain U.S.-made dialysis machines and ophthalmologic sonar equipment already in use throughout the island. (Schwab 1999: 74)

A study in the *American Journal of Public Health* concluded that U.S. sanctions against Cuba had impacted negatively on the Cuban healthcare system by raising the costs of medicines and other related material (Garfield and Santana 1997). Importations of food, textbooks, school supplies, and basic necessities have also been severely affected. As Robert Torricelli, the U.S. Congress member who sponsored the CDA, stated, the goal of U.S. economic measures is to "wreak havoc on that island" (Franklin 1997: 289).

The sanctions regime was further strengthened by the passage, in 1996, of the *Cuban Liberty and Democratic Solidarity Act* (CLDSA), widely referred to as the Helms–Burton Bill (United States Statutes 1997). The significance of the Helms–Burton Bill lies in the fact that it cements into law the U.S. policy of hostility towards the Cuban Revolution, while deepening the sanctions (for a detailed analysis see Alarcón 1997). Indeed, it was designed to be the *coup de grace* to the Cuban Revolution. The CLDSA establishes that the sanctions against Cuba will not be lifted if either Fidel or Raúl Castro are part of the Cuban government. Before there can be a normalization of relations between the two countries, there must be very specific political and economic changes in Cuba, namely the introduction a political process deemed "democratic" by Washington and the installation of a free-market capitalist economy. The CLDSA further establishes that the U.S. government will provide financial and other means by which to assist individuals and groups opposed to the Cuban Revolution. Jessie Helms, the main sponsor and promoter of the legislation, summed up its thrust as simply "adios, Fidel" (quoted in Schwab 1999: 50).

Under the CLDSA, the U.S. extends in law the sanctions against Cuba to include any international institution — such as the International Monetary Fund, the World Bank or the Inter American Development Bank — that provides financial aid. If an agency extends financial assistance to Cuba, the U.S. will reduce its funding to that organization by the exact amount given to Cuba. The reprisals are not only limited to international institutions, as "access to the U.S. sugar quota was denied to countries that did not certify that they were not importing Cuban sugar that could find its way to the U.S." (Schwab 1999: 47). The CLDSA establishes that any foreign company operating on the island whose business activity involves expropriated U.S. property will be liable to litigation in U.S. courts. Also, the U.S. government is empowered to refuse visas to members of those foreign companies. Ian Delaney, the chief executive officer of the Canadian company Sherritt, was barred from entry into the United States because of his company's joint ventures in Cuba.

The Helms–Burton Bill has provoked heated opposition from the European Union, due to its undisguised extra-territoriality and its violations of the general precepts of international law, specifically the General Agreement on Tariffs and Trade (now subsumed in the World Trade Organization). By "creating a legal framework to force other nations to abide by" the sanctions against Cuba, Washington had publicly announced that it could "foist its foreign policy objectives on other nations [notably the European Union] through the threat and actual imposition of trade sanctions" (Schwab 1999: 47). However, in response to the vocal international opposition, U.S. presidents have so far exercised their prerogative to suspend the operation of the section that would initiate legal suits against those corporations carrying on business in Cuba. Nevertheless, the possibility of being exposed to U.S. legal action and denied access to the U.S. market operates as a deterrent to potential investors in Cuba, as a regime is set in place by which to launch future reprisals against those parties engaged in business on the island.

Despite some recent temporary openings that have allowed the direct sale of foodstuffs to Cuba from U.S. companies, the edifice of the sanctions remains unchanged. Cuba is still denied access to funds from international funding agencies, forcing the Cuban government to seek loans from private lenders at higher-than-normal interest rates. Moreover, the campaign to sever the island's financial and commercial ties continues apace. Fidel Castro has categorized the nature of U.S. sanctions as:

> An economic war against Cuba.... It is the tenacious, constant persecution of any Cuban economic deal made anywhere in the world. The United States actively operates, through its diplomatic channels, through its embassies, to put pressure on any country that wishes to trade with Cuba; or any business interest wishing to make commercial links with or invest in Cuba; to pressure and punish any boat transporting cargo to Cuba. It is a universal war, with an immense imbalance of power in its favour, against the economy of our country, going to the extreme of taking action against individuals who attempt to undertake any economic activity with our country. (1996a: 14)

EMIGRATION

Emigration policy is another avenue through which the U.S. has an immense impact on Cuba. The media is flooded with reports and stories of the "countless" Cubans "fleeing" the island, risking their lives on the high seas to reach the United States and "freedom." The popular image of the Cuban refugee is of someone escaping political persecution and a veritable prison (Rodriguez Chavez 1999: 83–84). Cuban emigration is treated as if it exists in a vacuum. Invariably, there is no analysis of Cuban emigration within the context of the Latin American region in general and U.S. immigration policy in relation to Cuba in particular.

The mass emigration of Latin Americans is a regional phenomenon. From 1999 to 2002, an estimated 600,000 people left Columbia. Between 1999 and 2001, in the case of Ecuador, 500,000 persons departed. At present, 20 percent of El Salvador's population has emigrated. In Argentina, as a direct consequence of the ongoing economic crisis, thousands queue up at foreign embassies seeking escape through emigration. In 1998, an estimated 7.5 million Mexicans were living in the United States, with an additional 300,000 entering illegally. Overall, 15 million Latin Americans now reside in the United States: 50 percent of the total immigrants (*The Economist* 2002b; Rodriguez Chavez 1999: 97–99).

The number of emigrants from Cuba — both in absolute and relative figures — is comparatively lower, although, with the economic downturn in recent years, the number of those seeking to leave the island — legally and illegally — has risen dramatically (Rodriguez Chavez 1999: 95–97). A 1994 report by the United States Interests Section in Havana (USINT), which was sent to the U.S. Secretary of State, the Central Intelligence Agency and the U.S. Immigration and Naturalization Service (INS) — demonstrates that the primary motivating factor in the decisions to leave Cuba are economic:

> In the processing of visa applications for refugees, there are still few solid cases. Most of those who file applications do so not out of real fear of persecution, but because of the deterioration of the economic situation. Particularly difficult for USINT and INS officials are the cases presented by human rights activists. Although we have done everything possible to work with the human rights organizations over which we have the greatest control, to identify those activists who are truly persecuted by the government, the human rights cases represent the least solid category within the refugee program. In recent months, accusa-

tions have persisted of fraudulent applications made by activists
and the sale of letters of support from human rights leaders. Due
to the lack of verifiable documentary evidence, generally USINT
officials and members of the INS have considered human rights
cases the most susceptible to fraud. (USINT 1994)

Critical to understanding Cuban emigration is locating it within the
overall U.S. strategy of undermining the Cuban Revolution. The Eisenhower administration encouraged the emigration of professionals and
skilled personnel as a means to deprive the Cuban government of the
expertise necessary to manage the economy and implement its development program. This effort to denude Cuba of essential competencies was
coupled with efforts to destablize the country and discredit the Revolution by inciting mass emigration, specifically an illegal flow of migrants.
Central to this objective is the *Act for the Adjustment of the Status of Cuban
Refugees* — commonly referred to as the Cuban Adjustment Act —
promulgated by the U.S. in 1966. As the famous case of Elián González
illustrated, the U.S. government adopts a unique approach to Cuban
immigrants. Under the Cuban Adjustment Act, preferential treatment is
accorded to Cuban citizens. Cubans arriving in the United States automatically, among other things, receive:

> 1. Immediate issuance of a work permit and a social security
> number; 2. Financial assistance for food, accommodation and
> education; and 3. Permanent residency status in the U.S. one year
> and a day after their arrival. (Rodriguez Chavez 1999: 99–100; see
> also United States Government 1967)

The Cuban Adjustment Act is atypical of U.S. immigration policy in that
Cubans are the only national group upon which these privileges are
conferred. As Felix Masud-Piloto, director of the Center for Latino
Research, notes, the U.S. in relation to other Latin American countries
uses "very different criteria than that used to accept Cubans" and has
"almost systematically denied asylum to refugees fleeing political repression in Latin America" (1999: 9). One has only to reflect on the different
treatment meted out to, for example, Haitian illegal immigrants — who
are detained and then sent back to their home country — to appreciate the
uniqueness of the Act and its intended consequences (Jones 2002). David
Abraham, an immigration law specialist at the University of Miami, notes
that for Cubans who opt for illegal migration: "There's always a risk

involved, but the rewards for those who reach the U.S. are so easy and so substantial" (quoted in Bauza 2003).

The Cuban Adjustment Act has served as a means by which to encourage illegal emigration. Cuban law is quite specific that those who choose to leave the island are free to do so once they have obtained the necessary legal authorization and documents from the country to which they are emigrating. The overwhelming country of choice is the United States. There have been several agreements between the Cuban and U.S. governments covering the facilitation of legal migration. However, Washington has consistently violated these agreements. Under the 1994 migration accords, the U.S. is obligated to grant a minimum of 20,000 immigration visas annually (Rodriguez Chavez 1999: 125). However, the number of visas granted often falls far below that minimum. For example, between October 1, 2002, and February 28, 2003, the U.S. issued 505 visas. In 2002, in total, 7,237 visas were granted; in 2001, 8,300; and in 2000, 10,860 (Pérez Roque 2003).

The refusal to grant the required number of visas directly leads to a build-up of migratory pressures, by heightening the frustrations of those who desire to migrate. By disabling the legal process of migration, U.S. policy encourages illegal departures. As noted, those who depart illegally will be granted the many privileges — denied to other would-be immigrants to the U.S. — automatically bestowed on Cubans who arrive on U.S. soil. This situation is further aggravated by the U.S. government-funded, Miami-based, Radio Martí, which, together with other stations, broadcasts hundreds of hours each week into the island, exhorting people to leave illegally.

Beyond the dangerous voyages across the Florida straits, U.S. policy provokes and stimulates hijackings. People who commit acts of armed hijacking and piracy are seldom prosecuted. Although the hijackers involved use weapons and violence to fulfil their objectives, often putting people's lives in danger, they are welcomed in the United States as heroes who have fled totalitarianism. In this way, Washington has divided hijackings into "good and bad hijackings" (Blum 1998: 186). The first half of 2003 witnessed several hijackings, and those hijackers who were successful in reaching the United States were not incarcerated but set free. These hijackings and similar acts illustrate how the U.S. government uses "immigration as a factor to destabilize the Revolution or as a way to propagandize that it is not viable" (Rodriguez Chavez 1999: 84).

Illegal emigration from Cuba is a product of the interrelation of the world economic crisis, which impacts on Cuba, the ongoing U.S.

economic sanctions and the political and military threats that continue to emanate from Washington. The Cuban government views the hijackings and U.S. immigration policy within the broader context of the unrelenting U.S. campaign to topple the Cuban Revolution. In response to the statement from the George W. Bush administration that an uncontrolled migratory flow from Cuba would be considered a threat to U.S. national security, an editorial in *Granma* (the newspaper of the Communist Party of Cuba) underlined that:

> the head of the United States Interests Section is at the forefront of a conscious plan to stimulate illegal emigration via acts of terrorism with the objective of casting aside the migratory agreements between the two countries and creating a chaotic situation. The objective is to stimulate mass migration, obliging Washington to take aggressive action to avoid it. (*Granma* 2003b)

CONCLUSION

The Cuban government and various mass organizations have consistently stated that the U.S. policies are violations of the inalienable and inviolable human rights of Cuban citizens, particularly the right to self-determination, which is enshrined in the United Nations Charter and other international conventions. Other rights violated include the right to food and medicine covered under Article 25 of the Universal Declaration of Human Rights and articles 11 and 12 of the International Covenant on Economic, Social and Cultural Rights. On May 31, 1999, several Cuban mass organizations filed a lawsuit in Cuban courts against the U.S. government, seeking compensation for the deaths and injuries caused by four decades of Washington's undeclared war. The suit detailed U.S. aggressions "ranging from backing for armed rebel groups within Cuba and the Bay of Pigs invasion in 1961, to subversion attempts from the U.S. naval base in Guatánamo and the planting of epidemics on the island" (Blum 2000: 228). Cuba demanded $181.1 billion in compensation for 3,478 people that had been killed and 2,099 who had been injured (Blum 2000: 228; Deutchsman and Ratner 1999). The U.S. did not deign to reply to or acknowledge the suit.

By challenging U.S. hegemony, Cuba has proven to be, to use William Blum's term, "the unforgivable revolution" (Blum 1998: 184). The U.S.'s "standing as a hegemonic power" was based "on its capacity to maintain and demonstrate control of its own hemispheric community" (Payne and Sutton 2001: 224). The Cuban Revolution was (and is) an "undeniable and visible breach of this system" (Payne and Sutton 2001: 224). Thus, a central objective of U.S. policy remains the destruction of "Cuba's government and to eradicate the revolution" (Erisman 1998: 91). Integral to this aim are "the propaganda and disinformation campaigns waged by the media under the direct or indirect control of the United States ... to isolate the Cuban Revolution in the hope of leaving it defenseless as a prelude to a final bellicose act" (Lechuga 1995: 1–2; for a detailed examination, see Elliston 1999). In July 2003, for example, Washington accused Cuba of jamming U.S. broadcasts to Iran. The Bush administration went so far as to declare that Cuba was "in league with the Iranian government" (BBC 2003b). In the wake of the war against Iraq and the increasing U.S. pressures on Iran, Havana considered these charges to be a serious provocation, dismissing them as part of "a new campaign of anti-Cuba lies ... adding to a long list of hostile and aggressive actions that the imperial administration of George W. Bush had taken against our country" (MINREX 2003 and Reuters 2003a). A subsequent investigation by Cuban authorities revealed that the jamming emanated from an Iranian diplomatic compound. The activity was promptly stopped and a note of protest sent by Cuba to the government of Iran (Safa 2003 and *VOA News* 2003).

Cubans keenly understand, as they have their history as a guide, that the unrelenting U.S. hostility is not simply a product of misguided policies: the tactical approach to the "Cuba problem" may change from U.S. administration to administration — from the military assault of a Kennedy to the *rapprochement* of a Carter back again to the hyper-aggressiveness of a George W. Bush — but the underlying logic driving the imperialist system remains the same, a lust for expansion and domination. What defines and determines this logic is the rush to secure and cement

> a worldwide "open door" for capital and commerce, the integration of societies within the capitalist political and economic orbit, and the maintenance of an American-dominated capitalist world. (Morley 1987: 305)

It is not policies that drive the system; they are the precipitates of its imperatives. The policy contestations in U.S. ruling circles are "within the common political and economic framework that shapes the universe" where these disputes occur (Morley 1987: 305). Thus, Cuba cannot afford to have — and does not have — illusions about the United States.

NOTE

1. A telling commentary on Washington's hypocritical, tacit and complicit role is the case Gerardo Hernández, Antonio Guerrero, Ramón Labañino, René González, and Fernando González. These five men are serving prison sentences of fifteen years to life in U.S federal maximum-security penitentiaries. They had been monitoring various groups in Miami that advocate and have carried out terrorist attacks against Cuba in order to provide information to the Cuban government. In June 2001 they were convicted of engaging in espionage activity and threatening U.S. national security. However, no evidence was introduced that substantiated that charge. Cuba has maintained that the only crime the five are guilty of is defending the island against terrorism. An international campaign has been launched to win their freedom (see *Miami 5* 2003 and Murphy 2003).

6. LESSONS AND FOOTPRINTS

As a country of the South, Cuba must deal with the same seemingly-intractable issues and problems that confront and afflict other so-called lesser-developed nations. The island, as Castro stated, cannot insulate itself from the world, as the Revolution does not exist "inside a glass case, isolated from the rest of the world and its problems" (quoted in Reed 1992: 35). With its increasing interaction with the capitalist world economy, Cuba was forced to reorient its development strategy in an effort to exploit what were its "competitive advantages." The necessity for efficiency, administrative flexibility and budgetary restraint in the utilization of material, financial and human resources came to the fore. With the implementation of a variety of economic measures, Cuba

> achieved a great deal considering that the difficult conditions caused more than one analyst to doubt its ability to survive. Growth recovered in 1994 and has been sustained for seven years, the country's international insertion has been substantially modified, the domestic economy is more dynamic and has greater macroeconomic equilibrium, new production and service sectors have been consolidated and the government has gained greater experience in managing economic policy in the new international conditions and under strong external pressures, especially the North American blockade. (Carranza 2002: 44)

Despite being far removed from the worst and desperate days of the Special Period, the economy has not recovered completely, standing at 80–85 percent of the level it had attained before the economic crisis (Carranza 2002: 39). Substantial economic hurdles still lie in its path. Energy continues to be the main vulnerability (Benjamin-Alvarado 2000). While domestic oil production is increasing, most of the island's energy requirements have to be imported. While the Cuban tourist industry has had remarkable growth, now accounting for 50 percent of foreign exchange earned, the vicissitudes of the world economy and the international situation have left it precariously perched, as are the tourist industries in other tourist-dependent countries. For example, Cuba's 2002 tourist numbers were down by 5 percent as a consequence of the decline in air travel following the September 11, 2001, attacks on New York City (*The Economist* 2002a: 36–37). However, in the first quarter of 2003 tourism rebounded, with almost 800,000 people visiting the island. This was a 19 percent increase over the same period in 2002 and 2 percent over 2001, the year that previously had recorded the highest visitation figures (Frank 2003b). The total number of tourists for 2003 is projected to be 1.9 million (Eaton 2003). The instability and unpredictability of commodity prices — especially sugar and nickel — have, along with tourism, accentuated the vulnerability of Cuba to the vagaries of the world market. The major restructuring of the sugar industry has led to forecasts that the 2003 harvest will only be 55 percent of the 2002 harvest: 2 million tons as opposed to 3.6 million tons (Frank 2003b). However, with the revival of tourism and the increase in nickel prices the growth of the Cuban economy for 2003 is expected to be 1.5 percent. Cuban economists and officials emphasize that, despite the vulnerabilities that exist, the Cuban economy is better insulated and prepared to face these economic challenges as a result of the restructuring initiated in the 1990s. There has been a shift to an economy that is markedly less dependent on the production of goods, one in which services account for approximately half of economic activity.

The external debt to the West continues to climb, in 1999 standing at $11.078 billion U.S. (*Cuba Business* 2000: 4; LeoGrande and Thomas 2002: 345–46; Hernández 2002: 23). Re-negotiating the debt and bringing it under control is critical to "reestablishing its international credit and making itself attractive to investors" (LeoGrande and Thomas 2002: 345). This situation has been exacerbated by Cuba's lack of access to medium and long-term credit, which forces the island to rely on short-term credit under onerous conditions. Cuba also is in negotiations with Russia regarding the debt it accumulated during the existence of the Soviet Union. The Russian government estimates that debt at $18–20 billion U.S. (LeoGrande and Thomas 2002: 345). The Castro government has countered that the Cuban economy suffered "more than $20 billion U.S. in damage as a result of the abrupt rupture of aid and trade in 1989–1991" (LeoGrande and Thomas 2002: 345).

The function of the U.S. dollar in the Cuban economy has stimulated much debate. Its role was considered both an unwelcome retreat from socialist methods and a temporary measure. In July 2003, a government directive established that state firms would no longer conduct their financial affairs using U.S. dollars. Instead they would use convertible pesos, which were created in the early 1990s as a new currency (BBC 2003a; Frank 2003c). As an equivalent to the U.S. dollar, the convertible peso operates as a third Cuban currency and a means by which to enhance the government's capacity to corral hard currency. The new directive was seen not only as an effort to conserve foreign exchange stocks but also as a step in the elimination of the U.S. dollar as the dominant currency in Cuba. Thus, the directive is viewed as a "step towards a single currency" (Frank 2003c). The creation of a new stable Cuban currency, while still a long-term goal, would place the island's economy and independence on much firmer ground.

The question of economic diversification — both in terms of exports and trading partners — remains a central task for the Cuban government as it seeks to avoid the over-reliance on one commodity as its major export earner. The decades preceding the disintegration of the Soviet Bloc were characterized by an over-reliance on sugar, leaving the island vulnerable, as events attested, to the sudden disappearance of its main markets and the collapse of prices. This underlines that

> Cuba does not exist in a vacuum and, whether socialist or capitalist, it is part of the global economy and is affected, like all nations, by the vagaries of world capital and its chaotic market. It is not literally, an island unto itself — it must export goods it produces, in order to acquire capital to buy what it does not have. This is simple basic economics and applies, in the current world situation, to socialist as well as capitalist states. (Koehnlein 2001)

Though Cuba may be of the Third World, its experiences and approaches to resolving difficulties and the results thereof are clearly atypical. For example, the "global technology revolution" has become emblematic of the North/South divide. To bridge this gap, the Cuban government has embarked on an ambitious effort to create a society that is computer and information literate. As a result, despite its limited resources, the government has achieved "access to computer and the internet" that "is relatively high in comparison with Cuba's neighbours in Central America and the Caribbean" (*Cuba Business* 2001d: 4). This has been achieved by promoting free access for all citizens in more than three hundred youth computer clubs throughout the country, coupled with a drive to ensure that every school has a computer laboratory. Complementing this educational program is the creation of several Cuban software design enterprises (*Cuba Business* 2001d: 5).

Cuba's development strategy has been conditioned by two fundamental imperatives: 1) the pursuit of social justice and 2) the preservation of Cuban sovereignty. It is a society with one of the highest indices of social justice and continues to make strides — without any assistance from and against the wrecking activity of the United States — in what are recognized in international law as fundamental and inviolable human rights, such as, among others, healthcare, education and social security. As a consequence, this Caribbean island nation stands in remarkable contrast to almost every other Third World country. Thus, while Cuba cannot be a template for other countries, there are key characteristics of the Cuban path that have profound implications for other countries. The Cuban developmental paradigm is rooted in socialism. It is defined by a strong state that guides the economy, protects the island's independence and guarantees citizen participation in decision-making; the socialization of the main means of production, which ensures the equitable distribution of wealth and resources; the promotion of social justice and equality; and the extension — nationally and internationally — of an ethos of solidarity. To elucidate this path, this chapter surveys Cuba's experience in four areas of crucial importance for developing countries: foreign investment, the environment, internationalism and social transformation.

FOREIGN INVESTMENT

On September 5, 1995, the Cuban National Assembly adopted a new law on foreign investment, *Law 77: Foreign Investment Act*, updating the existing legislation, passed in 1982, which established the framework and conditions for the development of economic associations and joint ventures between Cuba and foreign companies. The first foreign investment was made in 1988, in tourism. By 1991, there was groundbreaking foreign investment in several sectors, such as mining, oil and citrus production (August 1999: 228; Kirk and Ritter 1995: 48; Perez-Lopez 1994). The 1982 law permitted joint ventures but limited foreign nationals to 49 percent ownership (August 1999: 228). The 1995 changes to the legislation reflected the needs of the Special Period. Important modifications were also made to the Cuban Constitution, particularly the specification that the "people own the strategic means of production," as opposed to "all the means of production" (*Constitution of the Republic of Cuba* 1993; Kirk and Ritter 1995: 48; Perez-Lopez 1994: 193). These changes widened the category of the forms of property that were recognized under Cuban law.

Law 77 was passed with the intention of attenuating the framework that governed foreign investment, bringing it in line with Cuban economic imperatives and international requirements. Protection of assets was guaranteed and the right to repatriate and move profits in hard currency was granted. In addition, investment to lease and develop real estate was allowed. The law gave retroactive approval to a 1994 executive decision to open almost all economic sectors to foreign capital, exceptions being defence, national security, healthcare and education (Article 10 of Law 77,1995, Economist Intelligence Unit 1995: 8–9; Susman 1998: 197). For the first time since the Revolution triumphed, majority foreign ownership of an enterprise in Cuba was permitted.

Cuba adopted a policy of aggressive pursuit of foreign investment. Cuban advantages and favourable conditions were outlined: The island is the largest and most populous in the Caribbean. It is politically and socially stable, with the most highly educated, disciplined and skilled workforce in Latin America and the Caribbean. Cuba has a well-developed infrastructure relative to other Latin American countries. Over 94 percent of the Cuban population is supplied with electricity. Also, there exists a wide network of roads, railways, civil aviation and port facilities. The telecommunication service is being modernized (Hernández 1997: 38; Garcia Bielsa 1997; Ross Leal 1997). In addition, the country has an estimated 28 percent of the world's nickel reserves (Hernández 1997: 34). The beaches are largely unspoiled, with the opportunity for considerable tourism development. Moreover, Cuban officials stressed the successful efforts at reorganizing the internal financial situation — the reduction of the budget deficit and growth in GDP — and the absence of institutionalized corruption.

Cuban officials have described the opening of the Cuban economy to foreign capital as a "necessary and unavoidable evil" (Martinez 1998). The Cuban government would have preferred to keep the development of the industry and natural resources solely on a national footing, without recourse to international capital. As President Castro expatiated:

> We are well aware that over several years we fought against foreign investments, that for several years we felt proud that the people were the owners of all their industries and all the country's wealth. However, given the existing conditions, we could not do without foreign investment on a larger scale because we needed capital, technology and markets. These are the determining factors. The opposite would be paralysis and stagnation for a very long time. (1996a: 78–79)

But the conditions of the Special Period — loss of markets, lack of capital and technology — "simply demanded the utilization of foreign capital and the acceptance of foreign investment" (Castro 1998b: 24). With the new approach to foreign investment,

> Cuba has been successful at acquiring technologies and management capacities, and has achieved industrial upgrading in those areas where it has a strong presence. This success should be a guide for improving the development of other sectors or areas for greater dynamism in world trade so that Cuba can insert itself in the world economy as it is evolving in the new economy. (Everleny Pérez 2002: 66)

While the important contribution of foreign capital to economic recovery is acknowledged, the Cuban government does not consider it to be the essential or decisive factor (Castro 1998b: 161; Lage 1996: 46). The whole package of economic measures has created an internal capacity for domestic growth. The state is still the dominant force directing the economy and determining the allocation of capital and resources, and officials are insistent that state-run enterprises will continue to be the strategic component of the overall economy.

It is necessary to appreciate that Havana's circumspect stance is reflective of the international debates in the 1950s, '60s and '70s, which centred on the benefits versus the disadvantages of foreign investment. Moreover, the government's position is firmly rooted in its understanding of the Cuban experience with foreign capital before the Revolution, when the absence of regulation of the economy and the investment process led to the subordination of the national interest to those of foreign investor. Foreign investors "were the absolute owners of all the means of production and of earnings, generally evading taxes and exerting negative control over the island's economic and political life" (Canton Navarro 2000: 259). Hence, the tight state control is intended to ensure that Cuban sovereignty and development goals are not infringed by foreign capital. President Castro has stated that the government recognizes "the important function that international capital plays at present in the world economy, but we cannot accept the dismantling of our sovereignty or renounce our national programs of development" (Castro 1998a: 7). Cuban officials argue that unless the state generates a coherent and comprehensive investment strategy, together with the complementary policy of directing investment to prioritized sectors, it is unlikely that foreign investment will contribute to the economic and social development of the recipient country (Figueras 1998: 30).

The Cuban government seeks to avoid an outflow of capital, the decimation of domestic industries, loss of a substantial portion of national savings, environmental degradation and — above all — a compromise of social development (Figueras 1998: 29). Therefore, the government aim is to ensure that foreign investors operate in a socially and publicly responsible fashion. *Law 77* establishes the requisite regulated and controlled basis for the role of foreign investment within Cuba's development strategy. Its purpose is the augmentation of traditional exports and stimulation of new ones; the introduction of advanced technologies and techniques; the creation of new employment and the contribution to national capital accumulation and formation. The overarching objective of Cuba's economic strategy is the generation of the capital and resources necessary to fund, preserve and expand the gains of the Revolution: free and universal healthcare and education and the extensive social security programs. Thus, *Law 77* is designed to construct the parameters necessary to constrain any contradiction between the dynamics of foreign capital and national development goals. Toward this end, each potential foreign investment deal is carefully studied, with the goal of fostering the conditions for continuance of the steady economic recovery, while not allowing foreign capital to gain too much influence or to cause too much social dislocation.

Commentators from both ends of the ideological spectrum have predicted that the increasing role of foreign investment in the Cuban economy will bring in its wake fundamental economic and political change, in fact, a return to capitalism. On the right, it is anticipated that the penetration of foreign capital will unleash new economic actors and lead to "the demise of the socialist system" (Kubalkova 1994: 101). These new actors will constitute a new political force, inevitably challenge the existing order and undermine socialist consciousness, eventually contributing to a dismantling of the current Cuban development paradigm (Smith 1996). On the left, it is argued that Cuba has already made too many concessions to international capital. Indeed, some assert that Havana has implemented a neoliberal agenda (Susman 1998). Thus, the present economic trajectory is viewed as antithetical to the goals of socialism. In this view, Cuba's reversion to capitalism is inexorable and ineluctable (Kirk and Ritter 1995: 213; Perez-Lopez 1994: 215; Smith 1996: 3; Susman 1998: 199–200). Intimately entwined with this argument is the old (but theoretically important) position that socialism in one country is impossible — especially in a small, poor and economically underdeveloped country (Castro 1996a: 74–80).

The Chinese and Vietnamese experiences are repeatedly invoked as touchstones (Brundenius 2002: 392–94; Diaz Vazquez 2002; Dapice 2002; Smith 1996;Susman 1998: 204–205). It is argued that those experiences demonstrate that the impact of foreign investment cannot be controlled. In order to maintain the level of investment, domestic economic liberalization is inevitable and unavoidable. Engagement with the world economy exposes a country to external influences from which insulation is impossible. The end result is the engendering of a series of systemic problems that eventually overwhelm the *ancien regime* and initiate a transition to an untrammelled free-market economy (Kirk and Ritter 1995: 213; Perez-Lopez 1994: 215; Smith 1996: 3; Susman 1998: 201). The argument goes that Cuba cannot reap the benefits of foreign investment and maintain its socialist system.

There are many who predict that privatization is the concomitant next step for the Cuban economy. They argue that foreign investment presages the complete opening of the economy and the subsequent dismantling of the state sector. However, in emphatic terms, the Cuban leadership has rejected privatization, a linchpin of neoliberal policies. They are resolutely opposed to "creating through privatization, a wealthy class in this country, which would subsequently acquire tremendous power and would begin to conspire against socialism" (Castro 1998b: 162). Accordingly, self-employed businesses are restricted at the level of family businesses and controlled by taxation. Havana has not abandoned socialist imperatives and still sees the consolidation of "social ownership of the basic means of production" as indispensable to national development (Valdes Vivo 1998: 7).

The Cuban experience challenges the validity of the "doomsday" prognosticators. The Cuban government, through *Law* 77, has confined foreign capital within definite boundaries. Moreover, basic principles of the overall economy have been safeguarded. The state sector — i.e., the socialization of the strategic heights — continues to be the dominant force. While Cuba is restructuring its economy, it is doing so with the intent of keeping the essence of the Revolution intact. The joint ventures and economic partnerships the Cuban state pursues with foreign capital are fundamentally different than similar activities in other countries. They are not carried out for private profit; rather, any profit that the Cuban state derives becomes part of the social redistribution of wealth to maintain the healthcare, education and social security systems. The historic path that the Cuban nation embarked on in 1959 is not being reversed. While the economic measures and the openings to foreign capital were necessary, the Cuban government remains, as Fidel Castro has stated, "open to all economic possibilities except the renunciation of socialism" (1998b: 22).

THE ENVIRONMENT

Cuban economic development in the 1990s did not occur at the expense of the environment. Indeed, the government pursued a policy of economic growth and improvement within the context of sustainable development. At the Earth Summit in Rio de Janeiro in 1992, Fidel Castro stated:

> Unequal trade, protectionism and the foreign debt assault the ecological balance and promote the destruction of the environment. If we want to save humanity from this self-destruction, wealth and the available technologies must be distributed better throughout the planet. Less luxury and less waste in a few countries would mean less poverty and hunger in much of the world. Stop transferring to the Third World lifestyles and consumer habits that ruin the environment. Make human life more rational. Adopt a more just international economic order. Use science to achieve sustainable development without pollution. Pay the ecological debt instead of the foreign debt. Eradicate hunger and not humanity.... Enough of selfishness. Enough of schemes of domination. Enough of insensitivity, irresponsibility and deceit. Tomorrow will be too late to do what we should have done along time ago. (1993: 4)

Cuba was the first country to incorporate the Rio Declaration into its Constitution. Article 27 of the Cuban Constitution iterates:

> The State protects the country's environment and natural resources. It recognizes its close link with sustainable economic and social development to make human life more rational and assure the survival, welfare and security of current and future generations. It corresponds to the competent institutions to apply this policy. It is a duty of citizens to contribute to the protection of water resources, the atmosphere, soil conservation, the flora and fauna, and all of nature's rich potential. (*Constitution of the Republic of Cuba* 1993)

In short, "while most of the nations that attended … forgot about its commitment [the Earth Summit's] to halt, the destruction of species, reduce poverty and prevent climate change," Cuba "sought to preserve the island's biodiversity" (Linden 2003: 98). Twenty-two percent of the island's land is covered by environmental protection regimes. Cuba has one of the highest levels of protected areas in the world, with a steady increase in the amount of protected wetlands. The island's forest cover now stands at 21 percent (in 2003) as compared to 14 percent in 1956. Among the Caribbean islands, Cuba's "ecosystems are in the best shape," and it "has the largest tracts of untouched rain forest, unspoiled reefs and intact wetlands" (Linden 2003: 94–96, see also 98, 102).

Several polluting factories operating near rivers were forced to implement ecologically favourable measures or relocate (Benjamin and Rossett 1994; Lopez Vigil 1999: 99–144). As part of a major clean-up campaign, oil tankers are no longer allowed to enter Havana Harbour. Economic investment and activity are assessed in terms of their potential ecological implications. These provisions also apply to foreign capital and are covered in the introduction and articles 54–56 of the 1995 *Foreign Investment Act*. Under this legislation, investment proposals that have a potential impact on the environment must be submitted for study to the Ministry of Science, Technology and Environment. The Ministry determines whether an environmental impact evaluation is required, and also grants the required environmental licences.

Once a licence is granted, the Ministry establishes a control and inspection program. Strictures exist governing land use consistent with sustainable development and waste processing and disposal. For example, "at the resort of Cayo Coco, hotels can be no more than four stories and must be set back from the beach" (World Watch Institute 2002: 123). Any company causing environmental damage must not only provide financial compensation but is also responsible for returning the area to its original condition. Thus, while Cuba endeavours to create an attractive climate for investment, it is, among other things, seeking to avoid associated ecological repercussions. This approach is captured by a prominent Cuban economist:

> Look, in the end it means there will be more interest in foreign investment rather than less. If you build a multi-million dollar hotel on a beach in Varadero, you want assurances that there won't be any chance of leaky oil tankers a half a mile down, from some company doing oil exploration. It's one of the advantages

of a centralized economy. We can actually make a company's investment more secure than it would be in an unregulated economy. (Gordon 1997: 4)

Cuba does face environmental degradation that has resulted from coastal development and exploitation of the fisheries. The size of the catches of some species of fish, such as groupers and mullet, has declined (Benchley 2002: 52). However, the Cuban government is determined to pursue a program of ecological preservation and renewal. John Thorbjarnarson, a scientist with the New York-based Wildlife Conservation Society, observed that Cuba "stands head and shoulders above anywhere else in the Caribbean in terms of government support for conservation" (quoted in Linden 2003: 97). The Minister of Science, Technology and the Environment, Rosa Elena Simeon, stated the government's resolve to "shut down any hotel, any factory, any investment opportunity that violates our environmental laws" (Benchley 2002: 53). The Cuban state's control of investment and supervision of economic activity enables the implementation of an effective ecological protocol.

The move toward a "green" economy is integral to Cuban agriculture, which has undergone the most far-reaching transition to organic methods of food production in the world (Auld 2001; Rosset 1997, 1998; Benjamin and Rossett 1994). The food crisis of the 1990s, together with the loss of the supply of pesticides and herbicides, led the Cuban government to initiate an extensive and intensive development of organic farming methods. Agricultural scientists in more than two hundred factories are developing organic forms of pest control. For example, a natural pesticide has been developed from the nee tree. Cuba has become "a leader in alternative farming approaches" (Auld 2001: 6).

Paralleling this organic "revolution" has been the program of urban and community gardens. Throughout Cuban cities and provinces, vacant lots, rooftops and other empty spaces have been converted into organic gardens. These gardens play a critical role in supplying vegetables and other produce to the island's population, especially in the cities. In Havana, five thousand acres of land have been devoted to 27,000 gardens, with an estimated annual production of a million tons. In the Province of Cienfuegos, there are more than 50,000 gardens, with 120 in the city of Cienfuegos. This urban and community garden phenomenon "is a popular movement that has been supported by the government as the only way to face the food crisis due to the collapse of the socialist bloc and the U.S. embargo" (Auld 2001: 7).

INTERNATIONALISM

One of the most remarkable aspects of the Cuban Revolution is the internationalist missions it has sent to other countries. Indeed, Cuba has left its footprints in Asia, Latin America and Africa. The island has sent thousands of doctors, teachers and other personnel on humanitarian assignments to various countries. In the mid-1990s, Cuba had three times as many doctors as the World health Organization (WHO) serving abroad and providing free medical treatment (Castro 1996a: 30–31). A special facility was established in the Ukraine where specialized care was administered to the more than 15,000 children who were victims of the Chernobyl nuclear disaster. There are several education and health projects throughout Africa and Latin America. Cuban doctors are serving throughout sub-Saharan Africa, for example, in The Gambia, Guinea-Bissau, Equatorial Guinea and South Africa. In Central America, Cuba was critical in the development of the Integral Health Program (PIS), which was created in 1998 as a response to the extensive destruction caused by Hurricane Mitch. More than 5,000 Cuban health workers have served in this program.

The Cuban government set up the Latin American School of Medicine to train doctors from across the developing world. These students are given Cuban government scholarships and attend on the condition that once they have graduated they will return to offer their services to their respective countries. At present, there are more than 6,000 students studying at the school (Martinez Puentes 2003: 405), and it is anticipated that by 2005, an estimated 1,400 physicians will have graduated. While students train in various specialities, they also participate in clinical practice in primary health care and community health programs in preparation for working in the most marginal areas of their home countries. The Latin America School of Medicine is not a unique program in Cuba, only one of the most recently implemented. This form of international assistance was instituted at the very beginning of the Cuban Revolution. Since the 1960s, more than 40,000 students from 120 countries have received education and training in Cuba. To facilitate this program, the Cuban government provided $500 million in scholarships over this period for foreign students.

Cuba plays a prominent role in challenging the present world economic and political order, often voicing publicly what other nations will not or are unable to state for fear of some form of retaliation, such as, an interruption in aid from and trade relations with metropolitan countries. Evidence of Cuba's prestige among Third World nations was its appointment in 2002, for a second time — the first being in 1979 — as Chair of the Non-Aligned Movement. In April 2003, Cuba was elected by acclamation to the United Nations Human Rights Commission, a membership it has held for the last fifteen years. Cuba has repeatedly called for the democratization of the United Nations, the cancelling of the debt owed by developing countries and a restructuring of international commercial and financial relations. At the Third World Conference against Racism, Racial Discrimination, Xenophobia and Other Related Intolerances, held in Durban, South Africa, Castro declared:

> May the arms race and the weapon commerce that only brings devastation and death truly end. Let it be used for development a good part of the one trillion U.S. dollars annually spent on the commercial advertising that creates false illusions and inaccessible consumer habits while releasing the venom that destroys the national cultures and identities. May the modest 0.7 percentage point of the Gross National Product promised as official development assistance be finally delivered. May the tax suggested by Nobel Prize Laureate James Tobin be imposed in a reasonable and effective way on the current speculative operations accounting for trillions of U.S. dollars every 24 hours, then the United Nations, which cannot go on depending on meagre, inadequate, and belated donations and charities, will have one trillion U.S. dollars annually to save and develop the world.... Given the seriousness and urgency of the existing problems, which have become a real hazard for the very survival of our species on the planet, that is what would actually be needed before it is too late.... There have been enough centuries of deception. From my viewpoint we are on the verge of a huge economic, social and political global crisis. Let's try to build an awareness about these realities and the alternatives will come up. History has shown that it is only from deep crisis that great solutions have emerged. The people's right to life and justice will definitely impose itself under a thousand different shapes. (2001f)

While condemning the September 11, 2001, attacks on New York City, Cuba has opposed Washington's "war on terrorism" as merely a pretext to impose U.S. dictates in international affairs. Cuba's opposition to the 2003 U.S.-led war on and military occupation of Iraq mirrors Havana's stance against the first U.S.-led war against Iraq, the preparations for which it opposed during its two-year term — from 1990 to 1991— on the U.N. Security Council. It also refused to endorse economic sanctions, condemning the denial of food and medicine to the Iraqi people as a violation of human rights (Castro and Alarcón 1990: 63–72). On August 7, 1990, President Castro sent a letter outlining Cuba's concern to all governments of the world, particularly Arab heads of state:

> I am writing to you because I am deeply concerned about the events that are now threatening the Arab world and humanity. I firmly believe that at this crucial time it is still possible for the leaders of the Arab nations to prevent the conflict that broke out between Iraq and Kuwait from leading to an adverse situation for the independence of many Arab states, to an economic catastrophe, and to a holocaust affecting a large portion of their people. Such is the threat, as we see it, caused by the growing and accelerated preparations for a direct military intervention by the Unite States and its allies. No less alarming is the evidence pointing to steps aimed at the creation, for the same interventionist purpose, of a multinational force whose composition reveals a new relationship of forces on a world scale against the interests of the Arab peoples.… The experience of history more than attests to how dominant powers like the United States are accustomed to imposing accomplished facts and unleashing processes difficult to reverse. (Castro and Alarcón 1990: 32 and 35)

The Cuban government and various mass organizations and professional associations have convened numerous international symposia to discuss, debate and oppose neoliberal globalization. This is a continuation of the Cuban struggle for a New International Economic Order, which was carried out in the 1970s and 1980s (Castro 1984). Since 1999, an annual conference for economists and other scholars — the International Meeting of Economists on Globalization and Problems of Development — is hosted in Havana. This conference brings together economic and development theorists and technocrats from across the ideological spectrum. While the Cuban government has its own very definite stance, it seeks to encourage a dialogue among and between the various schools of thought. Representatives of institutions that adhere to worldviews diametrically opposed to the Cuban government, such as the World Bank, the International Monetary Fund and the Inter-American Development Bank, participated. Beyond these gatherings of scholars and technocrats, several conferences of social, political and trade union activists from across the world and, in particular Latin America, have been held. For example, in 1997 and 2001, Havana hosted the International Meeting of Workers against Neoliberalism and Globalization. In 2001 and 2002, the Hemispheric Meeting against the Free Trade Area of the Americas was convoked. These conferences brought together hundreds of activists with the goal of forging a common program of action to confront the neoliberal agenda. Thus, Cuba has been an active and dynamic force for unity and justice in the South.

Cuba's most outstanding example of internationalism has been its aid to several national liberation, anti-colonial and anti-imperialist movements. While this internationalist spirit has been immeasurably amplified under the Cuban Revolution, it is important to note that it has deep roots in the island's history, epitomized by the life of José Martí, who

> was not simply fighting to overthrow the Spanish and win political independence for Cuba but was also fighting as an international revolutionary to secure the liberation of his continent, and indeed of the world. (Kirk 1983: 15)

For example, diplomatic solidarity, training, military aid and other forms of concrete material assistance were provided to the National Liberation Front of Algeria in its struggle for independence from France; Che Guevara led a guerrilla group in the Congo; and training material, aid and medical personnel were given to Guinea-Bissau's liberation struggle against Portugal. Extensive assistance was provided to Nicaragua during the struggle of the Sandinistas against the Anastasio Samoza dictatorship. Once the Sandinistas triumphed, Cuba sent construction workers, doctors, teachers and technicians to aid in the reconstruction and development of Nicaragua. Similar help was rendered to the Grenadian Revolution from 1979 to 1983. The island has also provided a safe haven for African American, Puerto Rican and other political exiles.

The most dramatic — and, arguably, significant — internationalist mission was Cuban military assistance to help the Angolan government repulse South African aggression. From 1975 to 1990, more than 300,000 Cuban volunteers participated in repelling several South African invasions, with more than 2000 Cubans losing their lives (Canton Navarro 2000: 245). The decisive defeat of the South African Defense Forces (SADF) at the town of Cuito Cuanavale in 1987–8 not only drove the apartheid army out of Angola, but also directly contributed to Namibian independence and accelerated the dismantling of apartheid in South Africa.

Ironically, Cuba's role in ending racist rule in South Africa is little known. Western views of Cuban involvement in Southern Africa have an almost paradoxical quality. On one hand, it has been repeatedly dismissed as surrogate activity for the Soviet Union, as an instrument of Soviet era expansionism. On the other, the crucial role of Cuba in securing Namibia's independence and expediting the demise of apartheid has been ignored and erased from collective memory. Yet, it is one of the most compelling stories of disinterested military intervention.

In a major work, *Conflicting Missions: Havana, Washington and Africa*, Piero Gliejeses, from the Johns Hopkins School of Advanced International Studies, has provided what has now been accepted as the definitive account of Cuba's involvement in Angola. The book is based on an assiduous study of archival material in the United States, Cuba, Britain, Belgium and Portugal. He interviewed more than 150 individuals, including CIA officers with knowledge of the conflict. His study unequivocally concludes that: 1) the Cuban government — as it had repeatedly asserted — decided to dispatch combat troops to Angola only after the Angolan government had requested Cuba's military assistance to repel a South African invasion. This refutes the position of the U.S. government — particularly, the Ford, Carter and Reagan administrations — that South African forces intervened in Angola only after the arrival of the Cuban forces; and 2) the Soviet Union had no role in Cuba's decision and were not even informed prior to deployment. In short, Cuba was not the puppet of the U.S.S.R. (Gleijeses 2001).

Cuba's involvement in Angola dates back to the 1960s, when relations were established with the Movement for the Popular Liberation of Angola (MPLA), the principal organization in the struggle to liberate Angola from Portuguese colonialism. In 1975, the Portuguese withdrew from Angola. However, in order to stop the MPLA from ascending to power, the U.S. government had already been funding several groups, in particular, the Union for the Total Independence of Angola (UNITA) led by Jonas Savimbi. Furthermore, Henry Kissinger — then Secretary of State — began to coordinate efforts with South Africa to defeat the MPLA (Saul 1993: 19). In October 1975, South African forces launched a major invasion of Angola with the objective of installing Jonas Savimbi in power (North 1986: 211; Seidman 1990: 51).

On November 5, in response to a request by Agostinho Neto, President of Angola, the Castro government initiated Operation Carlota, beginning the deployment of troops. Cuban military assistance was decisive not only in stopping the South African drive to Luanda, the capital, but in pushing them back over the Angolan border. The Cuban effort attained such a scale that

> there were so many ships anchored in the Bay of Luanda, that President Agostinho Neto, counting them from his window, felt a very characteristic shudder of modesty. "It's not right," he said to a functionary personally close to him. "If they go on like that, the Cubans will ruin themselves." (Garcia Marquez 1989: 41)

After the South Africans were driven out, Cuban forces stayed for almost fifteen years at the request of the Angolan government, because of repeated South African invasions and continued aggression (Brittain 1988: 68; Seidman 1990: 50). The Cuban government viewed its military assistance not only as aiding an independent country in its defence against a foreign invader but also as a historical debt owed by Cuba to Africa as a result of slavery and the slave trade. Castro observed:

> That those who once enslaved man and sent him to America perhaps never imagined that one of those peoples who received slaves would one day send their fighters to struggle for freedom in Africa. (1989: 69)

During this period, Cuba provided extensive development assistance, sending physicians, teachers, technicians and construction workers, many of whom were victims of terrorist attacks by UNITA (Canton Navarro 2000: 245). Also, hundreds of Angolans received technical and professional training in Cuba (Henderson 1979: 260). The other independent African countries supported the presence of Cuban troops in Angola as both a prerogative of Angola as an independent state and protection against South African aggression (Harris 1987: 247). Kenneth Kaunda, then President of Zambia, stated:

> Britain and the United States joined forces with the Soviet Union to defeat Hitler during World War II. What is wrong now that our countries receive similar help as we confront another version of Hitler here in Southern Africa? (quoted in North 1986: 211)

In 1987, the FAPLA, the Angolan armed forces, launched an offensive against UNITA in the southwestern part of the country, despite the Cubans' advice that it would create the opportunity for a significant South African invasion. Indeed, the South African government, with the support of the U.S., launched its largest military invasion of Angola since 1975 (Brittain 1998: 34) and succeeded in stopping and throwing back the Angolan forces.

The battle between the South African and Angolan forces became centred on the South African determination to capture the town and strategic military base of Cuito Cuanavale, which was important as a forward airbase to patrol and defend southern Angola (Brittain 1998: 35). At Cuito Cuanavale "the South Africans were tempted into an ill-fated effort to score a knock-out blow against the MPLA" (Heberstein and Evenson 1989: 171). Toward this goal, Pretoria committed its best troops and most sophisticated military hardware. In late 1987, the South Africans were "convinced they were close to a decisive victory which would change the course of the war" (Brittain 1998: 35), a victory which would have cemented Pretoria's control over the southern African region.

As the situation for Angolan troops became critical, the Cuban government was asked by the Angolan government to intervene. Cuba decided to bolster the Angolan defence of Cuito Cuanavale by sending fresh detachments (Minter 1994: 49). The battle that then ensued, as South Africa repeatedly tried to seize the town, was the largest military engagement on the African continent since the Battle of El Alemain during the Second World War. At Cuito Cuanavale, the SADF were dealt a decisive defeat (Brittain 1998: 36). Consequently, the military balance of power in the region was altered (Moorcraft 1990: 208). As the South Africans withdrew, the Cubans, together with Angolan and SWAPO forces, advanced toward the Namibian border, an action which exposed the insecurity and vulnerability of the South African troops in northern Namibia (Minter 1994: 49). By May 1988, the Cuban forces were so close to the Namibian border that "white South Africa's nightmare had become a reality" (Heberstein and Evenson 1989: 173). Such was their vulnerability that a senior South African officer stated: "Had the Cubans attacked [Namibia] they would have over-run the place. We could not have stopped them" (Cliffe 1994: 59).

The victory at Cuito Cuananvale transformed it into "a symbol across the continent that apartheid and its army were no longer invincible" (Brittain 1998: 36). The defeat shattered the confidence of the South African military, and with the approach of Cuban forces toward Namibia, Pretoria sought a means by which to extricate their troops "without humiliation and alive" (Brittain 1998: 37). Thus, the Battle of Cuito Cuanavale was instrumental in paving the path to negotiations (Brittain

1998: 36–37; Dominguez 1992: 70; Hodges 2001: 11–12; Saul 1993: 46). In December 1988, an agreement was reached between Cuba and Angola on one side and South Africa on the other, which provided for the gradual withdrawal of Cuban troops from Angola and the establishment of an independent Namibia.

Cuba's role in Angola had been "undeniably pivotal in ending South Africa's control of Namibia" (Erisman 1995: 235). Since 1920, South Africa had occupied Namibia, a former German colony, under a mandate granted by the League of Nations. In 1966, the UN revoked South Africa's Mandate. The UN General Assembly also passed several resolutions declaring South Africa's occupation illegal. In 1978, the United Nations Security Council adopted Resolution 435 on Namibian independence, recognizing SWAPO as the sole legitimate representative of the Namibian people. However, South Africa continued its occupation, violating and defying the UN resolutions and international law. Had it not been for its defeat at Cuito Cuanavale:

> South Africa had no serious intention of leaving Namibia. The government had never really accepted Resolution 435 and was determined to put off the evil day when the "suidwes" [South African settlers and business interests] would "go back." But once the SDAF had invested its prestige in capturing the airfield of a remote Angolan town, and failed, the chemistry of the sub-continent changed. Like it or not, the non-victor had to abide by the rules of the game. (Heberstein and Evenson 1989:175)

Besides securing Namibia's independence, the victory at Cuito Cuanavale stymied Pretoria's campaign to secure southern Africa as its exclusive zone of control. By transforming the regional ratio of power, South Africa's defeat quickened the end of apartheid. In 2001, Thabo Mbeki, President of South Africa, recalled:

> the period in our region which ended just over a decade ago, which saw the involvement of apartheid South Africa in a massive and concerted effort to impose its will on the region and thus extend the life of the apartheid crime against humanity. Cuba's contribution to the defeat of that campaign of aggression and destabilisation against independent Africa was, of course, particularly exemplified by its decisive involvement in the military struggle to defeat apartheid forces that had invaded Angola soon

after that country's independence from Portugal. The Cuban forces were to stay in Angola over a decade. That stay ended only when, after defeat at Cuito Cuanavale, the apartheid invaders understood that they would never be able to realise their objectives and that the Angolan people should have the freedom to determine their future. With that realisation came the understanding in Pretoria that it could not dictate to the independent African states through the use of force. Neither could it hold back the tide leading to the independence of Namibia and the liberation of South Africa. (Mbeki 2001)

During a 1991 visit to Cuba, Nelson Mandela outlined the significance of the island's contribution:

The Cuban people hold a special place in the hearts of the people of Africa. The Cuban internationalists have made a contribution to African independence, freedom and justice unparalleled for its principled and selfless character.... We in Africa are used to being victims of countries wanting to carve up our territory or subvert our sovereignty. It is unparalleled in African history to have another people rise to the defense of one of us.... The defeat of the apartheid army was an inspiration to the struggling people in South Africa! Without the defeat of Cuito Cuanavale our organizations would not have been unbanned! The defeat of the racist army at Cuito Cuanavale has made it possible for me to be here today! Cuito Cuanavale was a milestone in the history of the struggle for southern African liberation! Cuito Cuanavale has been a turning point in the struggle to free the continent and our country from the scourge of apartheid! The decisive defeat of Cuito Cuanavale altered the balance of forces within the region and substantially reduced the capacity of Pretoria to destabilise its neighbours. This in combination with our people's struggle within the country, was crucial in bringing Pretoria to realise it would have to talk. (Mandela 1993: 119, 121 and 124)

SOCIALISM ON ONE ISLAND

Cuba has managed to create a society with high levels of social and human development in spite of being denied access to loans from either the International Monetary Fund or the World Bank and in the face of unbridled hostility from the United States. Thus, a central question, as posed by Felix Greene, is:

> Why was it possible only after the Cuban people overthrew the bloody Batista regime and his American-paid army and stooges, and only after they took over the enterprises owned by foreigners that the Cuban people could begin to establish schools and hospitals … to eliminate illiteracy and unemployment — and this in spite of every hindrance put in their way by the United States? (Greene 1970: 191)

As noted in the introduction to this book, the Cuban experience is much ignored. At the very least, Cuba demonstrates that a viable alternative approach does exist, one that has achieved much greater success than the prevailing dominant model, which continues to result in greater degrees of marginalization between and within nations. However, the Cuban experience also brings to the fore "old" questions about the requisites for development. Thus, while there are no universal models, Cuba forces us to revisit these debates from the 1960s, 1970s and early 1980s. The Cuban Revolution raises the central proposition of whether the establishment of revolutionary power committed to digging "up the roots of imperialism and prevent the operation of neo-colonialism" is essential to harnessing a country's resources and wealth for the benefit of its citizens (Woddis 1971: 44–45). The issue of state power and who wields it is set front and centre.

Closely coupled with this proposition is the relevance of socialism as a realistic option. Since the collapse of the Soviet Bloc, discussions on the pertinence and viability of socialism have dominated the discourses that endeavour to banish the socialist project from any emancipatory agenda. Cuba offers profound insights on the issue of the viability of socialism as a counter-project to the neoliberal triumphalism. Nevertheless, even on the left, the Cuban socialist project remains neglected and maligned. For Antonio Blanco, Cuba constitutes a socialist experiment that "has something new to say about the model of sustainable human development that is urgently needed by the ecosystem and humanity" (1997: 110).

With the onset of the crisis of the 1990s, Cuba's socialist project was put under intense pressure. The very question of what type of socialist society would be possible under those conditions became a central point of debate. For some, the dimensions of the crisis required "that while elements of socialism remain in place in Cuba, the possibility of building a fully socialist society has to be put on hold, for the time being or perhaps permanently" (Beverly 2002: 4). In the midst of the crisis, Castro stated:

> We talk about saving the gains of socialism, because we cannot say at this time that we are building socialism but rather that we are defending what we have done, we are defending our achievements. (1996a: 28)

Entwined with the question of what kind of socialism could be built was the old debate on whether it was possible to construct socialism in one country, much less a small underdeveloped island. This question has occupied Marxist scholars in Cuba, and in 1995, Castro addressed it in some detail at the closing of the Cuba Vive International Youth Festival:

> You are all aware that the whole question of whether socialism in one country is possible or not has been amply discussed; or if it is possible once the revolution has broken out in the most industrialized countries, in relation to Germany, England or in the other European nations. This was discussed over many, many years; but Marxism didn't stop with Marx, and the doctrines of socialism moved on from Marx and Engels.... There was Lenin, and it has to be said that Lenin and those who made the October Revolution all believed that the European Revolution was a prerequisite for creating socialism. When the European revolution didn't take place, then came the moment when they took the decision that had to be made: "Well we can't surrender; we have to create socialism in one country." Of course, talking of one country is relative, given that it was one country of 22 million square kilometers. We are one country of 111,111 square kilometers. (1996a: 75)

He went on to address the economic measures Cuba had implemented to meet the crisis, contrasting Cuba's program with the New Economic Policy (NEP) instituted by the Bolsheviks in the wake of foreign interventions and the 1918–20 civil war. The NEP was a retreat that permitted the development of capitalism in order to revive the Russian economy. Castro asserted:

> They [the Bolsheviks] had to do it. They had to move toward a new economic policy, the famous NEP, during one historic period. But there is something more. At certain points Lenin also

planted the idea of building capitalism under proletarian leadership. For your peace of mind, of course, I can tell you that we are not thinking of doing anything of the kind. And it's not because we are in disagreement with Lenin, but because the circumstances are different, since our process, which was able to rely on assistance from the socialist camp and from the Soviet Union, has made great advances. It has very strong forces and does not have to raise the question in those terms. I have already said, or tried to tell you before, that if we were a country with significant oil or similar resources, perhaps, we wouldn't have gone for large-scale tourism development. From experience, we know all the consequences of large-scale tourism development. However, given the existing conditions in our country, we couldn't do without it, since given those conditions we couldn't do without foreign investment.... Some of our friends have advised us to say no, that we are doing this because it's a very good thing. We have to be honest. We have gone down this road basically because it was the only alternative for saving the Revolution and saving the conquest of socialism. We had to establish joint ventures in a relatively short time period. We had to accept foreign investment. We had to do what we did in respect to the decriminalization of convertible currency, and you can be sure that doing the last pained us greatly, very greatly. We are aware of the inequalities that it created, the privileges it created, but we had to do it, and we did it. (1996a: 78–79)

Cuba's concessions on the economic front are not necessarily capitalist concessions *per se*, but concessions that may lead to capitalism under particular circumstances. For some, this might seem to be a risible distinction, a meaningless splitting of hairs. But it is a critical point. The economic measures that have been implemented might be unpalatable — generating equally unwelcome results — but they have occurred within a socialist framework and have not altered the underlying structures. Thus, while there has been a transformation of the landholding structure (the transfer of land in *usufruct*) and the introduction of joint ventures with international capital, there has been no alienation of property, no privatization of the natural patrimony. What have emerged may, perhaps, be categorized as new forms of socialist property that represent new configurations, as opposed to the mass sale of public assets that has unfolded globally.

The necessary introduction of "capitalist reforms and elements" does not alter the reality that in Cuba the main means of production had been nationalized and socialized, and remain in the hands of the people. The island maintains its sovereignty, especially in the face of U.S. pressures, projecting an internationalist, anti-imperialist and anti-capitalist position globally. It remains a profoundly collectivist society. Despite the negative social phenomena that have emerged, the country continues to be defined by an ethos of human solidarity — an ethos encapsulated in the struggle to build a nation based on the ethic of being rather than the ethic of having, a nation where "human happiness does not reside in our unlimited capacity to consume but in our unlimited capacity to give solidarity to our fellow human beings" (Blanco 1997: 103).

Central to Cuba's capacity to resist has been the conquest of state power by the working people of Cuba. This has always been the crux, the fulcrum of the Revolution. As Fidel Castro iterated:

> We are making changes but without giving up the real principle of a government of the people, by the people and for the people; which if translated into revolutionary language, is the government of the workers, by the workers and for the workers. It's not a government of the bourgeoisie, by the bourgeoisie and for the bourgeoisie; nor a government of the capitalists, by the capitalists and for the capitalists; nor a government of the transnationals, by the transnationals and for the transnationals; nor a government of the imperialists, by the imperialists, for the imperialists. (1996a: 30)

The Cuban state operates to enhance the well-being of the Cuban people, through the distribution of the social surplus and the meaningful integration into the decision-making process of the citizenry. While the capitalist state exists to ensure and augment corporate sector profits, the Cuban state redistributes wealth. For example, while profit does accrue to the foreign investor, other revenues are not appropriated by a Cuban oligarchy but are ploughed back into the social system. Also, while workers may not always agree with the government, any debates and disagreements are within a non-antagonistic framework, in which workers have very real power to influence state policy.

However, Cuba illustrates an inherent tension in socialist projects. On one hand, changes have been instituted in the Cuban political system to devolve greater decision-making power to the community level. This is in accord with the Marxist conception that the state will eventually wither away, disappearing as the central and overweening structure in society. In this view, socialism is conceptualized as a process that sets the stage for the dissolution of the state. Frederick Engels framed the state as:

> nothing but a machine for the oppression of one class by another, and indeed in the democratic republic no less than in the monarchy; and at best an evil inherited by the proletariat after its victorious struggle for class supremacy, whose worst sides the proletariat ... cannot avoid having to lop off at the earliest possible moment, until such a time as a new generation reared in new and free social conditions, will be able to throw the entire lumber of the state on the scrap-heap. (Engels 1940: 22)

While aiming at ever-greater social justice and political empowerment and participation of citizens, Cuba must also contend with an incessant imperialist onslaught "mounted on various fronts and at different levels to undermine and destabilize established regimes that challenge global capitalist hegemony" (Saul 1990: 77). Moreover, with the intense international economic pressures that increasingly relegate developing countries to marginal positions in the "international division of labour," it is essential to have a coherent national structure with the power to marshall resources and capital behind the country's development. The patterns of foreign direct investment (FDI) illustrate this trend to marginalization. In 1997, 58 percent of FDI went to industrial countries, while more than 80 percent of the FDI that went to the South in the 1990s was concentrated among just twenty countries (UNDP 1999: 31, 38). Operating in the world economy exposes the island to the very same mechanisms that transfer value (wealth) from developing countries to the dominant capitalist countries. Cuba must contend with "the unequal exchange inherent in international commerce" (Carchedi 2001: 161), a process that inevitably results in an appropriation of value from the national economy. To mitigate this loss and retain as much value as possible within the country requires a tight trade and commercial regime, which, in turn, necessitates a strong state.

Intimately interconnected with the subordination of the developing world within neoliberal globalization is the continuing undermining of national sovereignty. Additionally, in Cuba, the legalization of the U.S. dollar, joint ventures with foreign capital and the creation of an entrepreneurial strata have generated problems of corruption in state enterprises and privileges for certain sectors. As the role and the weight of these groups in society have increased, it has been necessary to curb their influence. Therefore, under the present political and economic — both international and domestic — conditions:

> a powerful state is necessary to confront uninterrupted, counterrevolutionary aggression (both internal and external, with the former supported by the latter), to centralize the available resources, to command programs of material change — a veritable epic struggle against underdevelopment — and to distribute/ redistribute the social wealth that is produced. (Lopez Garcia 1999: 43)

A key problem that confronts the Cuban socialist project is the issue of equality. While socialism does not prescribe full equality — the "from each according to ability, to each according to work" principle — it does promote and guarantee greater equality. The goal of full equality lies in the communist stage of society, where the principle of "from each according to work, to each according to need" operates. While socialism, as the transition phase from capitalism to communism, does not promise or posit full equality, any inequality should stem from different levels of contribution to building socialism, as opposed to activities leading to private gain. At present, the "new rich" not only do not make a contribution to the socialist project — except indirectly through fees and taxes — but actually engender an anti-socialist consciousness.

The revolution's goal of building a just and equitable society, in the spirit of José Martí's vision of a Cuba "with all and for the good of all," has always faced daunting obstacles (Martí 1999: 144). The material transformation of an underdeveloped country is a titanic task. A small, poor island has extreme limitations on what it can accomplish, even without an economic blockade by the world's most powerful country. Yet, as Fidel Castro underscores, the Revolution remains unbowed in its pursuit of the just society:

> There are marginal neighbourhoods; there are hundreds of thousands of people who live in marginal neighbourhoods, and not only blacks and mixed race people, but whites as well. There are marginal whites, too, and all this we inherited from the previous social system. I told you that our country is on its way to a new era. I hope someday to be able to speak to you of the

things we are doing today and how we are going to continue to do them. We do not have the money to build housing for all the people who live in what we could call marginal conditions. But we have lots of other ideas which will not wait until the end of times and which our united and justice loving people will implement to get rid of even the tiniest vestiges of marginality and discrimination. I have faith that we will succeed because that is the endeavour today of the leaders of our youth, our students and our people. I shall not say more, I am simply saying that we are aware that there is still marginality in our country. But, there is the will to eradicate it with the proper methods for this task to bring more unity and equality to our society. (Castro 2000a: 59)

The unavoidable introduction of "capitalist elements" has not altered the collectivist trajectory of the Revolution. Despite the inequalities and the negative social phenomena, the island is still defined by an ethos of human solidarity. Within this context, the island has embarked on a battle of ideas: an ideological struggle that challenges the existing global order, asserting its inherent injustice and unsustainablity. It is an ethos encapsulated in the struggle between building a nation based on the "ethic of being" rather than the "ethic of having." This struggle is based on actively resisting the "ethics" and "values" of the market that have risen on the base of the "dollar economy," reinforced by world capitalism: in short, a very definite domestic contradiction between the socialist character of Cuban society — resting upon socialized property and workers' power — and the concessions to capitalism. The new network of international economic relations that Cuba was compelled to accept has exposed it to the pressures that emanate from the logic of the global capitalist market.

While some on the left may dispute the characterization of Cuba as a socialist society (see, for example, Binns and Gonzalez 1981; Reyes 2000, 2003; Vann 1999), it is indisputably a profoundly collective community. All the main means of production and resources have been nationalized and the benefits socialized. The island has eliminated U.S. imperial control and established Cuban sovereignty. Cuba has built and continues to build a humane, collectivist society, which is, necessarily, anti-capitalist.

CONCLUSION

The Cuban Revolution culminated over a century of struggle for independence, human dignity and social justice. Cuban scholars insist that the Revolution is an organic part of this process (e.g., Alzugaray Treto 1989; Blanco 1997; Canto Navarro 2000; Le Riverend 1997). Fidel Castro asserted that:

> When you come right down to it, our fight for independence began way back in 1868 and it has taken us almost a hundred years of continuous struggle to achieve the freedom we have today. (quoted in Scheer and Zeitlin 1964: 35)

For Cubans, history has not yet met its "end." The present is not detached from what has preceded it. This is the context that frames the oft-repeated slogan, "Socialism or death!" — a rallying cry that signifies a central leitmotif of Cuban history. To those unaware of Cuban history, it appears to be a suicide pact with an aging "despot." While it most obviously expresses the resolve to defend the socialist system, there is also a less understood meaning. It posits that the Cuban nation has only two alternatives: through socialism it can maintain its independence and project of social justice, or it can renounce socialism and revert to being a neocolony of the United States, signifying the death of the Cuban nation (Durand 1998). This understanding under-girds the Cuban proclamation to defend the Cuban Revolution. Cuba is determined not to sacrifice its social achievements. As Castro has emphatically stated,

> There is no alternative to socialism in this country, there is no alternative to the Revolution, because anything else would not only mean taking away our social achievements, but also our independence. (1996b: 1)

Thus, the struggle to affirm Cuba's independence and sovereignty is inextricably bound up with the socialist project. The Cuban people see socialism "not only as the outcome of the struggle for and the means to ensure independence, but also as the outcome of the struggle for and means to ensure social justice" (Durand 1998).

The economic crisis of the 1990s arrested the ongoing material transformation of the society. While the country would have preferred not to adopt market mechanisms, make concessions to capitalism and create openings to foreign capital, these measures were essential for the stimulation of production and the acquisition of capital, markets and technologies that generate the funds that sustain the social achievements. The government is intent on not returning to the past, where as a dependent capitalist country, it was subjected to external domination. Cubans have very strong memories of this history. Those who predict the inevitable demise of Cuban socialism and a capitalist resurrection have misunderstood the Cuban Revolution and the Cuban people.

Of course, many argue that intentions often clash with reality and that the central question is whether Cuba can survive as a lone socialist island in a capitalist sea. In the case of foreign investment, the problem is thus posed: Will foreign investment translate into autonomous accumulation and development or merely generate dependence and the foreign appropriation of the country's economic surplus? The argument is that while the Cuban government may attempt to set limits on the role and impact of international capital, the objective processes will inevitably overwhelm state constraints. The legal controls that exist on paper may mean nothing in actual practice. Quite often the query is posed whether tourism will provide the imperialist and capitalist beachheads that could ultimately undermine the Revolution. However the situation may unfold, it is clear that the Cuban Revolution will not remain passive in the course of events and has many surprises in store, especially for the doomsayers of both right and left.

When I have asked Cubans — be they intellectuals, government officials, Communist Party activists or friends negotiating the difficult economic circumstances — whether the Cuban project of national independence and socialist development can survive, invariably they reply that there are no guarantees, that this question will only be resolved in the crucible of struggle. All they pledge is to do their utmost to defend what they have built. They are keenly aware that the United States seeks to reverse the process initiated in 1959. Washington's hostility to the revolutionary project continues unabated, with the singular objective of the overthrow of the Revolution, the elimination of socialism and the restoration of capitalism and U.S. tutelage.

As a counter, Cubans have heeded Lenin's call to erect the most durable barriers to capitalist restoration by carrying out the Revolution "in the most far reaching, consistent and determined manner possible. The more far reaching the revolution the more difficult will it be to restore the old order" (Lenin 1936: 327). In Havana, there was a well-known billboard, based on a quote taken from the 1996 address to the UN General Assembly by Cuban Vice-President Carlos Lage, that simply stated: *Each day in the world 200 million children sleep in the streets. Not one is Cuban.* Perhaps, this best sums up what Cuba is and strives to be, what Cubans are — in the face of immense obstacles — building and defending.

BIBLIOGRAPHY

Agee, Philip. 2003. "Terrorism and Civil Society as Instruments of U.S. Policy in Cuba." Havana. Available at http://www.antiterroristas.cu/index.php?tpl=noticia/anew&noticiaid=932&noticiafecha=2003-05-21

Aitsisselmi, Amin. 2002. "Despite U.S. Embargo, Cuban Biotech Booms." *NACLA Report on the Americas* XXXV, 5 (March/April).

Alarcón, Ricardo. 1999. "The Cuban Miracle and its Future." *Tricontinental* 141.

_____. 1997. *Helms-Burton*. Havana: Editorial José Martí.

Allen, Theodore. 1994. *The Invention of the White Race*. New York: Verso.

Alvarado Godoy, Percy Francisco. 2003. "Target: Cabaret Tropicana: The most ambitious terrorist plan against Cuba in the 1990s." *Granma International* May 23.

Alvarez, Miguel. 1999. *Note on Foreign Investment in Cuba*. Ottawa: Embassy of Cuba.

Alzugaray Treto, Carlos. 1989. "Problems of National Sovereignty in the Cuba–U.S. Historic Breach." In Jorge I. Dominguez and Rafael Hernández (eds.) *U.S.-Cuban Relations in the 1990s*. Boulder, CO: Westview.

Amnesty International. 2003. *Amnesty International Report 2003*. London: Amnesty International. Available at web.amnesty.org/report2003/index-eng

_____. 1998. *Amnesty International Human Rights Report*. London: Amnesty International.

Arboleya Cervera, Jesús. 2003. "Neighbours to the South: An Examination of U.S. Criticism of Cuba." *Radio Progreso*, Havana. May 2. Available at http://www.rprogreso.com/2003/05May/02week/Arboleya.htm

_____. 2000. *The Cuban Counter Revolution*. Ohio: Center for International Studies, Ohio University.

Arias Fernández, Francisco. 2003. "Curacao Network: Various drug traffickers sentenced." *Granma International* July 9.

Associated Press. 2003a. "Cuba Unmasks Spies Among Dissidents." April 12.

_____. 2003b. April 10.

_____. 2002. "Cuba justice in case of exile." November 27.

Augier, F.R., S.C. Gordon, D.G. Hall and M. Reckford. 1971. *The Making of the West Indies*. London: Longman.

August, Arnold. 1999. *Democracy in Cuba and the 1997–98 Elections*. Havana: Editorial José Martí.

Auld, Alison. 2001. "Linking people to the land: Cuba turns to Mother Earth." *Shunpiking* Halifax. May/June.

Aylward, Carol A. 1999. *Canadian Critical Race Theory: Racism and the Law*.

Halifax: Fernwood.

Azcri, Max. 2000. *Cuba Today and Tomorrow: Reinventing Socialism.* Miami: University Press of Florida.

_____. 1988. *Cuba: Politics, Economics and Society.* London: Pinter.

Baerg, William R. 1993. "Judicial Institutionalization of the Revolution: The Legal Systems of the Peoples's Republic of China and the Republic of Cuba." *Loyola of Los Angeles International and Comparative Law Journal* 15.

Bains, Hardial. 1993a. *A Power to Share: A Modern Definition of the Political Process and a Case for its Democratic Renewal.* Ottawa: Canadian Renewal Party.

_____ (ed.). 1993b. *Blockade: U.S Policy of Siege Against Cuba — Reference Material.* Toronto: New Magazine Publishing.

Baker, Christopher. 2000. *Havana Handbook.* Emoryville, CA: Avalon Travelling.

Baker, Judy L. 1997. *World Bank Discussion Paper No.366: Poverty Reduction and Human Development in the Caribbean: A Cross-Country Survey.* Washington, DC: World Bank.

Bamford, James. 2001. *Body of Secrets: Anatomy of the Ultra-Secret National Security Agency.* New York: Doubleday.

Bardach, Anna Louise. 2002. *Cuba Confidential: Love and Vengeance in Miami and Havana.* New York: Random House.

Barry, Tom, Beth Wood and Deb Preusch. 1984. *The Other Side of Paradise: Foreign Control in the Caribbean.* New York: Grove Press.

Bauza, Vanessa. 2003. "Cuba says the U.S. to blame for boat hijackings." *Sun-Sentinel,* July 16.

BBC. 2003a. "Cuba starts to ease out the dollar." July 29.

_____. 2003b. "Cuba denies jamming broadcast." July 19.

_____. 2002. "Cuba backs permanent socialism." June 27.

Benchley, Peter. 2002. "Cuba Reefs: A Last Caribbean Refuge." *National Geographic* February.

Bengelsdorf, Carollee. 1994. *The Problem of Democracy in Cuba: Between Vision and Reality.* Oxford: Oxford University Press.

Benjamin, Medea, and Peter Rosset. 1994. *The Greening of the Revolution: Cuba's Experiment with Organic Agriculture.* Melbourne: Ocean Press.

Benjamin–Alvarado, Jonathan. 2000. *Power to the People: Energy and the Cuban Nuclear Program.* New York: Routledge.

Bennett Jr., Lerone. 1988. *Before the Mayflower: A History of Black America.* New York: Penguin.

Berman, Harold J., and Van R. Whiting. 1980. "Impressions of Cuban Law." *American Journal of Comparative Law* 28.

Bernstein, Paul. 1993. "Cuba: Last Look at an Alternative Legal System." *Temple International and Comparative Law Journal* 7.

Beverly, John, (ed.). 2002. *Boundary 2: From Cuba.* Durham: Duke University Press.

Bigman, David. 2002. *Globalization and the Developing Countries: Emerging*

Strategies for Rural Development and Poverty Alleviation. The Hague: International Service for National Agricultural Research.

Binns, P., and Gonzalez, M. 1981. *Castro, Cuba and Socialism: The Economics of State Capitalism.* Cleveland: Hera Press.

Blackburn, Robin. 2000. "Putting the Hammer Down on Cuba." *New Left Review* 4 (July/August).

Blanco, Juan Antonio. 1997. *Talking about Revolution.* Melbourne: Ocean Press.

Blum, William. 2000. *Rogue State: A Guide to the World's Only Superpower.* Monroe, Maine: Common Courage Press.

_____. 1998. *Killing Hope: U.S. Military and CIA Interventions Since World War II.* Montreal: Black Rose.

Bogdan, Michael. 1989. "Thirty Years of Cuban Revolutionary Law." *Review of Socialist Law* 4.

Boron, Atilo A. 1995. *State, Capitalism and Democracy in Latin America.* London: Lynne Rienner.

Brady, James. 1982. "A Season of Startling Alliance: Chinese Law and Justice in a New Order." In Piers Beirne and Richard Quinney (eds.) *Marxism and Law.* New York: John Wiley and Sons.

Bravo, Ernesto Mario. 1998. *Development Within Underdevelopment: New Trends in Cuban Medicine.* Havana: Editorial José Martí.

Bravo, Olga Miranda. 1996. *The U.S.A. Versus Cuba: Nationalizations and Blockade.* Havana: Editorial José Martí.

Brigos Garcia, Jesús. 2002. Discussions between the author and Jesús Garcia Brigos in Havana. June.

Brittain, Victoria. 1998. *Death of Dignity: Angola's Civil War.* Trenton, NJ: African World Press.

_____. 1988. *Hidden Lives, Hidden Deaths: South Africa's Crippling of a Continent.* London: Faber and Faber.

Broadle, Anthony. 2003a. "Castro Agents Infiltrated Dissidents, Envoy's Home." Reuters. April 10.

_____. 2003b. "Cuba Sentences Dissidents to 15 to 25 years." Reuters. April 7.

Brock, Lisa, and Otis Cunningham. 1991. "Race and the Cuban Revolution: A Critique of Carlos Moore's 'Castro, the Blacks, and Africa'." Available at www.afrocubaweb.com/brock2.htm

Brundenius, Claes. 2002. "Whither the Cuban economy after recovery?" *Journal of Latin American Studies* 34 (Spring).

Calvo, Hernando, and Katlijn Declercq. 2000. *The Cuban Exile Movement: Dissidents or Mercenaries?* Melbourne: Ocean Press.

Campbell, Al. 2001. "Review: People's Power: Cuba's Experience with Representative Government." *Science and Society* 65, 2 (Summer).

Canada Commission of Inquiry Concerning Certain Activities of the Royal Canadian Mounted Police. 1981. *Freedom and Security Under the Law.* Second Report, Vol. 2. Ottawa: Supply and Services.

Canton Navarro, Jose. 2000. *History of Cuba: The Challenge of the Yoke and the Star.*

Havana: SI-MAR S.A. Publishing House.

Carchedi, Guglielmo. 2001. "Imperialism, Dollarization and the Euro." In Leo Panitch and Colin Leys (eds.) *Socialist Register 2002: A World of Contradictions*. London: Merlin.

Carr, Robert K. 1979. *The House Committee on Un-American Activities*. New York: Octagon.

Carranza, Julio. 2002. "The Cuban Economy During the 1990s: A Brief Assessment of a Crucial Decade." In Monreal.

Castro, Fidel. 2003a. "The Malign Idea is to Provoke an Armed Conflict Between Cuba and the United States." *Granma International* May.

_____. 2003b. "In Miami and Washington they are now discussing where, how and when Cuba will be attacked." *Granma International* May.

_____. 2003c. Closing Speech at the Pedagogy 2003 Conference. Havana: Council of State. February 15.

_____. 2002a. "Speech by Dr. Fidel Castro Ruz, President of the Republic of Cuba, at the International Workers' Day Celebration in Revolution Square, Havana, May 1, 2002." New York: Permanent Mission of the Republic of Cuba to the United Nations.

_____. 2002b. "Sooner rather than later, the world will change!" *Granma Internacional: Special Supplement* March 7.

_____. 2002c. "Roundtable on the Mexico Embassy Incident," New York: Permanent Mission of the Republic of Cuba to the United Nations. March 12.

_____. 2002d. *Closing of the 4th International Meeting on Globalization and Problems of Development*. Havana, Cuba, February 15. Author's notes.

_____. 2001a. *Closing of the 18th Congress of the Confederation of Cuban Workers*. Havana, Cuba, April 30. Author's notes.

_____. 2001b. *Commentary at a working session of 18th Congress of the Confederation of Cuban Workers*. Havana, Cuba, April 28. Author's notes.

_____. 2001c. "Estamos mas unidos y fuertes que nunca y mucho major preparados para enfretar esta situación." *Granma* November 3.

_____. 2001d. Speech given on the 40th Anniversary of the Declaration of the Socialist Character of the Cuban Revolution. Havana: Cuban Council of State. April 16.

_____. 2001e. Speech at the Plenary Session of the 105th conference of the Inter-Parliamentary Union, Havana, April 5, 2001. Havana: Cuban Council of State.

_____. 2001f. Speech at the Third World Conference Against Racism, Racial Discrimination, Xenophobia and Other Related Intolerances. Durban, South Africa. Available at http://www.afrocubaweb.com/wcr.htm#Fidel%20Speech

_____. 2000a. Speech at the Cuban Solidarity Rally, Riverside Church, Harlem, New York. Havana: Cuban Council of State. September 8. Available at http://www.afrocubaweb.com/fidelcastroriversidespeech.htm

_____. 2000b. *Capitalism in Crisis: Globalization and World Politics Today.* Melbourne: Ocean Press.

_____. 1999. Speech to the Pedagogia Congress. Havana. February.

_____. 1998a. "The Caribbean is Incomplete Without Cuba." *Granma International* August 30.

_____. 1998b. *Main Report and Speech at the Closing: 5th Congress of the Communist Party of Cuba (1997).* Havana: Editoria Política.

_____. 1996a. *Cuba at the Crossroads.* Melbourne: Ocean Press.

_____. 1996b. "Some Ideas Put Forward by the First Secretary of the Party." *5th Plenum of the Central Committee of the Communist Party of Cuba.* Havana: Editoria Política.

_____. 1993. *Tomorrow Is Too Late: Development and the Environmental Crisis in the Third World.* Melbourne: Ocean Press.

_____. 1992a. "The case of Cuba is the case of all underdeveloped countries." In Alice Waters (ed.) *To Speak the Truth: Why Washington's 'Cold War' against Cuba Doesn't End.* New York: Pathfinder.

_____. 1989. "An African Girón." In David Deutchsman (ed.) *Changing the History of Africa: Angola and Namibia.* Melbourne: Ocean Press.

_____. 1986. *Main Report: Third Congress of the Communist Party of Cuba.* Havana: Editoria Política.

_____. 1984. *The World Economy: Its Economic and Social Impact on the Underdeveloped Countries.* London: Zed.

_____. 1961. *Speech on the Eighth Anniversary of the Attack on Moncada.* Houston, University of Texas: Castro Speech Data Base.

Castro, Fidel, and Ricardo Alarcón. 1990. *U.S. Hands off the MiddleEast! Cuba speaks out at the United Nations.* New York: Pathfinder.

Caute, David. 1978. *The Great Fear: Under Truman and Eisenhower.* New York: Simon and Schuster.

Cawthorne, Andrew. 2001. "Cuba sees less growth, calls U.S. war 'terrorist.'" Reuters. October 28.

CEPAL. 1996. *Desarrollo con Equidad.* Caracas: Editorial Nueva Sociedad.

Chomsky, Noam. 2002. *Pirates and Emperors: New and Old International Terrorism in the Real World.* Toronto: Between the Lines.

_____. 2000. *Rogue States: The Rule of Force in World Affairs.* Cambridge, MA: South End.

_____. 1992. *Deterring Democracy.* New York: Hill and Wang.

Chossudovsky, Michel. 1998. *The Globalisation of Poverty: Impacts of imf and World Bank Reforms.* London: Zed.

Churchhill, Ward, and Jim Vander Wall. 1990. *Agents of Repression: The fbi's Secret War against the Black Panther Party and the American Indian Movement.* Boston: South End.

Cirules, Enrique. 2002. *The Mafia in Cuba.* Melbourne: Ocean Press.

Cliffe, Lionel. 1994. *The Transition to Independence in Namibia.* London: Lynne Rienner.

Coburn, Forrest D. 2002. *Latin America at the End of Politics*. Princeton: Princeton University Press.

Cockburn, Cynthia. 1982. "People's Power." In Griffiths and Griffiths.

Cole, Johnetta. 1986. *Race Toward Equality*. Havana: José Martí Publishing.

Cole, Ken. 1998. *Cuba: From Revolution to Development*. London: Pinter.

Communist Party of Canada. 2000. "Statement of the Central Executive Committee." January 24.

Communist Party of Cuba. 1997. *The Party of Unity, Democracy and the Human Rights We Defend*. Havana: Editoria Política.

"Conscience of the World." 2003. *Porcuba*. Available at http://www.porcuba.cult.cu

Constance, Paul. 2002. "A call to action in the classroom: Ground-breaking study takes a hard look at student achievement in 11 countries." In *IDB America: Magazine of the Inter American Development Bank* Washington: IADB. January 10.

Constitution of the Republic of Cuba. 1993. Havana: Editoria Política.

Cotayo, Nicanor Leon. 1978. *Crime in Barbados*. Budapest: Interpress Publishing.

Coy, Peter. 2002. "Economic trends." *Business Week Online* June 17.

Cramer, Mark. 1998. *Culture Shock: Cuba*. Portland: Graphics Art Center Publishing.

Creedy, John. 1998. *The Dynamics of Income Inequality and Poverty*. Northampton, MA: Elgar.

Cuba Business. 2001a. "Ill Wind Adds to Fears of Austerity." Vol. 15, nos. 8/9 (October/November).

———. 2001b. "Despite September 11th Havana Trade Fair is as Attractive as Ever." Vol. 15, nos. 8/98 (October/November).

———. 2001c. "Cuban Scientists Plan to Test AIDS Vaccine." Vol. 15, nos. 8/9 (October/November).

———. 2001d. "Cuba's Nascent Information Society." Vol. 15, no. 3 (April).

———. 2001e. "'Slave Labour' Threat to Foreign Firms." Vol. 15, no. 3 (April).

———. 2000. "No quick fix for Cuba's foreign debt." September.

———. 1998a. Vol. 12, no. 10 (December).

———. 1998b. Vol. 12, no. 2 (February).

———. 1997. Vol. 11, no. 9 (November).

———. 1993. "Shake-Out at the Habana Libre." Vol. 7, no. 8 (October).

Cuban Armed Forces Review. 1997. *Cuba-Military Expenditures, Armed Forces, GNP, Central Government Expeditures and Population, 1987–1997*. Available at http://www.cubapolidata.com/cafr/cafr_expenditures.html

D'Estefano, Miguel A. 1989. "International Law and U.S.-Cuban Relations." In Jorge Dominguez and Rafael Hernández (eds.) *U.S.-Cuban Relations in the 1990s*. Boulder, CO: Westview.

Dahl, R.A. 1971. *Polyarchy*. New Haven: Yale University Press.

Dallas Morning News. 2003. "Cuba disputes terrorist label." May 8.

Dapice, David. 2002. "Vietnam: So Much Done, So Much to Do! A Subtle

Footnote on Comparative Development Prospects." In Monreal.

Davidson, Basil. 1980. *Black: Mother: Africa and the Atlantic Slave Trade*. New York: Penguin.

Davies, Joseph E. 1943. *Mission to Moscow*. New York: Garden City.

Davis, David Brion (ed.). 1971. *The Fear of Conspiracy: Images of Un-American Subversion form the Revolution to the Present*. Ithaca: Cornell University Press.

Davis, James. 1991. *Who Is Black? One Nation's Definition*. University Park: Pennsylvania State University.

de la Fuente, Alejandro. 2001. *A Nation for All: Race, Inequality and Politics in the Twentieth Century*. Chapel Hill: The University of North Carolina Press.

de Rivero, Oswaldo. 2001. *The Myth of Development: The Non-Viable Economies of the 21st Century*. London: Zed.

Deere, C.D., P. Antrobus, L. Bolles, E. Melendez, P. Phillips, M. Rivera, and H. Safa. 1990. *In the Shadows of the Sun: Caribbean Development Alternatives and U.S. Policy*. Boulder, CO: Westview.

Dei, George J.S. 1996. *Anti-Racism Education in Theory and Practice*. Halifax: Fernwood.

Dei, George J.S., and Agnes Calliste (eds.). 2000. *Power, Knowledge and Anti-Racism Education*. Halifax: Fernwood.

Deutchsman, David (ed.). 1989. *Changing the History of Africa: Angola and Namibia*. Melbourne: Ocean.

Deutchsman, David, and Michael Ratner. 1999. *Washington on Trial: The People of Cuba v. The Government of the United States*. New York: Ocean.

Diamond, Larry, Juan J. Linz and Seymour Martin Lipset (eds.). 1990. *Politics in Developing Countries: Comparing Experiences with Democracy*. Boulder, CO: Lynne Rienner.

Diaz Vasquez, Julio. 2002. "Markets and Reform in China, Vietnam and Cuba." In Monreal.

Dominguez, Jorge I. 1995. "The Caribbean in a New International Context: Are Freedom and Peace a Threat to its Prosperity?" In Anthony T. Bryan, *The Caribbean: New Dynamics in Trade and Political Economy*. Coral Gables, Florida: North-South Center, University of Miami.

Dominguez, Jorge I. 1992. "Pipsqueak Power." In *The Suffering Grass: Superpowers and Regional Conflict in Southern Africa and the Caribbean*. London: Lynne Rienner.

Dotres, Carlos. 1996. "Balance del MINSAP del Año 1996." *Granma* March 4.

Driedger, Leo, and Shiva S. Halli (eds.). 2000. *Race and Racism: Canada's Challenge*. Montreal: McGill-Queen's University Press.

Durand, Cliff. 1998. *Cuban National Identity and Socialism*. Chicago: Red Feather Institute.

Dzidzienyo, Anani, and Lourdes Casal. 1979. *The Position of Blacks in Brazilian and Cuban Society*. London: Minority Rights Group.

D'Zurrilla, William T. 1981. "Cuba's 1976 Socialist Constitution and the Fidelista Interpretation of Cuban Constitutional History." *Tulane Law*

Review 55.

Eaton, Tracey. 2003. "Travel to Cuba grows after post-September 11 slump." *Dallas Morning News*, July 7.

ECLA/ECF. 1997. "The Cuban Economy: Structural reforms and performance in the nineties." Montevideo: United Nations Economic Commission on Latin America and the Caribbean and the Economic Culture Fund.

Eckstein, Susan. 1994. *Back from the Future: Cuba under Castro*. Princeton; Princeton University Press.

Economist Intelligence Unit Limited. 1995. *Country Report: Cuba: 4th Quarter*. London.

Editorial José Martí. 1989. *Case 1/1989: End of the Cuban Connection*. Havana.

Edwards, Michael. 1982. "Urban and Rural Planning." In *Cuba: The Second Decade*. London: Writers and Readers.

EFE News. 2003. "Castro: Executions needed to foil U.S. war plan." Mexico City. May 17.

Eisenberg, Leon. 1997. "The Sleep of Reason Produces Monsters: Human Costs of Economic Sanctions." *New England Journal of Medicine* 336, 14 (April).

Elijah, Sofia. 2000. "Lessons from our neighbours to the south: The Cuban prison system — reflective observations." AfroCubaWeb. Online: http://www.afrocubaweb.com/elijah.htm

Elliston, Jon. 1999. *Psy War on Cuba: The Declassified History of U.S. Anti-Castro Propaganda*. New York: Ocean.

Emergencies Act. 1988. S.C./29. Passed by the Parliament of Canada.

Engels, Frederick. 1985. "The Origin of the Family, Private Property and the State." *Selected Works*. Moscow: Progress.

Engels, Frederick. 1940. "Introduction." In Karl Marx *The Civil War in France*. New York: International.

Erisman, H. Michael. 2000. *Cuba's Foreign Relations in a Post-Soviet World*. Gainesville, FL: University Press of Florida.

———. 1998. "Cuba and the Caribbean Basin: From Pariah to Partner: Review Essay." *Journal of Interamerican Studies and World Affairs* 40, 1 (Spring).

———. 1995. "The Odyssey of Revolution in Cuba." In Anthony Payne and Paul Sutton (eds.) *Modern Caribbean Politics*. Kingston, Jamaica: Ian Randle.

Escalante, Fabian. 1995. *The Secret War: CIA Covert Operations Against Cuba, 1959–62*. Melbourne: Ocean.

Escalante, Fabian. 1994. *CIA Targets Fidel: The Secret Assassination Report*. Melbourne: Ocean.

Espín, Vilma. 1991. *Cuban Women Confront the Future*. Melbourne: Ocean.

Evenson, Debra. 2002a. Varela Project Memo. Unpublished.

———. 2002b. *Workers in Cuba: Union and Labor Relations*. Detroit: The National Lawyer's Guild/Maurice and Jane Sugar Law Centre for Economic and Social Justice.

———. 1994. *Revolution in the Balance: Law and Society in Contemporary Cuba*. San Francisco: Westview.

Everleny Perez, Omar. 2002. "Foreign Direct Investment in Cuba: Recent Experience and Prospects." In Monreal.

Ewan, Arthur. 1981. *Revolution and Economic Development in Cuba.* New York: St. Martin's.

Fariello, Griffin. 1995. *Red Scare: Memories of the American Inquisition.* New York: Avalon.

Fernández, Olga. 1993. *Cuba: Reevaluate Democracy From a Third World Perspective.* Havana: Instituto de Filosofia. Unpublished.

Fernández de Cossío, Carlos. 2003. Unpublished letter. April 10.

_____. 2001. "Cuba: The Struggle of the 1990s." *Shunpiking* May/June.

Fernández Robaina, Tomas. 1997. "The 20th century black question." In Pérez-Sarduy and Jean Stubbs (eds.) *AfroCuba: An Anthology of Cuban Writing on Race, Politics and Culture.* Melbourne: Ocean.

Fields, Barbara. 1990. "Slavery, Race and Ideology in the United States of America." *New Left Review* May/June.

Figueras, Miguel Alejandro. 1998. "Effects of Foreign Direct Investment on Economic Development." *Business Tips on Cuba* 5, 12, (December).

Financial Times of London. 2001. March 6.

Fitzgerald, Frank T. 1994. *The Cuban Revolution in Crisis: From Managing Socialism to Managing Survival.* New York: Monthly Review Press.

Fleras, Augie, and Jean L. Elliott. 1990. *Unequal Relations: An Introduction to Race and Ethnic Dynamics in Canada.* Toronto: Prentice-Hall.

Florida Today. 2001. "Cubans deal with dollars: American currency builds second tier in communist economy." November 12.

Fodor's Travel Publications Inc. 1998. *Exploring Cuba.* New York.

Foner, Eric. 1983. *Nothing But Freedom: Emancipation and its Legacy.* Baton Rouge: Louisiana State University Press.

Foner, Philip. 1988. *José Martí: Political Parties and Elections in the United States.* Havana: José Martí Publishing House.

Foster, William Z. 1951. *Outline Political History of the Americas.* New York: International.

Frank, Marc. 2003a. "Castro shuffles cabinet as Cuban economy stagnates." Reuters. June 21.

_____. 2003b. "Cuba Economy Flat as Tourism Booms and Sugar Crashes." Reuters. May 5.

_____. 2003c. "Cuba sets rule on dollar use by state companies." Reuters. July 21.

_____. 2002a. "Cuba reports record oil and gas production." Reuters. December 22.

_____. 2002b. "Castro warns energy crisis looms in Cuba." Reuters. December 22.

_____. 2001a. "Cuba bracing for bleak economic new year." Reuters. December 23.s

_____. 2001b. "Cuban Sugar Minister sees 'very complex' Harvest." Reuters.

December 9.

_____. 2001c. "Cuban Sugar Minister sees slightly improved crop." Reuters. October 15.

_____. 1993. *Cuba Looks to the Year 2000*. New York: International Publishers.

Franklin, Jane. 1998. "The War Against Cuba." *Covert Action Quarterly* 66 (Fall).

_____. 1997. *Cuba and the United States: A Chronological History*. Melbourne: Ocean.

Fuller, Linda. 1992. *Work and Democracy in Socialist Cuba*. Philadelphia: Temple University Press.

Gaceta Oficial de la República de Cuba. 1999. "Preamble: Ley 88/99 Ley de Protección de la Independencia Nacional y de la Economía de Cuba." March 4.

_____. 1996. "Law 80: Reaffirmation of Cuba Dignity and Sovereignty Act." June 25.

_____. 1994. "Ley 5/77 Ley de Procedimiento Penal (Actualizada)." August 13.

Galeano, Eduardo. 2003. "Cuba Hurts." *New Internationalist* 258, July.

Garcia Bielsa, Fernando. 1997. Interview with Fernando Garcia Bielsa. June 12.

Garcia, Anna-Maria. 2003. "Cuban oil production distances the spectre of power cuts." *Granma International* July 9.

Garcia Luis, Julio. 2001. *Cuban Revolution Reader*. Melbourne: Ocean.

Garcia Marquez, Gabriel. 1989. "Operation Carlota." In Deutchsman.

Garfield, Richard, and Sarah Santana. 1997. "The impact of the Economic Crisis and the U.S. Embargo on Health in Cuba." *American Journal of Public Health* 87, 1 (January).

Gilmore, John. 2000. *Faces of the Caribbean*. London: Latin American Bureau.

Glazer, H. 1989. "The Building Industry in Cuba." In Wilber A. Chaffee, Jr. and Gary Prevost (eds.) *Cuba: A Different America*. New York: Monthly Review Press.

Gleijeses, Piero. 2001. *Conflicting Missions: Havana, Washington and Africa, 1975–1976*. Chapel Hill: University of North Carolina Press.

Globe and Mail. 2003a. "Dictators take heed: Democratization nigh." Toronto. April 11.

_____. 2003b. "Locked up in Cuba with Castro's key." Toronto. April 8.

Godfried, Eugène. 2000. "Reflections on Race and the Status of People of African Descent in Revolutionary Cuba." Available at http://www.afrocubaweb.com/eugenegodfried/eugenegodfried.htm#Reflections

Goldstein, Robert Justin. 1978. *Political Repression in Modern America*. Boston: Schenkman Publishing.

Gomer Sunahara, Ann. 1981. *The Politics of Racism: The Uprooting of Japanese Canadians During the Second World War*. Toronto: James Lorimer

Gordon, Joy. 1997. "Cuba's Entrepreneurial Socialism." *The Atlantic Monthly* January.

Granma. 2003a. January 10.

_____. 2003b. April 16.

_____. 2002. October 28.

_____. 2001. December 22.

_____. 1999a. July 28.

_____. 1999b. July 8.

_____. 1999c. "Who Are the So-Called Dissidents and Prisoners of Conscience in Cuba?" March 4.

_____. 1999d. March 2.

_____. 1999e. February 7.

_____. 1999f. January 6.

_____. 1998. December 15.

Granma International. 2003a. April 18.

_____. 2003b. "Nickel at $8,495 per ton." February 3.

_____. 2002a. "Unemployment Down to 3.3%." December 20.

_____. 2002b. October 22.

_____. 2002c. "Oil production." August 8.

_____. 2002d. "Alternatives in the sugar industry." July 4.

_____. 2002e. January 21.

_____. 2001. "Island to produce 90% of its own electricity by year's end." April 27.

_____. 1999a. February 10.

_____. 1999b. January 25.

Gray, Patricia. 2002. *Latin America: Its Future in the Global Economy.* London: Palgrove.

Green, Duncan. 1998. *Hidden Lives: Voices of Children in Latin America and the Caribbean.* London: Latin America Bureau.

Greene, Felix. 1970. *The Enemy: What Every American Should Know About Imperialism.* New York: Random House.

Griffiths, John, and Peter Griffiths (eds.). 1979. *Cuba: The Second Decade.* London: Writers and Readers Writing Co-operative Publishing.

Grogg, Patricia. 2001. "Male Enrolment Challenges Gender Equity in Cuba." Inter Press Service. March 24.

Guardian. 2003. "Regimes who worry that they will be next." London. April 11.

Guillén, Nicolas. 1995. *The Great Zoo and Other Poems.* Havana: Editorial José Martí.

Gunn, Gillian. 1993. *Cuba in Transition: Options for U.S. Policy.* New York: Twentieth Century Fund.

Harnecker, Marta. 1979. *Cuba: Dictatorship or Democracy?* Westport: Lawrence Hill and Co.

Harney, Stefano. 1996. *Nationalism and Identity: Culture and the Imagination in the Caribbean Diaspora.* London: Zed.

Harris, Joseph E. 1987. *Africans and Their History.* New York: Penguin.

Harris, Olivia. 1983. *Latin American Women.* London: Minority Rights Group.

Harrison, Paul. 1983. *Inside the Third World.* London: Penguin.

Heberstein, Denis, and John Evenson. 1989. *The Devils Are Among Us: The War for Namibia*. London: Zed.

Helg, Aline. 1995. *Our Rightful Share: The Afro-Cuban Struggle for Equality, 1896-1912*. Chapel Hill: The Univerity of North Carolina Press

Heller, Celia S. 1969. *Structured Social Inequality*. Toronto: Macmillan.

Henderson, Lawrence W. 1979. *Angola: Five Centuries of Conflict*. Ithaca: Cornell University Press.

Hernández, Carmen. 1997. *100 Questions and Answers about Cuba*. Havana: Pablo de La Torriente.

Hernández, Rafael. 2002. "Frozen Relations: Washington and Cuba After the Cold War." *NACLA: Report on the America*. XXXV, 4 (January/February).

Hickle, William, and William Turner. 1981. *The Fish is Red: The Story of the Secret War against Castro*. New York: Harper and Row.

Hodges, Tony. 2001. *Angola: From Afro-Stalinism to Petro-Diamond Capitalism*. Bloomington: Indiana University Press.

Hoffmann, Bert. 1998. "The Helms–Burton Law and its Consequences for Cuba, the United States and Europe." Delivered at the meeting of the Latin American Studies Association. Chicago. Unpublished.

Holthuis, Annemieke E. 1991. *The Emergencies Act, The Canadian Charter of Rights and Freedoms and International Law: The Protection of Human Rights in States of Emergency*. Unpublished paper. Faculty of Law: McGill University.

Huberman, Leo, and Paul Sweezy. 1969. *Socialism in Cuba*. New York: Monthly Review Press.

———. 1960. *Cuba: Anatomy of a Revolution*. New York: Monthly Review Press.

Hurlich, Susan. 2002. "Democracy in Cuba: An Overview of Elections and the Structure of Government." Unpublished paper. Havana.

IADB. 2000. *Development Beyond Economic: Economic and Social Progress in Latin America, 2000 Report*.

IBRD. 2001. *World Development Indicators*. Washington: World Bank.

Insight Guide: Cuba. 1999. London: APA Publications.

Izquierdo Canosa, Raúl. 1998. *La Reconcentracion 1896–1897*. Havana: Ediciones Verde Olivo.

James, Winston. 1998. *Holding Aloft the Banner of Ethiopia: Caribbean Radicalism in Early Twentieth Century America*. London: Verso.

Jatar-Hausmann, Ana Julia. 1996. "Through the Cracks of Socialism: The Emerging Private Sector in Cuba." *Cuba in Transition* 6. (August).

Jorquera, Roberto. 1998. "Cuba: Showing How To Defeat Racism." *Venceremos!* 57.

Jones, Alberto. 2002. "What others say." *The News-Journal* Florida. October 31.

Kapica, Antoni. 1996. "Politics in Cuba: Beyond the Stereotypes." *Bulletin of Latin America Research* 15, 2.

Karol, K.S. 1970. *Guerrillas in Power: The Course of the Cuban Revolution*. New York: Hill and Wang.

Karon, Tony. 2001. "Cuba Contemplates Life Without Castro." *Time.Com*. August 14.

Kirk, John. 2000. "Foreword." In Max Azcri, *Cuba Today and Tomorrow: Reinventing Socialism*. Miami: University Press of Florida.

_____. 1983. *José Martí: Mentor of the Cuban Nation*. Tampa: University Presses of Florida.

Kirk, John, and Archibald Ritter. 1995. *Cuba in the International System*. London: MacMillan.

Kivel, Paul. 2002. *Uprooting Racism: How White People Can Work For Racial Justice*. Vancouver: New Society.

Knight, Franklin W. 1996. "Ethnicity and social structure in contemporary Cuba." In Gert Oostinde (ed.) *Ethnicity in the Caribbean*. London: Macmillan Education Ltd.

Knox, Paul. 2003. "Graham protests against Cuban trials." *Globe and Mail*. Toronto. April 8.

Koehnlein, B. 2001 *The Cuban Revolution in 2001: A Short Look*. Available at http://www.blythe.org/nytransfer-subs/2001rad/The_Cuban_Revolution_in_2001

Kohn, Stephen M. 1994. *American Political Prisoners: Prosecutions Under the Espionage and Sedition Acts*. Westport: Praeger.

Krinski, M., and D. Golove (eds.). 1993. *U.S. Economic Measures against Cuba*. Northhampton, MA: Aletheia Press.

Kubalkova, Vendulka. 1994. "The Experience of Eastern Europe: Seven Lessons for Cuba." In Jiame Suchlicki and Antonio Jorge (eds.) *Investing in Cuba: Problems and Prospects*. London: Transaction.

La Riva, Gloria. 1996. "Cuban Labor Congress to meet in Havana." *Workers World News Service*. April 25.

Lage, Carlos. 1996. Speech. *5th Plenum of the Central Committee of the Communist Party of Cuba*. Havana: Editoria Política.

Lago, Armando. 1997. *An Economic Evaluation of the Foreign Investment Law of Cuba*. Miami: Association for the Study of the Cuban Economy.

Landau, Saul. 2003. Email to author. May 4.

Lappe, F., and P. Du Bois. 1994. *The Quickening of America: Rebuilding Our Nation, Remaking Our Lives*. San Francisco: Jossey-Bass.

Latin American Monitor: Caribbean. 2002. Vol. 19, 8 (August).

Latin American Weekly Report. 2002. "For millions another lost half-decade." November 12.

_____. 2001. "Climbing the Human development ladder." July 17.

_____. 1993. March 11.

Law 73: The Tax System Law. 1994. Havana: *Gaceta de la República de Cuba*.

Law 77: Foreign Investment Act. 1995. Havana: Editoria Política.

Lechuga, Carlos. 1995. "Preface." In Escalante.

Lenin, V.I. 1977. "The State and Revolution." *Collected Works*. Moscow: Progress. Vol. 25.

_____. 1936. "The Agrarian Programme of Social Democracy in the First Russian Revolution." *Selected Works*. Vol. III. London: Lawrence and

Wishart Ltd.

LeoGrande, William M. 2000. "A Politics Driven Policy: Washington's Cuba Agenda is Still in Place — for Now." *NACLA: Report on the Americas* November/December.

LeoGrande, William M., and Julie M. Thomas. 2002. "Cuba's Quest for Economic Independence." *Journal of Latin American Studies* 34 (Spring).

Leon Cotayo, Nicanor. 1978. *Crime in Barbados*. Budapest: Interpress.

Le Riverend, Julio. 1997. *Brief History of Cuba*. Havana: Editorial José Martí.

Lerner, Michael P. 1973. *The New Socialist Revolution: An Introduction to its Theory and Strategy*. New York: Dell.

"Ley 87 Modificación Código Penal Extraordinaria No. 1. 1999." *Gaceta Oficial de la Republica de Cuba*. Havana: Ministerio de Justicia.

"Ley 5/77 Ley de Procedimiento Penal (Actualizada)." Havana. August 13, 1977.

Linden, Eugene. 2003. "The Nature of Cuba." *Smithsonian* May.

Linger, Eloise, and John Cotman (eds.). 2000. *Cuban Transitions at the Millennium*. Largo, MD: International Development Options.

Liss, Sheldon B. 1987. *Roots of Revolution: Radical Thought in Cuba*. Lincoln, Nebraska: University of Nebraska Press.

Lobe, Jim. 2001. "Learn from Cuba, says World Bank." Inter Press Service. April 30.

Lopez García, Delia Luisa. 1999. "Economic Crisis, Adjustments, and Democracy in Cuba." *Cuba in the 1990s*. Havana: Editorial José Martí.

Lopez Vigil, Maria. 1999. *Cuba: Neither Heaven Nor Hell*. Washington: Epica.

Lorimer, Doug. 2000. *The Cuban Revolution and Its Leadership*. Newtown, Australia: Resistance.

Loury, Glenn C. 2002. *The Anatomy of Racial Inequality*. Cambridge: Harvard University Press.

Lumumba-Kasongo, Tukumbi. 1992. *Nationalistic Ideologies, Their Policy Implications and the Struggle for Democracy in African Politics*. Lewiston: Edwin Mellen.

Lussane, Clarence. 2000. "From Black Cuban to Afro-Cuban: Issues of Race Consciousness and Identity in Cuban Race Relations." In Linger and Cotman.

Lutjens, Sheryl. 2000a. "Schooling and 'Clean' Streets in Socialist Cuba: Children and the Special Period." In Mickelson.

_____. 2000b. "Restructuring Childhood in Cuba: The State as Family." In Mickelson.

Mace, Rodney. 1982. "Housing." In Griffiths and Griffiths.

MacKenzie, J.B. 1972. "Section 98, Criminal Code and the Freedom of Expression in Canada." *Queen's Law Journal* 4.

MacKinnon, Peter. 1977. "Conspiracy and Sedition as Canadian Political Crimes." *McGill Law Journal* 23.

Madan, N., B. Zaballa, A.R. Gort, I. Aguirrechu and A. Aguila. 1993. *Extraordinary Circumstances Bring People Together: Cuban Electoral Process*

(November 1992 — March 1993). Havana: Editoria Política.

Makhijani, Arjun. 1992. *From Global Capitalism to Economic Justice: An Inquiry into the Elimination of Systemic Poverty, Violence and Environmental Destruction in the World Economy.* New York: Apex.

Mandela, Nelson. 1993. *Nelson Mandela Speaks: Forging a Democratic Non-racist South Africa.* New York: Pathfinder.

Mannix, Daniel, P. 1977. *Black Cargoes: A History of the Atlantic Slave Trade.* New York: Penguin.

Marable, Manning. 2000. In Hisham Aidi, *Is Cuba a "Racial Democracy?"* January 28. Available at: http://www.Africana.com/DailyArticles/index_20000320.htm

_____. 1996. *Speaking Truth to Power: Essays on Race, Resistance and Radicalism.* Boulder, CO: Westview.

Marquis, Christopher. 2001. "Cuba leads Latin America in Primary Education, Study Finds." *New York Times* December 14.

Martí, José. 1999. *José Martí Reader: Writings on the Americas.* Melbourne: Ocean.

_____. 1977. *Our America: Writings on Latin America and the Struggle for Cuban Independence.* New York: Monthly Review.

Martinez, Osvaldo. 1998. "The State of the Cuban Economy." Presentation at the First Cuba–Canada Meeting of Friendship and Solidarity, Havana, August 8.

Martinez Puentes, Silvia. 2003. *Cuba: Mas Alla de Los Suenos.* Havana: Editorial José Martí.

Martinez Reinosa, Milagros. 2001. "Women and Cuban Foreign Policy: An Approximation to the Study of the Topic in the Decade of the Nineties." In Colleen Lundy and Norma Vasallo Barrueta (eds.) *Cuban Women: History, Contradictions, and Contemporary Challenges.* Ottawa: Carleton University.

Martinussen, John. 1999. *Society, State and Market: A Guide to Competing Theories of Development.* London: Zed.

Masud-Piloto, Felix. 1999. "Foreword." In Ernesto Rodriguez Chavez (ed.) *Cuban Migration Today.* Havana: Editorial José Martí.

Mbeki, Thabo. 2001. "Letter from President Thabo Mbeki." *ANC Today.* March 30–April 5. Available at http://www.afrocubaweb.com/southafrica.htm

McAuslan, Fiona, and Norman Matthew. 2000. *The Rough Guide to Cuba.* London: Rough Guides.

McManus, Jane. 1989. *Getting to Know Cuba.* New York: St. Martin's.

McNally, David. 2002. *Another World Is Possible: Globalization and Anti-Capitalism.* Winnipeg: Arbeiter Ring.

McNaught, Kenneth. 1974. "Political Trials and the Canadian Political Tradition." *University of Toronto Law Journal* 24.

Mensah, Joséph. 2002. *Black Canadians: History, Experience, Social Conditions.* Halifax: Fernwood.

Mesa Redonda. 2003. *Nuestra Única Alternativa es la Victoria.* January 17.

Mesa–Lago, Carmelo. 1998. "Assessing Economic and Social Performance in the

Cuban Transition of the 1990s." *World Development* 26, 1–6.

_____. 1994. *Cuba in the 1970s: Pragmatism and Institutionalization.* Albuquerque: University of New Mexico Press.

_____. 1993. "The Economic Effects on Cuba of the Downfall of Socialism in the USSR and Eastern Europe." In Carmelo Mesa-Lago (ed.) *Cuba After the Cold War.* Pittsburgh: University of Pittsburgh Press.

_____. 1974. *Cuba in the 1970s: Pragmatism and Institutionalization.* Albuquerque: University of New Mexico Press.

Miami 5 2003. Website available at www.granma.cu/miami5/ingles/index.html

Miami Herald. 2003. "Where Truth Is a Crime: Release Jailed Cuban Dissidents." April 2.

_____. 1999. July 10.

Michalowski, Ray. 1997. "Cuba." In Graeme R. Newman (ed.) *World Fact Book of Criminal Justice Systems.* Washington: U.S. Department of Justice. Available at http://www.ojp.usdoj.gov/bjs/pub/ascii/wfbcjcub.txt

Mickelson, Rosslyn Arlin (ed.). 2000. *Children on the Streets of the Americas: Homelessness, Education and Globalization in the United States, Brazil and Cuba.* New York: Routledge.

Miller, Judith, Stephen Engelberg and William Broad. 2001. *Germs: Biological Weapons and America's Secret War.* New York: Simon and Schuster.

MINREX. 2003. "Cuba refutes U.S. charges of interfering with its satellite signals to Iran." *Granma International* July 21.

Minter, William. 1994. *Apartheid's Contras: An Inquiry into the Roots of War in Angola and Mozambique.* London: Zed.

Monreal, Pedro. (ed.). 2002. *Development Prospects in Cuba: An Agenda in the Making.* London: Institute for Latin American Studies.

Montanaro, Pam. 1999. "Inside Cuba's legal system." *San Francisco Bay Guardian.* November 3.

Moorcraft, Paul L. 1990. *African Nemesis: War and Revolution in Southern Africa.* London: Brassey's.

Moore, Dennison. 1995. *Origins and Development of Racial Ideology in Trinidad: The Black View of the East Indian.* Tunapuna, Trinidad: Chakra Publishing.

Moore, John Norton, Frederich S. Tipson and Robert F. Turner. 1990. *National Security Law.* Durham: Carolina Academic Press.

Morgan, Edmund Sears. 1979. *American Slavery, American Freedom: The Ordeal of Colonial Virginia.* New York: Norton.

Morley, Morris H. 1987. *Imperial State and Revolution: The United States and Cuba, 1952–1986.* Cambridge: Cambridge University Press.

Morray, J.P. 1968. "The United States and Latin America." In James Petras and Maurice Zeitlin (eds.) *Latin America: Reform or Revolution: A Reader.* New York: Fawcett.

Morton, J.R. 1979. "Agriculture and Rural Development." In Griffiths and Griffiths.

Munck, Ronaldo. 1988. *The New International Labour Studies: An Introduction.*

London: Zed.

Murphy, Terry. 2003. "Who, exactly, are the Cuban Five." *Canadian Dimension* July/August.

Murray, Mary. 2003. "Cuba admits drugs are a problem." *MSNBC.* March 7.

_____. 1993. *Cruel and Unusual Punishment: The U.S. Blockade against Cuba.* Melbourne: Ocean.

National Information Service. 1988. *The CIA's War against Cuba.* Havana.

New Internationalist. 2003. May.

New York Times. 2003. "Official: Cuba can prosecute dissidents." March 31.

_____. 2002. "Cuba Parliament begins economic review." December 22.

_____. 1998. "A bomber's tale: A Cuban exile details the 'horrendous matter' of a bombing campaign." July 12.

Ng, Roxane, Gillian Walker and Jacob Muller (eds.). 1990. *Community Organization and the Canadian State.* Toronto: Garamond.

North, James. 1986. *Freedom Rising.* New York: Macmillan.

Nuñez Sarmineto, Marta. 2001. "Cuban Strategies for Women's Employment in the 1990s: A Case Study of Professional Women." *Socialism and Democracy* 15, 1 (Spring–Summer).

O'Donnell, Guillermo A., Phillipe Schmitter and Lawrence Whitehead. 1986. *Transitions from Authoritarian Rule: Latin America.* Baltimore: Johns Hopkins University Press.

Office of the President of the United States of America. 2002. *The National Security Strategy of the United States of America.* Washington.

Oramas, Joaquin. 1998. "Sustained Recovery in Basic Industry." *Granma International* February 22.

Otero, Lisandro. 1987. *Dissenters and Supporters in Cuba.* Havana: Editorial José Martí.

Pages, Raisa. 2003. "44th Anniversary of the First Agrarian Reform Act." *Granma International.* May 23.

_____. 2000. "On Gender and Racial Equality." *Granma International.* March 18.

Pastor Jr., Manuel, and Andrew Zimbalist. 1998. "Has Cuba Turned the Corner?" *Cuban Studies* 27.

Patterson, Thomas G. 1994. *Contesting Castro: The United States and the Triumph of the Cuban Revolution.* New York: Oxford University Press.

Payne, Anthony, and Paul Sutton. 2001. *Charting Caribbean Development.* London: Macmillan.

Peppin, Patricia. 1993. "Emergency Legislation and Rights in Canada." *Queen's Law Journal* 18.

Pérez Jr., Louis A. 1999. *On Becoming Cuban: Identity, Nationality and Culture.* New York: Harper Collins.

_____. 1988. *Cuba: Between Reform and Revolution.* New York: Oxford University Press.

Pérez Lopez, Jorge. 1994. *Cuba at a Crossroads: Politics and Economics after the Fourth Party Congress.* Miami: University Press of Florida.

Pérez Roque, Felipe. 2003. "Press Conference." April 9. Available at http://www.canadiannetworkoncuba.ca/Documents/Roque-Dissidents-Apr03.html

Pérez-Sarduy, Pedro. 1995. "What do Blacks Have in Cuba, and an Open Letter to Carlos Moore." Available at www.afrocubaweb.com/whatdoblacks.htm

Pérez-Sarduy, Pedro, and Jean Stubbs (eds.). 1997. *AfroCuba: An Anthology of Cuban Writing on Race, Politics and Culture.* Melbourne: Ocean Press.

_____. 2000. *Afro-Cuban Voices: On Race and Identity in Contemporary Cuba.* Miami: University Press of Florida.

Pérez Villanueva, Omar Everleny. 1997. *Cuba's Social Performance in the Economic Crisis.* Havana: FLACSO, University of Havana.

Petras, James. 2003. "The Responsibility of the Intellectuals." *Canadian Dimension* 26, 4 (July/August).

_____. 1981. *Class, State and Power in the Third World.* London: Zed.

Petras. James, and Morris Morley. 1992. *Latin America in the Time of Cholera: Electoral Politics, Market Economics and Permanent Crisis.* London: Routledge.

Petras, James, and Henry Veltmeyer. 2001. *Globalization Unmasked: Imperialism in the 21st Century.* London: Zed.

Pieterse, Jan N. 1992. *White on Black: Images of Africa in Western Popular Culture.* New Haven: Yale University Press

Philippine Star. 2003. April 24.

Polanyi Levitt, Kari. 2000. "The Right to Development." Fifth Sir Arthur Lewis Memorial Lecture, Saint Lucia, November 22.

Porcheron, Michel. 2001. "Seven Days." *Granma International* June 14.

Prada, Pedro. 1995. *Island Under Siege: The U.S. Blockade of Cuba.* Melbourne: Ocean.

Prensa Latina. 2003. "Cuba Will Confront Internal Subversion Financed by the U.S." April 10.

_____. 2001. "Report from Tourism Minister Ibrahim Ferradaz to National Assembly." August 4.

Proenza, Christiana. 2000. "What Colour is Cuba? Complexities of Ethnic and Racial Identity." In Linger and Cotman.

Puma, Enrique S. 1996. "Labour Effects of Adjustment Policies in Cuba." *Cuba in Transition* 6.

R. v. Bartle. 1994. *Supreme Court Reports.* Canada. Vol. 3.

R. v. Boyles. 1991. *Supreme Court Reports.* Canada. Vol. 3.

R. v. Feeny. 1997. *Supreme Court Reports.* Canada. Vol. 2.

R. v. Herbert. 1990. *Supreme Court Reports.* Canada. Vol. 2.

R. v. Jones. 1994. *Supreme Court of Canada.* Vol. 1.

R. v. Oickle. 2000. *Canadian Criminal Courts.* Vol. 147.

R. v. Stillman. 1997. *Supreme Court Reports.* Canada. Vol. 1.

R. v. Van Haarlem. 1992. *Supreme Court Reports.* Canada. Vol. 1.

R. v. Wooley. 1998. *Canadian Criminal Courts.* Vol. 40. 3rd Edition.

Radio Havana Cuba. 2002. "Social Security: Guaranteed by the Cuban Revolution." January 7.

_____. 2001a. "Economy Continues to Recover Despite World Economic Recession." December 31.

_____. 2001b. "Cuba's Social Achievements Immune to World Economic Crisis." December 28.

_____. 2001c. "Foreign Investment in Cuba Continues to Grow, Despite Global Economic Crisis." December 27.

_____. 2001d. "Cuban President evaluates recovery efforts following Hurricane Michelle." December 20.

Ramy, Manuel Alberto. 2002. *The Varela Project: Its Juridical and Legal Viability.* Havana: Progresso Weekly.

Randall, Margaret. 1981. *Women in Cuba: Twenty Years Later.* New York: Smyrna.

Reckford, Barry. 1971. *Does Fidel Eat More Than Your Father?* New York: Praeger.

Reed, Gail. 1992. *Island in the Storm: The Cuban Communist Party's Fourth Congress.* Melbourne: Ocean.

Remigio-Ferro, Ruben. 1999. "Cuban Law: How Workers Deal with Crime." *Workers World* December 9.

Remigio-Ferro, Ruben, and Mayda Goite. 2000. "The Cuban Criminal Law System and the Social Role of Cuban Prisons." *Guild Practitioner* 57, 1 (Winter).

Reuters. 2003. "Canadian Jailed for 25 Years in Cuba for Sex Crime." April 28.

_____. 2003a. "Cuba denies jamming U.S. broadcasts." July 19.

Reyes, Hector. 2003. "Cuba, Democracy and the Bush Doctrine." *International Socialist Review* 30, Summer.

_____. 2000. "Cuba: The Crisis of State Capitalism." *International Socialist Review* 11 (Spring).

Ricardo, Robert. 1994. *Guantanamo: The Bay of Discord: The Story of the U.S. military base in Cuba.* Melbourne: Ocean.

Robinson, Linda. 1998. "What we didn't do to get rid of Castro." *U.S. News and World Report* October 26.

Rodney, Walter. 1972. *How Europe underdeveloped Africa.* London: Bogle-L'Ouverture.

Rodriquez, Andrea. 2002. "En Cuba, la población negra es la menos favorecida." Associated Press. Havana. December 3.

Rodriguez Chavez, Ernesto. 1999. *Cuban Migration Today.* Havana: Editorial José Martí.

Roman, Gustavo. 1995. "On Politics and Health: An Epidemic of Neurologic Disease in Cuba." *Annals of Internal Medicine* 122, 7 (April).

Roman, Peter. 1999. *People's Power: Cuba's Experience with Representative Government.* Boulder, CO: Westview.

_____. 1995. "Worker's Parliament in Cuba." *Latin American Perspectives* 22, 87 (Fall).

Rosenthal, Peter. 1991. "The New Emergencies Act." *Manitoba Law Journal* 20.

Ross Leal, Pedro. 1997. Presentation. Havana. May 3.

Rosset, Peter M. 1998. "Alternative Agriculture Works: The Case of Cuba." *Monthly Review* July/August.

_____. 1997. "The Greening of Cuba." In Helen Collinson (ed.) *Green Guerrillas: Environmental Conflicts and Initiatives in Latin America and the Caribbean*. Montreal: Black Rose.

Rous Manitas, Nita. 1983. "Cuba and the Contemporary World Order." *Newer Caribbean*. Philadelphia: Institute for the Study of Human Issue.

Ryan, Selwyn, Roy McCree and Godfrey St. Bernard. 1997. *Behind the Bridge: Poverty, Politics and Patronage in Laventille, Trinidad*. St. Augustine, Florida: ISER, University of the West Indies.

Safa, Haeri. 2003. "Cuba blows the whistle on Iranian jamming." *Asia Times*. August 22.

Salas, Luis. 1983. "The Judicial System of Postrevolutionary Cuba." *Nova Law Journal* 8.

_____. 1979. *Social Control and Deviance in Cuba*. New York: Praeger.

Sandels, Robert. 2003. "Cuba Crackdown: A Revolt against the National Security Strategy." *Counterpunch*. April 26.

Saul, John S. 1993. *Recolonization and Resistance in Southern Africa in the 1990s*. Toronto: Between the Lines.

_____. 1990. *Socialist Ideology and the Struggle for Southern Africa*. Trenton: Africa World Press.

Schapp, Bill. 1982. "The Cuba Dengue Fever Epidemic." *Covert Action Information Quarterly* 17 (Summer).

Scheer, Robert, and Maurice Zeitlin. 1964. *Cuba: An American Tragedy*. London: Penguin.

Schuyler, George. 2000. *Venezuela and Cuba in the Age of Globalization: Healthcare and Development*. Working Paper no. 00.10.4. Halifax: International Development Studies, Saint Mary's University.

Schwab, Peter. 1999. *Cuba: Confronting the U.S. Embargo*. New York: St. Martin's Griffin.

Seager, Joni. 2000. *The State of Women in the World Atlas*. New York: Penguin.

Seed, Tony. 2000. Interview with Tony Seed. March 28.

Seers, Dudley (ed.). 1964. *Cuba: The Economic and Social Revolution*. Chapel Hill: University of North Carolina Press.

Seidman, Ann. 1990. *Apartheid, Militarism and the U.S. South East*. Trenton: Africa World Press.

Senate Select Committee to Study Government Operations with Respect to Intelligence Activities, Part B. 1975. *Alleged Assassination Plots Involving Foreign Leaders: An Interim Report*. Washington: Government of the United States.

Serviat, Pedro. 1997. "Solutions to the black problem." In Pérez-Sarduy and Stubbs.

_____. 1986. *El Problema Negro En Cuba y Su Solución Definitiva*. Havana: Editoria Política.

Shakur, Assata. 2003. *Assata Shakur: The Interview*. Detroit: The Pan-African Research and Documentation Centre.

_____. 1999. "Race and Revolution: Interview with Assata Shakur." *SOULS Magazine* (Spring).

_____. 1996. "In a society based on justice things can change." *Fight Racism! Fight Imperialism!* London. June/July.

Shutt, Harry. 2001. *A New Democracy: Alternatives to a Bankrupt World Order*. London: Zed.

Silber, Irwin. 1994. *Socialism: What Went Wrong? An Inquiry into the Theoretical and Historical Sources of the Socialist Crisis*. London: Pluto.

Silverman, Bertram (ed.). 1971. *Man and Socialism in Cuba: The Great Debate*. New York: Monthly Review.

Sinclair, Minor, and Martha Thompson. 2000. *Cuba: Going against the Grain: Agricultural Crisis and Transformation*. Washington: Oxfam America.

Slottje, Daniel Jonathan, and Raj Baldev. 1998. *Income Inequality: Poverty and Economic Welfare*. New York: Physica-Verlag.

Smith, Wayne. 2003a. "Provocation, war spawned Cuba crackdown." *Baltimore Sun*. April 15.

_____. 2003b. "Why the crackdown?" *L.A. Times*. April 7.

_____. 2003c. "Dissidents in Cuba." *New York Times*. March 26.

_____. 1996. "Cuba's long reform." *Foreign Affairs* 75, 2 (March/April).

Snow, Anita. 2003. "Critics say anti-Castro aid ends up hurting." *Seattle Times*. April 14.

_____. 2002. "Cuba's economic growth slows." *Associated Press*. December 21.

Snowden, Frank M. 1983. *Before Color Prejudice: The Ancient View of Blacks*. Cambridge, MA: Harvard University Press.

Spalding, Hobart. 2003. "People's Power in Cuba." *Monthly Review* (February).

Stubbs, Jean. 1989. *Cuba: The Test of Time*. London: Latin America Bureau.

Suarez Salazar, Luis. 1991. *Cuba: Isolation or Reinsertion in a Changed World*. Havana: Editorial José Martí.

Sullivan, Kevin. 2003. "Cuban dissidents reel under wave of repression." *Washington Post Foreign Service*. April 6.

Sunahara, Ann Gomer. 1981. *The Politics of Racism: The Uprooting of Japanese Canadians During the Second World War*. Toronto: Lorimer.

Susman, Paul. 1998. "Cuban Socialism in Crisis: A Neoliberal Solution?" In Thomas Klak (ed.) *Globalization and Neoliberalism: The Caribbean Context*. London: Routledge.

Sweezy, Paul M. 1990. "Cuba: A Left U.S. View." *Monthly Review* 42, 4 (September).

Sweig, Julia, and Kai Bird (eds.). 1997. *Denial of Food and Medicine: The Impact of the U.S. Embargo on Health and Nutrition in Cuba*. Washington: American Association for World Health.

Tanner, William Randolph. 1971. *The Passage of the Internal Security Act of 1950.* Ph.D. Thesis, University of Kansas.

Thomas, Clive Y. 1988. *The Poor and the Powerless: Economic Policy and Change in the Caribbean.* London: Latin American Bureau.

The Economist. 2002a. "The Caribbean: Trouble in Paradise." November 23.

_____. 2002b. "Emigration from Latin America: Making the most of an exodus." February 21.

Tigar, Michael E. 2000. *Law and the Rise of Capitalism.* New York: Monthly Review.

Tovar, Carlos Mendez. 1997. *Democracy in Cuba?* Havana: Editorial José Martí.

TransAfrica Forum. 1999. "Forty Years of Hostility: Consequences of the United States Economic Embargo on Cuba." Online: http://transafricaforum.org/reports/print/cuba_print.shtml

Treverton, Gregory F. 1989. "Cuba in U.S. Security Perspective." In Jorge I. Dominguez and Rafael Hernández (eds.) *U.S.-Cuban Relations In The 1990s.* Boulder, CO: Westview.

Tucker, Cynthia. 2001. "Communism After Fidel Castro: Q &A with Cuba's Ricardo Alarcón." *The Atlantic Journal and Constitution.* July 8.

Turnbull, Charles. 2000. "Economic Reforms and Social Contradictions in Cuba." *Cuba in Transition* 10 (August).

Ulysses Travel Publications. 1999. *Cuba.* Montreal.

UN Wire. 2002. "UNICEF Says Country Hits Lowest Infant Mortality Rate in 40 Years." January 3.

UNDP. 2003. *Human Development Report.* New York: United Nations Development Programme.

_____. 2002. *Human Development Report.* New York: United Nations Development Programme.

_____. 1999. *Human Development Report.* New York: United Nations Development Program.

_____. 1998. *Human Development Report.* New York: United Nations Development Program.

_____. 1996. *Human Development Report.* New York: United Nations Development Program.

UNODC. 2003. *Caribbean Drug Trends 2001–2002.* Barbados: United Nations Office on Drugs and Crime. Available at http://www.unodc.org/pdf/barbados/caribbean_drug-trends_2001-2002.pdf

United Nations. 1997. *United Nations World Statistics Pocketbook.* New York: United Nations.

_____. 1971. *Declaration on Principles of International Law Concerning Friendly Relations and Co-operation Among States in Accordance with the Charter of the United Nations.*

United States Government. 1967. *An Act to Adjust the Status of Cuban Refugees to that of Lawful Permanent Residents of the United States and for Other Purposes. Public Law 89-732.* November 1, 1966, United States Statutes at Large. Vol.

80, Part 1. Washington: U.S. Government Printing Office.

———. 1997. *Cuban Liberty and Democratic Solidarity Act, 104th Congress Session 1996 Public Law 101-114 of March 12, 1996.* Washington: U.S. Government Printing Office.

USAID. 2002. *Cuba Program: Objective: Increase Flow of Information on Democracy, Human Rights and Free Enterprise, To, From, and Within Cuba.* U.S. Agency for International Development. May 2002. Available at http://www.usaid.gov/regions/lac/cu/upd-cub.htm

U.S. Congress. 1998. *Report to the Congress by the Chairmen of the House Committees on Appropriations and International Relations and the Senate Committees on Foreign Relations and Appropriations.* Washington.

U.S. Department of State. 2003. *Patterns of Global Terrorism.* Washington. Available at http://www.state.gov/s/ct/rls/pgtrpt/2001/html/10249.htm

USINT. 1994. *Current Situation of Cuban Refugee Program.* Havana: United States Interest Section.

Valdes Vivo, Raul. 1998. "Why Cuba says no to Privatization." *Granma International* January 11.

Valencia, Marelys. 2002. "Slates for the Provincial Assembly of People's Power and deputies to Parliament approved." *Granma International.* December 2.

Vann, Bill. 1999. "Castroism at forty: The dead-end of petty-bourgeois nationalism." World Socialist Web Site, January 20. Available at http://www.wsws.org/articles/1999/jan1999/cuba-j20.shtml

Vasallo Barrueta, Norma. 2001. "Cuba Women and Economic Changes: The Impact on Women's Personal Experience." In Colleen Lundy and Norma Vasallo Barrueta (eds.) *Cuban Women: History, Contradictions, and Contemporary Challenges.* Ottawa: Carleton University.

Veltmeyer, Henry. 2001. "Globalization and the Restructuring of Labour in Latin America." Unpublished paper.

———. 1999. *The Labyrinth of Latin American Development.* New Delhi: A.P.H. Publishing.

Vienna Convention on Diplomatic Relations and Other Protocols, April 18, 1961. Available at http://www.mfa.gov.tr/grupe/ed/eda/eda02e.htm

VOA News. 2003 "Cuba stops Iran from jamming U.S. broadcasts." August 20.

Wald, Karen. 2003a. "Dissecting the NY Times Spin on Cuba's 50th anniversary." Email article. July 15.

———. 2003. Unpublished letter. April 3.

———. 1999a. "Widespread organic farming could help boost Cuba's sagging agricultural sector." *Cuba News* November.

———. 1999b. "Popes, Prostitutes and Prisoners." *Peace Review* 11:1 (March).

Walton, Richard J. 1972. *Cold War and Counterrevolution: The Foreign Policy of John F. Kennedy.* New York: Viking.

Waters, Mary Alice, 1994. "Defending Cuba, Defending Cuba's Socialist Revolution." *New International: A Magazine of Marxist Politics and Theory* 10.

Watson, Hilbourne. 2001. "Theorizing the Racialization of Global Politics and the Caribbean Experience." *Alternatives* 26.

White, Gordon. 1987. "Cuban Planning in the Mid-1980s: Centralization, Decentralization and Participation." *World Development* 15, 1.

Whitney, William, et al. 1996. *U.S. Embargo: Cuba's Affliction*. Brunswick, ME: Let Cuba Live.

WHO. 2000. "WHO Issues New Healthy Life Expectancy Rankings." Press Release. World Health Organization. June 4.

_____. 1998a. "Citation: Award of the World Health Organization Health For All Gold Medal to His Excellency Dr. Fidel Castro, President of the Republic of Cuba." World Health Organization. A51/D1/7, May 15.

_____. 1998b. "WHO Turns 50: 51st World Health Assembly Opens in Geneva." Press Release. World Health Organization, May 8.

Williams, Eric. 1984. *From Columbus to Castro: The History of the Caribbean*. New York: Random House.

_____. 1983. *Capitalism and Slavery*. London: Andre Deutsch.

Woddis, Jack. 1971. *Introduction to Neo-colonialism: The New Imperialism in Asia, Africa and Latin America*. New York: International

World Watch Institute. 2002. *State of the World 2002. A World Watch Institute Report on Progress Towards a Sustainable Society*. New York: W.W. Norton.

Wroughton, Lesley. 2003. "Western nickel producers differ on market outlook." *Reuters*. May 5.

Yu-lan Price, Alana, and Jessica Leight. 2003. "OAS right to reject U.S. bullying of Cuba." *Baltimore Sun* June 17.

Zatz, Majorie S. 1994. *Producing Legality: Law and Socialism in Cuba*. New York: Routledge.

Zetlin, Maurice. 1967. *Revolutionary Politics and the Cuban Working Class*. Princeton: Princeton University Press.

Zinn, Howard. 1995. *A People's History of the United States, 1492–Present*. New York: Harper Perennial.

INDEX